Timothy Green Beckley's

KNIFE-WIELDING DEMONS

AND

MURDEROUS GHOSTS

Uncovering the Truth About Terrifying Homicidal Poltergeists

INNER LIGHT/GLOBAL COMMUNICATIONS

P.O. Box 753
New Brunswick, NJ 08903

mrufo8@hotmail.com

Timothy Green Beckley's

**Knife-Wielding Demons and Murderous Ghosts:
Uncovering the Truth About Terrifying Homicidal Poltergeists**

Contributors:

Timothy Green Beckley, Sean Casteel, Scott Corrales, Maria D'Andrea, Paul Eno, Hercules Invictus, William Kern, Michele Lowe, Shawn Robbins, Adele Casales Rocha, Carol Rodriguez, Brad Steiger, Tim R. Swartz, Joshua Warren, Butch Witkowski

Copyright © 2019 by Timothy Green Beckley
dba Inner Light/Global Communications

All Rights Reserved

No part of these manuscripts may be copied or reproduced by any mechanical or digital methods and no excerpts or quotes may be used in any other book or manuscript without permission in writing by the Publisher, Inner Light/Global Communications, except by a reviewer who may quote brief passages in a review.

Published in the United States of America By
Inner Light/Global Communications
Box 753, New Brunswick, NJ 08903

Staff Members

Timothy G. Beckley, Publisher
Carol Ann Rodriguez, Assistant to the Publisher
Sean Casteel, General Associate Editor
Tim R. Swartz, Layout, Graphics and Editorial Consultant
William Kern, Editorial and Art Consultant

Sign Up For Our Free Weekly Newsletter and Mail Order Version of Conspiracy Journal and Bizarre Bazaar

www.ConspiracyJournal.com

Order Hot Line: 1-732-602-3407

PayPal: MrUFO8@hotmail.com

CONTENTS

- SOME HEADS ARE GONNA ROLL 7
- THE DANGEROUS WRATH OF THE POLTERGEIST 19
- VENGEFUL GHOSTS AND SPITEFUL DEMONS 29
- TERROR-FILLED NIGHTS AND DISTURBING DAYS 43
- THE "EVIL WITCH" OF HAMPTON BEACH — GOODY COLE, NEW HAMPSHIRE'S TROUBLING POLTERGEIST 57
- THE POLTERGEIST REVOLUTION OF THE 1960s – SO WERE THEY SMOKING WEED IN THE SPIRIT WORLD? 69
- HERE THERE BE MONSTERS 91
- THE MOOR 97
- A MURDER/SUICIDE AND A CHILLING SOUTHERN HAUNTING 111
- ALONE OVERNIGHT IN AMERICA'S MOST HAUNTED BEDROOM 119
- MOST ASTONISHING POLTERGEIST CASES OF MODERN AMERICA 131
- HOBGOBLINS AND UNFRIENDLY REALMS 151
- THE POLTERGEIST EFFECT! 165
- CRYPTIDS – A NEW WAVE OF "HAUNTINGS" 177
- DOING BATTLE WITH ULTRA-TERRESTRIALS - ATTACK OF THE ALIEN POLTERGEIST 185
- SERVANTS OF THE DARK SIDE: CULTS THAT KILL 209
- WHEN THE POLTERGEIST FINDS ITS VOICE 221
- THE PASSING OF BRAD STEIGER – NOW A PART OF "THE OTHER" 237
- KNOCK, KNOCK – THERE ARE DEMONS IN THE HOUSE 241
- THE AMHERST POLTERGEIST – A KNIFE-WIELDING SPIRIT 253
- THE HAUNTED HOUSE: A True Ghost Story 255

Knife-Wielding Demons and Murderous Ghosts

SOME HEADS ARE GONNA ROLL
By Timothy Green Beckley

About Editor and Publisher Timothy Green Beckley – UFO and Paranormal Pioneer

Tim Beckley has had so many careers that even his own girlfriend doesn't know what he does for a living. Timothy Green Beckley has been described as the Hunter Thompson of UFOlogy by the editor of UFO magazine, Nancy Birnes.

From an early age, his life has more or less revolved around the paranormal. At the age of three, his life was saved by an invisible force. The house he was raised in was thought to be haunted. His grandfather saw a headless horseman. Beckley also underwent out-of-body experiences starting at age six.

He saw his first of three UFOs when he was but ten, and has had two more sightings since - including an attempt to communicate with one of these objects. Tim grew up listening to the only all night talk show in the country that revolved around the strange and unexplained.

Long John Nebel's guests included the early UFO contactees who claimed to have visited other planets and built time machines in the desert. Tim was fascinated by everything that went bump in the night - or even in the daylight for that matter.

Years later, Tim was to appear on Long John's show numerous times and over the years has been a frequent guest on hundreds of programs which have come and gone just like ghosts in the night.

He is a popular guest on Coast to Coast AM, has appeared on William Shatner's *"Weird Or What?"* and was featured in an episode of *"UFO Hunters"* regarding the dreaded Men In Black. He has his own podcast, "Exploring the Bizarre" and his YouTube channel: Mr. UFO's Secret Files.

Knife-Wielding Demons and Murderous Ghosts

Photo of Tim Beckley by Jeff Goodman taken sometime in the Seventies. Writing and editing and publishing a book like this – maybe Mr. UFO shouldn't be opening an umbrella in the house. "If necessary. it could be used for a weapon," he insists, though how it would affect a spirit is hard to say.

* * * * * * * * *

Have you ever contemplated the notion that you might suffer a heart attack if you encountered a ghost or a deranged spirit in the dead of night?

Most of us think of ghosts as frightening entities, but I'm really not sure why. I mean the majority of ghostly entities and spirits are like will-o-the-wisps. They may drift out of the cobwebs of your attic or a damp cellar corner, but for the most part they don't really do anything dramatic or harmful except perhaps throw a chair in the air, or shake a bed till it rocks, or step heavily on the floor boards in your house alerting you to their presence. Now I've seen doors open and close by themselves, lights go on and off and dishes drop to the floor without breaking. But after watching hours upon hours of your favorite ghost hunters' show, I really can't get as excited as I was at age four when I thought I saw a full body apparition in my room surrounded by a brilliant aura.

TV and the movies portray ghosts and the esoteric in general in a more aggressive tone. You have "Ghostbusters" with its slime and "The Exorcist's" star Linda Blair spitting pea soup and defaming her mother with a reference to oral sex and what she can do while in hell. Nothing like a good nail biting horror story like *"Pet Semetary"* to prompt us to hide under the covers and leave on the night light next to the bed. It doesn't matter in these instances if we are five or fifty; a good scare is a good scare!

So boo to you!

But good scares in real life as far as ghosts go are pretty much a rarity, except for those occasional cases which are guaranteed to make you wet your pants and scare the bejesus out of you.

For purposes of this work we naturally decided not to include your average, mundane ghost story. Such "let's not try to yawn to these accounts" are a dime a dozen, or a bit more pricy these days – long gone is the fifty cents cover price, which I used to pay for *Fate Magazine* in 1956 or 67, anxious to turn to their "My Proof of Survival" feature, which I considered really frightful at the time.

I have never actually considered myself a ghost hunter per se. And I can't claim to be a parapsychologist, either, since I don't profess to have any sort of degree. I have always more or less identified myself as a Fortean researcher, someone who follows the tenants of the late Charles Fort, who spent most days in the library going through old journals and newspaper files digging up the dirt on a wide range of paranormal phenomena. If you had to buttonhole me, I would accept the mantle of an archivist of the strange and unknown, which can best be described in my mind's eye as encompassing a wide sweep of the supernatural paint brush.

What we are concerned with at the moment are incidents which can be categorized as the most diabolic of poltergeist experiences, as well as skirmishes with the most gruesome and alarming phantoms you are likely to deal with.

Previously, I have written about the house alongside Loch Ness in Scotland where Led Zeppelin's Jimmy Page resided and where the controversial, self-professed "black magician," Aleister Crowley, once performed rituals to bring back the dead.

Known as Boleskine House, the place is decidedly haunted, no doubt about it. Proclaimed by the media as the "wickedest man in the world," Crowley described the Boleskine property in which he cast his "demonically perceived" spells this way: "The house is a long low building. I set apart the south-western half for my work. The largest room had a bow window, and here I made my door and constructed the terrace and lodge. Inside the room, I set up my oratory proper. This was a wooden structure, lined in part with the big mirrors which I had brought from London."

Knife-Wielding Demons and Murderous Ghosts

Boleskine House

Now quoting from: http://findingzoso.blogspot.com/ –

Jimmy Page was a noted Crowley disciple and in 1971, when on the search for a new home, his eye immediately settled on his former residence in Scotland. Right after moving in, Page relayed in an interview in 1975 the strange vibes that he picked up from inside the home. While it was in his possession, the house included an entrance hall, five bedrooms, three bathrooms, a drawing room, dining room, family room, kitchen, utility room, and the cellars. The total size of the grounds equaled out to about 47 acres.

When Jimmy purchased Boleskine House, it was in less than stellar condition as Malcolm Dent, Jimmy's hired caretaker would later relate. "It was a wreck. It had been more or less abandoned. There'd been at least one fire there, parts of the building were missing and it had been badly patched up. The grounds, which at one time had been very nicely laid out, were gone to hell, so the main task I took on was getting them into some sort of shape." He later remarked on the views seen from the house, "All the main rooms look out across the loch and you're 300 feet up so you have some dramatic views."

Jimmy Page stands before the haunted Boleskine House where heads often roll.

"Strange things have happened in that house that had nothing to do with Crowley. The bad vibes were already there. A man was beheaded there and sometimes you can hear his head rolling down. I haven't actually heard it, but a friend of mine, who is extremely straight and doesn't know anything about anything like that at all, heard it. He thought it was the cats bungling about. I wasn't there at the time, but he told the help, 'Why don't you let the cats out at night? They make a terrible racket, rolling about in the halls.' And they said, 'The cats are locked in a room every night.' Then they told him the story of the house. So that sort of thing was there before Crowley got there. Of course, after Crowley, there have been suicides, people carted off to mental hospitals."

Now that's some pretty wild shit admittedly and I can personally attest to the fact that something pretty hellish was going on inside that house.

I was visiting Loch Ness back in the early 1980s while on a trip to the UK to make a presentation for the House of Lords UFO club, an unofficial group inside the halls of Parliament organized by my late friend Brinsley Le Poer Trench. The 8th Earl of Clancarty, the proud Briton, long before Disclosure with a capital D, was pushing for Her Majesty's Government to release its UFO files to the public.

After delivering an unscripted talk to the group made up of approximately 80 – 100 listeners from the hallowed halls of Britain's officialdom, I ventured to Loch Ness via train. While I looked for Nessie, I stayed at a very lovely bed and breakfast owned by a quite feisty elderly lady who was most impressed when I told her about my proclamation inside the House of Lords. She made several calls and I found myself being introduced to several locals, including a minister who had seen several UFOs in the area surrounding the Loch, and the milkman, who had established a routine of driving around the Loch to deliver his product to those who found themselves a bit out-of-the-way of a supermarket to do their shopping.

Now, the gentleman knew nothing about Led Zeppelin, Jimmy Page, Aleister Crowley or even rock and roll, but he did have an interesting story to tell.

"I honestly don't like to drive past that place," he stated, referring to the Boleskine property. "I was delivering milk on several occasions, driving by the place, and my dog, which always traveled with me, would suddenly start to act crazy. He would start barking and would try to dig a hole under the front seat. I knew I had to either leave him home or take another route."

One of my favorite bands, Judas Priest, says in their hit song, "Some Heads Are Gonna Roll," and I believe they did so at one time inside Boleskine House, which is now off limits to tourists, with the current owners requesting their privacy.

IT'S A BLOODY MESS INSIDE THE TOWER OF LONDON

I have also written about the ghosts said to haunt the Tower of London. I'm told you can stack the decapitated heads up here as well, and tourists have seen blood dripping from the walls and felt cold clammy hands upon their body. Trust me, it wasn't Joe Biden.

Says one informed source: "Anne Boleyn was beheaded in 1536 for treason against Henry VIII; her ghost supposedly haunts the Church of St. Peter ad Vincula in the Tower, where she is buried, and has been said to walk around the White Tower carrying her head under her arm. This haunting is commemorated in the 1934 comic song 'With Her Head Tucked Underneath Her Arm.' Other reported ghosts include Henry VI, Lady Jane Grey, Margaret Pole, and the Princes in the Tower. In January 1816, a sentry on guard outside the Jewel House claimed to have witnessed an apparition of a bear advancing towards him, and reportedly died of fright a few days later. In October 1817, a tubular, glowing apparition was claimed to have been seen in the Jewel House by the Keeper of the Crown Jewels, Edmund Lenthal Swifte. He said that the apparition hovered over the shoulder of his wife, leading her to exclaim: 'Oh, Christ! It has seized me!' Other nameless and formless terrors have been reported, more recently, by members of the night staff at the Tower."

WATCH OUT FOR THOSE GHOSTLY WINGERS

Paranormal researcher Paul Dale Roberts is a buddy. He has been a guest on our "Exploring the Bizarre" program several times and has contributed to some of our vast catalogue of books. He is a topnotch field investigator who takes on all sorts of cases, some of them pretty weird.

Recently Paul told us about a phenomenon he dubbed "ghostly Wingers." Thinking back, I have myself run into reports of this nature encompassing some really weird – I guess you would call them "creatures," for lack of a better name. One couple, for example, were driving across country when their automobile was invaded by some very nondescript entities who wouldn't leave them alone, pestering them for hundreds of miles along a desolate highway late at night. Another time, a long haul truck driver was returning home when he was besieged by objects that started out as other vehicles on the highway only to shape-shift into some really bizarre forms and attack his 18-wheeler with him inside behind the steering wheel.

Paul Dale Robert's report is really a spine-tingling tale:

4/14/2019: "This was a confidential investigation. The family, which I will simply call the Lonnies, contacted me on my paranormal hotline. The family consists of Mr. Lonnie and his wife Ms. Lonnie and their three children (two boys and one girl). Mr. Lonnie tells me that his daughter two years ago was caught saying incantations from a black magic book. Mr. Lonnie burned the book and scolded his daughter. Mr. Lonnie says that his daughter claims she has not practiced black magic anymore. Mr. Lonnie feels like a portal opened in his home. A string of strange entities have entered his home and he does not know what can be done. Mr. Lonnie did not want an investigation, but merely wanted his home cleansed.

"On one particular night, it was storming. Ms. Lonnie says that Mr. Lonnie was working late that night and it was just her and the kids. The house started trembling and Ms. Lonnie could hear distant thunder. Ms. Lonnie felt the house

was trembling more in the daughter's bedroom. Ms. Lonnie opened the bedroom door and to her surprise she saw the bedroom window rattling and the screen flew off. To Ms. Lonnie's horrified shock, she saw black flying creatures come through the window. Ms. Lonnie describes the creatures as having long slick black wings that come to a point at the end. The creatures, which she calls Wingers, were completely jet black. About 20 flew through the window and into the house. At first Ms. Lonnie felt they were bats, but she could see the long wings and on the outside of the wing facing forward were three claws on each wing. The creatures have a body with no feet, legs or head. Ms. Lonnie freaked out and grabbed her son's baseball bat and started swinging. Ms. Lonnie was horrified to see that the baseball bat was going right through the creatures and some of the creatures were flying through the wall and into the next room. All of a sudden Ms. Lonnie's daughter started screaming as she was curled up next to her bedroom closet. Ms. Lonnie sees all kinds of scratches on her daughter and immediately starts praying to God loudly, asking God to dispel these foul creatures. When Ms. Lonnie prayed out loud, the creatures dispersed out of the window. Ms. Lonnie says she never seen these creatures again."

www.cryptic916.com

Sacramento Paranormal Help

www.facebook.com/HaloParanormalInvestigations

Email: jazmaonline@gmail.com

LA LLORONA KILLS CHILDREN

If you get a chance, you should hop on over to the local cinema or watch "The Curse of La Llorona" when it becomes available "On Demand," through your local cable provider.

This is a big screen version of a most horrendous specter, a weeping woman who terrorizes and snatches children to claim as her own and takes them to the afterlife.

The tale is a very popular Latino folktale and, whether it is true or not, it has been used to soil the knickers of kids for more than a century.

The story is told of a wealthy landowner who went on business trips which kept him away from his wife for long periods. His wife often became restless and, during one of his absences, had an illicit affair. As a result, she bore a child.

Knowing that she would not be able to convince her husband that the baby was his, she went to the river and drowned the child. The legend of La Llorrona, whose name is Spanish for "the weeping woman," tells that this woman has been cursed by God since then and now sits disconsolately on a rock by a river or creek combing her long, wavy black hair and crying pitifully, hoping to inspire the mercy of those who hear her.

The movie version of La Llorrona is quite frightening. Just ask author Tim Beckley!

A slightly different version of the legend can be found courtesy: *"Characters and Caricatures in Belizean Folklore"* In this variation, La Llorrona seems to direct hostility toward men more so than to children. (Does that make her less evil?).

Stories of La Llorona are popular in Belize, especially in the district of Orange Walk, and also in the neighboring countries of Mexico and Guatemala. Although LA LLORONA and XTABAI have traditionally become merged into one legend and, as enchantresses, are said to be variations of the same lore, each possesses distinct characteristics and behaviors.

Though seen most often near the water, LA LLORONA can also be found inland, at the roadside or under an almond or a breadfruit tree. On dark, lonely nights, her haunting cries and her appearance of helplessness give her an alluring charm which draws men to her. She also attracts a man's attention by allowing fire or a glowing light to come from her fingers, and as the man gets nearer, LA LLORONA appears to float in the air, moving farther and farther away as the man follows her. Men, who encounter her at midnight near rivers, or at crossroads, may witness her turning into a two-tailed serpent. She then sticks her tails into the victim's nostrils and squeezes. Travelers or drunks who have lost their way can become her unfortunate victims, and their greatest fear is to be wrapped in her thick, long hair and taken over the water to a region from where no one can return.

As is to be expected, the film version has its own twist and turns and has been adapted to the silver screen with enough frightening moments to scream to your heart's content. On the red carpet, to promote the release of the film, several of the stars talked about the importance of telling La Llorona's tale on the big screen, while also relaying their own creepy experiences from the set.

According to the male lead, Raymond Cruz, he had known all about the legend and as a child was afraid to go out after dark because the lady in white was vengeful and was known to come after very bad children. "It was known that she could get you. Drown you. She would try to kill you."

Cruz is a firm believer that the spooky lady was on the set when his beaded bracelet shattered off his wrist and flew all over the place.

In addition, one of the leading ladies said she wanted the role so bad that she wrote her desires down on a slip of paper and concentrated upon it till she did get the role.

Hey, as far as I'm concerned, stories such as these would even make the likes of Edgar Allan Poe jump. You can take them with a grain of salt if you like – but I wouldn't!

SUGGESTED READING

ALIEN STRONGHOLDS ON EARTH

SECRET EXPLOITS OF ADMIRAL RICHARD E BYRD: THE HOLLOW EARTH?

SCREWED BY THE ALIENS

UFO BLOOD LUST

UFO HOSTILITIES

BLOG AND AUTHOR'S AMAZON PAGE

https://www.amazon.com/Timothy-Green-Beckley/e/B000APJFWY

"Exploring the Bizarre," KCORradio.com - Thursday's 10 PM Eastern

YouTube.com "Mr. UFO's Secret Files" -- Over 400 interviews

Knife-Wielding Demons and Murderous Ghosts

Knife-Wielding Demons and Murderous Ghosts

This photo shows the ghostly figure of a young boy hiding at the top of the landing in the Amityville house. Could this be the spirit of one of the Defeo youths killed inside the house?

The original ghost hunter Hans Holtzer says the Amityville house was filled with terror.

Did a poltergeist cause Ronald Defeo Jr. to commit six grisly murders?

THE DANGEROUS WRATH OF THE POLTERGEIST
By Shawn Robbins and Timothy Green Beckley

A nasty poltergeist is nothing to joke about. They can do irreparable harm to body, mind and spirit.

They have even been known to kill!

Witnesses tell of heavy objects flying across the room. A multitude of curse words are sometimes spoken and houses have even been set ablaze by these fiery demons. Yes, that's the truth, and it's also true that far worse has been accomplished by an excitable spook who wants nothing more than to toy with humans and rip their hearts out.

Though, thank God, such cases are seemingly rare, there have been instances where a poltergeist has been known to murder a person in order to take them back with them to the other side.

In fact, there has been a rise in such occurrences in Asia, particularly among Laotian and Taiwanese men, who have been dying in their sleep in increasing numbers after being possessed by nocturnal visitors known in their culture as the "pee mae mai," or "Widow Ghosts." Placed in the category of malicious poltergeists, the spirits are said to be females who seek the companionship of men and stalk their victims just like Freddy Krueger – when the household is most silent. They then snuff out the life of their victims, who have gone to bed not suspecting that they will die in their nightmares. Recently 18 men are said to have succumbed to this menace in one village alone. To ward off and trick the Widow Ghosts into thinking they are females, they have taken to wearing fingernail polish and lingerie and dangling fake wooden penises over the headboard on the other side of the bed. Talk about a cold hearted woman. The term "black widow" certainly takes on a new meaning these days.

DAVE GARROWAY'S POLTERGEIST

Most of those who have thought ahead and purchased this book will know that for many years that I, Shawn Robbins, worked with the great parapsychologist and ghost hunter Hans Holtzer. Hans (January 26, 1920 – April 26, 2009) was an American paranormal icon and author. He wrote well over 100 books on supernatural and occult subjects for the popular market, as well as several plays, musicals, films, and documentaries, and hosted a television show, "Ghost Hunter." Frequently, he would call upon me to assist him as a psychic and medium on cases he was looking to validate.

For many years Hans was a darling of the media, both radio and television. In those days there were not dozens of newbie parapsychologists scrambling to be known. There were a few "professionals" like Dr. Nandor Fodor and Stanley Krippner, who made scholarly presentations. And then there was Hans, who was more of a pop culture icon from whom the general public enjoyed learning about ghosts and poltergeists. Hans ranked a little above everyone else because he managed to "explain" the phenomena in clear and easy to digest terms but also in a colorful way that put a bit of a scare into his audience. After all, what is a good ghost story for if it isn't to titillate the senses and get a person's blood running cold?

I guess that Hans met the host of NBC's "Today Show" early on while he was making the rounds promoting one of his paperback potboilers. I remember Hans telling me he liked David Garroway because he didn't take his celebrity status to heart.

But I think what struck Hans even more about the host known for his assortment of colorful bow ties was the fact that Dave was all too familiar with the subject matter because he had had to deal with a poltergeist of his own.

Garroway was living in a cozy brownstone on Manhattan's fashionable Upper East Side that was once owned by Rudyard Kipling's sister and her physician husband. But David admitted that despite all the amenities he was fearful about residing there because he was convinced that the townhouse was infested with poltergeists. He was afraid to leave his children there when he went out because he had heard that poltergeists can not only toss heavy objects around – which could maim someone – but were also known for setting fires as they went about their sordid business of haunting a place.

Knife-Wielding Demons and Murderous Ghosts

We don't know what sort of problems Dave's poltergeist challenged the TV personality with, but something very tragic did happen to Garroway some years later – he committed suicide with the help of a gunshot. Friends said they did not know that he was depressed, though he did seem despondent for a long time after his second wife died by taking a lethal overdose of pills.

There is no way we can say with certainty that Garroway's personal problems were tied in with his bout with a poltergeist or two running rampant in his living quarters, but nothing can be ruled out when you consider the headlines made by a shotgun wielding killer who murdered his entire family in what was to become America's number one spook house located in Amityville, Long Island.

Hans usually called after the supper hour so as to converse without being disturbed. This one evening I remember he sounded agitated, as if something was weighing heavily on his mind. There seemed to me to be a sense of urgency in his voice that I hadn't noticed before. I could almost hear his ticker pumping like in Edgar Allen Poe's *"A Telltale Heart."* Little did I suspect that I was about to be transported to a dark and dangerous place that should remain off limits even to the most otherworldly wise.

The famous ghost hunter told me that he had to see me as soon as I had a couple of hours to devote to what he had to tell me. Being that Hans seemed all "jacked up," I told him that I would be over to see him the very next day. Upon arriving at his spacious Riverside apartment, the kind with the extra high ceilings that were built around 1910, Hans ushered me into his library where he had a series of photos laid out on his large oak desk which had been cleared of all other items.

Dr. Holzer, who taught a course on parapsychology at the New School, knew I had worked on previous occasions with police departments in and around New York. He handed me one of the photos and said he wanted me to get into the mind of the individual in the glossy print. When I touched the photograph I immediately recoiled and must have made some comment like, "There is something really wrong here, Hans!"

You've heard it all before – chills ran up and down my spine and the hairs on the back of my neck stood up. I was almost in a state of shock. Looking down at the photograph I had been handed, I knew that I was looking at the face of a murderer, a man consumed by the darkest of thoughts, the kind that only a demon could possess. Little did I know at that moment that I was holding the photo of Ronald DeFeo, the tortured and twisted mass murderer who would come to international recognition when later linked to a house full of evil, a house where he had killed six members of his immediate family. He shot them to death, putting a bullet through each of their heads as if he had been shooting squirrels along the riverbank. The backdoor of the house would soon be identifiable to many millions through a bestselling book and no less than twenty motion pictures.

I admit that my reaction at the time was a bit more overwhelmed than usual when called upon to validate or otherwise get directly involved in a criminal investigation. Forty years later I still felt some of the original terror that had taken over my emotions. I knew I was looking into the eyes of a possessed man who was living in an alternate reality. At this point Hans revealed the person's identity to me. DeFeo had shot and killed his mother, father, and four of his young siblings, execution style, claiming that he had been possessed by evil spirits. Some said the house located on Ocean Avenue in Amityville had been constructed directly over an old Native American burial ground, though this could never be verified to everyone's satisfaction and remains a contentious issue even now. Hans had always believed there was a direct connection. Through a voice medium he had brought to the house it was determined that one of the spirits of the deceased was a young brave those horse had fallen on him and crushed him to death as he was trying to make the steed do a particularly dangerous jump. "People get to fighting with each other but they don't know why. They're driven to it because they are taken over by the one with the long jaw."

Known as "Butch" to his friends, Ronald DeFeo had an uneven disposition. Whenever he got mad at someone in the family he would often hurl a chair or some other object at them. To make matters worse, he drank a lot and liked to "play" with firearms.

He was, I felt, a human powder keg ready to blow his top – which he did on the night of November 13, 1974.

The neighbors heard the commotion even though they were some distance away. The police were called and they couldn't believe the amount of blood. There was blood everywhere; on the floor, the walls and even the ceiling, where it had sprayed with ease. At trial, when asked if he loved his family and what could possibly cause him to commit such a hideous crime, the teenage DeFeo said quite simply, "I didn't want to kill them. To be quite honest, it's not what I wanted to do. I had no choice. I had to do it."

Fade to black.

Knife-Wielding Demons and Murderous Ghosts

Butch was convicted of the crime and must spend the rest of his life incarcerated.

The following summer, along came an unsuspecting family looking for a place to settle down. They loved the house on Ocean Avenue and couldn't resist making an offer for the residence. The real estate broker, citing full disclosure, told the family what had transpired earlier in the house. George and Kathleen Lutz were a bit uncertain, but they didn't really believe in ghosts. So, after a chat between husband and wife, they decided to put down a deposit, preparing to move in at the earliest feasible moment.

They may have made the wrong decision it turns out!

A friend, who said he knew about "such things," suggested that, because of the mass murder that had taken place in the house, a priest be called in to bless the dwelling and remove any spirits which might be wandering about – be they Native Americans or the troubled souls of those shot to death on that fateful night in 1974.

In the words of Kathy Lutz, this is what transpired next, according to AmityvilleFiles.com –

Due to the property's grim reputation, a friend of George's suggested the house should be blessed by a Catholic priest. "I was a Methodist, so this was new and foreign to me at the time," recalls George. "Father Ray showed up shortly after we were in the process of moving in. I waved, he waved, and he went on in the house and went about blessing it. When he was done, I tried to pay him but he wouldn't take money. He said, 'No, you don't charge for this, and you don't charge friends for this.'

I thought that was a very kind thing to say, and then he said, 'You know, I felt something really strange in that one upstairs bedroom,' and he described the bedroom. And we said that's what we were going to use as a sewing room. We weren't going to use it as a bedroom.

He said, 'That's good, as long as no one sleeps in there.' And that's all he said, and he left.

"Strange occurrences began almost immediately. Cold spots were discovered in random spots throughout the house. Eerie vibes pervaded the atmosphere. Jolting sounds would wake the family during the night. The escalating chain of events took their toll on the Lutzes, resulting in drastic personality changes. George, who began to seclude himself from the *family, obsessed over the fireplace that never seemed to warm him enough. Kathy also began to undergo a series of unnerving events.*

On more than one occasion, she described being touched by an unseen person. And most dramatically, Kathy claims that after waking from a deep sleep, her face was that of an old hag that took hours to dissipate. Even the Lutz children began to argue more than usual, resulting in terrible beatings from their parents. The youngest child, Missy, described speaking to "an angel" that was living in her room. This angel, Missy claims, was named "Jodie." Jodie was able to present itself as a "large pig" to Missy and change shape and form at will.

George and Kathy claimed to have witnessed two red eyes peering in at them from the upstairs bedroom window. Missy believed it was Jodie wanting to come inside.

"I just didn't want to leave the house," George says. "We would invite people over instead of going to see them. There came a point when we would invite people over to see whether we were crazy or not. Because when our friends sat in the kitchen, they could hear the people walking around upstairs after the kids had been put to bed. We'd all go up and find the kids fast asleep. There was no way it was the kids – and when your friends confirm that for you, you almost want to break down and say out loud, 'I'm not crazy. They hear it too!' That is such an emotional moment when someone else confirms for you what you're hearing and that it's not just you hearing it – it's not your imagination."

Coming back to Ocean Avenue, the families that I found had resided in that dwelling place appeared to have a calamity within each one," recalls Kathy. The final night the Lutz family spent in the house was, in George's words, "the reason not to stay there anymore."

"I was lying in bed and everyone was asleep, and Kathy lifts up off the bed and starts to slide away from the bed and away from me," Lutz said. "I feel something get in the bed with us. I'm unable to move; I hear the kids' beds continually slamming up and down on the floor and being dragged. We heard these pigeons on the air conditioner top overhead from the master bathroom, and they're fluttering all night long and yet there are no pigeons there the next morning – or any nest or anything like that. The lights flickered. We brought the dog up to stay right by the bedroom. We

tied him right to the doorknob and he's up, going in circles, and throwing up all night.

"The boys came down in the morning absolutely frightened. They were unable to get down to me, and I was unable to get up to them. Missy came in and just asked, what was that all about? And Kathy had no memory of much of it. That day we spent trying to get ahold of Father Ray, and he said all the right words."

The family fled the house the following afternoon on January 14, 1976.

For the remainder of their lives, George and Kathleen Lutz maintained that their experiences in Amityville were real.

WHY THEY KILL

Whether the demon – the poltergeist – that possessed Butch was real or the work of a sick mind is up to personal interpretation. The fact is that DeFeo killed in cold blood. According to author Jean E. Blashfield, as he roamed the house upset because he had thought the dinner he had been served was "shit in a bowl," the demon which inhabited the young man began to make him suspect that the family was conspiring to harm him. "We'll wait until he goes to sleep and then get him," he was certain that he heard the others say.

In "***Why They Kill***" Blashfield describes the forthcoming bloodbath accordingly:

"At about 3 A.M., with the light glaring in the house, twenty-two-year old Ronald DeFeo, Jr. – or something that had taken possession of his body and mind – put the family sheepdog outdoors, where it proceeded to bark for the next fifteen minutes. Then he grabbed his expensive .35-caliber Marlin rifle and crept into his parents' bedroom. He fired two shots at his sleeping father's back, and then, as his mother, Louise DeFeo, awoke and started to rise, he fired two more shots at her. His father probably lived long enough to move around somewhat in the bed before dying.

"The young man, who had never done anything calmly in his life, calmly moved on to the thirteen-year-old Allison's room. She, too, looked into the muzzle of the gun with sleepy eyes, only to have a bullet smash her face and enter her brain, destroying it. Crossing the hall to the bedroom of his youngest brothers, twelve-year-old Mark and seven-year-old John Matthew, Butch stood between the twin beds and fired first at one, then the other, from less than two feet away. It's likely that Mark, who had been seriously injured in a football accident and could not turn over of his own accord, was turned onto his stomach after death.

As the heavyset young man reloaded his rifle while climbing the stairs to the third floor, where his sister Dawn slept, the eighteen-year-old probably woke up. It is also likely that brother and sister spoke together, with him calming her fears enough to send her crawling back into bed before he shot her at the base of her skull, Oddly enough, investigators found unburned gunpowder particles on her nightgown, which may indicate that Dawn herself had fired a gun. One of the stories that DeFeo told after he was arrested was that Dawn had killed their siblings after he had killed his parents and before he killed her, but there was no other evidence that this might have been the case. DeFeo did, however, confess later to an incestuous sexual relationship with his sister.

At this point, according to Blashfield, the gun-toting murderer threw up in reaction to what he had done, then took a shower and got dressed in his normal work clothing. He threw the rifle into the canal behind the house and went about his business as if nothing had happened – until the police showed up. They found him making the rounds of the nearby bars the very next afternoon, as if nothing "out of the ordinary" had happened the night before.

No killing.

No murder.

No guilt.

No remorse.

And so the story of the Amityville Horror goes. It's become a legend. Without a doubt the most famous possession-by-a-poltergeist tale in modern American history.

But we pretty much know all this. It's been duly reported in every manner of media across the globe. I am certain there are very few places one might venture where the story of the DeFeo murders is not known to one degree or another. It's a tragic event and one that has been, in a sense, a curse upon the field of paranormal research as it brings in death and utter insanity that cannot be found in most other cases – thank God.

Knife-Wielding Demons and Murderous Ghosts

Like the terrifying incidents on Long Island, this book delves into the bottom of the human psyche in its quest to determine the truth about destructive poltergeists and other paranormal phenomena. But it also treads where no other book on the subject has gone before (keywords indicate a strong "Star Trek" influence). For the authors selected to contribute material herein cover a wide variety of explanations for poltergeists – from what has become the acceptable "norm" to more radical thinking on the subject. The result is a mixed bag of entities and creatures who possess and dominate their human targets but whose points of origin are incredibly weirder and more varied than anything you have ever been confronted with before.

You can still, of course, find the possessions, the hauntings and the blood-soaked walls left by the insane Mister DeFeo, but venture causally on tiptoes as you make yourself comfortable and proceed to turn the pages ahead, just like the sands of time.

Medium and "top ten psychic" Shawn Robbins was used by parapsychologist Hans Holtzer to get into the mind of the killer.

SUGGESTED READING

WICCAPEDIA – A MODERN DAY WHITE WITCH'S GUIDE

AHEAD OF MYSELF – CONFESSIONS OF A PROFESSIONAL PSYCHIC

SHAWN ROBBINS' PROPHECIES FOR THE END OF TIME

Knife-Wielding Demons and Murderous Ghosts

28

VENGEFUL GHOSTS AND SPITEFUL DEMONS
By Sean Casteel

EDITOR'S NOTE: Putting your best ecto-plasmic foot forward is not something every ghost or spirit can lay claim to. There are some pretty nasty "hobgoblins" out there, as contributor Maria D' Andrea refers to them. It seems some of these apparitions just want to torment us to the point where we might have a mental breakdown. I am sure there are even cases where demonic predators have caused the living to turn to drinking and to drugs (i.e. see our edition of "***Thirty Years Among The Dead***.")

There are many different ways for spiteful spirits to manifest themselves, but we want to center our attention at the moment on what can be identified in ghostly parlance as those of a "vengeful" nature," who are looking to get even. They might do so by doing something as mundane as pulling down your pants or as whacked out as throwing a shiv at your ass. Worse yet, they have been known to play a part in beheadings, such as in the Tower of London, where blood-soaked holding cells offer up evidence that ghosts can be damn detrimental to your health and spiritual well-being.

* * * * * * * * *

In mythology and folklore, the vengeful ghost is thought to be the spirit of a dead person who returns from the afterlife to seek retribution for a cruel, unnatural or unjust death. In certain cultures, where funeral and burial or cremation rites are important, such vengeful spirits may also be considered as unhappy ghosts of individuals who were not given a proper funeral.

The concept of a vengeful ghost seeking retribution for wrongs it suffered as a living person goes back to ancient times and is part of many cultures. According to such legends and beliefs, these spirits wander the world of the living

Knife-Wielding Demons and Murderous Ghosts

as restless spirits, seeking to have their grievances redressed. This kind of spirit will not be satisfied until they have succeeded in punishing either their murderers or their tormentors. In certain cultures, vengeful ghosts are mostly female, said to be women who were unfairly treated in their lifetime.

Exorcisms and appeasement are among the religious and social customs practiced by various cultures in relation to the vengeful ghost. For example, some of the natives of Paraguay cremated old people thought to harbor dangerous vengeful spirits rather than give them a customary burial. In cases where the person had been killed and the body improperly disposed of, the corpse might be exhumed and reburied according to the proper funerary rituals in order to appease the spirit.

VENGEFUL SPIRITS IN VARIOUS CULTURES

In Roman mythology, Lemures are vengeful spirits not afforded proper burial.

In ancient Roman mythology, creatures called Lemures are the wandering and vengeful spirits of those not afforded proper burial, funeral rites or affection from the living.

In ancient Grecian mythology, vengeful spirits who suffered a violent or cruel death are called a Keres.

The Green Lady is a restless female spirit said to haunt certain locations in Scotland, to include Crathes Castle, Knock Castle (Isle of Skye) and Ashintully Castle. In some tales, she was murdered in a green dress and then stuffed unceremoniously up the chimney by a servant. It is said that her footsteps can still be heard as she walks in a given castle in sadness.

There are also comparable Chinese spirits, such as Mogwai, a vengeful ghost or demon in Chinese mythology, as well as Yuan Gui – literally "ghost with grievance" – the spirits of persons who have died wrongful deaths. In Japan, one finds the "Kuchisake-onna," the vengeful ghost of a woman mutilated by her husband.

In South America, a female spirit named Patasola appears as a beautiful woman. She attracts men and lures them to the depths of the rain forest, where she turns into a beast and devours her victims. Not merely vengeful and violent but also cannibalistic.

A HORRIFYING RESIDUAL HAUNTING CRIME SCENE

There are also vengeful spirits who were not wronged innocents in life but were instead violent and wicked in their time among the living. The following story can be found online at: backpackerverse.com/ghost-serial-killer-story

The article is headlined *"The Ghost of a Serial Killer Lurks within This Farmhouse."* The author identifies himself as a ghost hunter who normally takes his cue from other paranormal investigators. But this case seemed to fall right into his lap. As he drove along to another location he had been told was haunted, his "spidey senses" alerted him to a rundown farmhouse somewhere in California.

"When I stopped in front of the property," the unnamed writer writes, "I could almost hear screams and growls in my head. Strangely enough, there were no signs blocking the entrance to the property, so I grabbed my equipment and went in. I found it odd that the majority of the trees and plants surrounding the old house were either dead or dying."

The house itself was decaying from the inside out. There were boards nailed across the door, which the ghost hunter said were flimsy and easy to tear down.

"The door opened on its own," he writes. "Creepy enough. But I had to remember that the dangers were more than structural. The familiar pricking up of my hairs and the chills hit me fast."

When he walked into the kitchen what he saw made him freeze in his tracks.

"A woman was slumped on the floor under the sink," he recounts, "with a large knife in her chest and trickling blood. I was able to see through her and I realized I was in the middle of a residual haunting, but then she looked up. The pain in her face was horrible, but she managed to raise her hand and point upwards. Then she screamed. I looked up, but no one was there, so I turned back as I trembled in fear to see the woman standing up.

"Still screaming," he continues, "she pointed up again. Her head began to twitch and shake uncontrollably with her mouth wide open. I knew that I had to investigate, even though I was nearly peeing in my pants, so I went out and ran up the stairs."

He arrived at the upstairs bedroom at the front of the crumbling house.

"Again, the door opened on its own, making my flesh crawl. Then I saw a small boy lying in a pool of his own blood. I couldn't help the tears falling down my face, but I was distracted by a nasty growl close to my right ear. Angry now, I turned around and yelled, 'Who are you?' but I didn't get a response. Then the boy sat up and yelled in his tiny voice, 'Help us!'"

In another bedroom, the door opened violently this time, smashing against the wall while the handle rattled. A teenage girl was flung across the old bed, with slashes all over her body.

"A river of blood ran under the bed. Then I heard menacing laughter in the distance, which fueled my anger. The girl slowly sat up and pointed to the left. Her pretty face was littered with gashes and bruises. I was weeping angry tears for this ghostly family, who had obviously been viciously attacked by a sadistic killer. I could still hear the screams from the mother and the little boy, along with the gurgling from the girl on the bed. It was clear that she had her throat slashed but she was trying to speak as she pointed to the back of the house. The gurgling, crying and screaming went on as I crept down the landing to the room at the back, shivering in fear."

The writer expected to face the killer responsible, but instead saw a grown man in a chair with an axe deep in his head. There was a pool of blood under the chair. It was the father, who also couldn't speak but slowly lifted his hand and began to point.

"A chill swept through my soul as I realized that his finger was pointing directly at me. Was I the killer? As I thought that, the father pointed more emphatically and the screams and noises from his family increased. While I stood there dumbstruck, wondering what he meant, I felt a blast of evil hit my back, freezing my body. Then a putrid stench wafted over me and the father continued to point anxiously – to the space behind me."

The ghost hunter turned around, coming face to face with the most evil entity he had ever encountered.

"Now I was only centimeters away from a murderous monster who had slaughtered an innocent family in cold blood. He looked like a big gorilla of a man who had escaped an insane asylum, with huge black eyes and an awful sneer."

The writer remembered a mini-Bible on his keychain, a gift from his late mother. He shoved the tiny Bible in the killer's ghostly face and yelled, "Leave them alone! Go to hell, where you belong!" The monster screamed like a demon splashed with holy water, then disappeared.

"I turned around, and the father was gone. When I raced through the house, I saw that the whole family was gone. The house was now empty but free from evil."

THE DEMONS THAT DROVE DAVID BERKOWITZ

Moving on from the residual haunting of a sadistic killer, we next examine the case of David Berkowitz, also called the Son of Sam and the .44 caliber killer, who shot 13 people during his reign of terror in New York City from 1976 to 1977.

In an article published by *"Psychology Today"* and written by Dr. Scott A. Bonn, Berkowitz's plea that "the devil made him do it" is given an objective psychological analysis.

"Visionary killers commit murder at the command of imagined internal or external voices," Bonn writes, "which they experience and perceive to be real. Such individuals are often suffering from either psychosis or some other form of mental illness. Visionary killers typically experience a psychotic break from reality that leads them to murder.

"While most serial killers have an ideal victim they seek out," Bonn continues, "e.g., white female prostitutes, visionary killers select their victims seemingly at random, based on logic that is indiscernible to either investigators or forensic psychologists. Their murderous agenda is entirely synchronized to their internal madness."

The belief that they are compelled to murder by someone else – saying their killing is "God-mandated" or "demon-mandated" – is also commonplace and well-documented.

David Berkowitz is often cited as a classic example of the visionary serial killer. As the killings were taking place, he sent handwritten letters to the police and the press claiming that Satan was ordering him to kill.

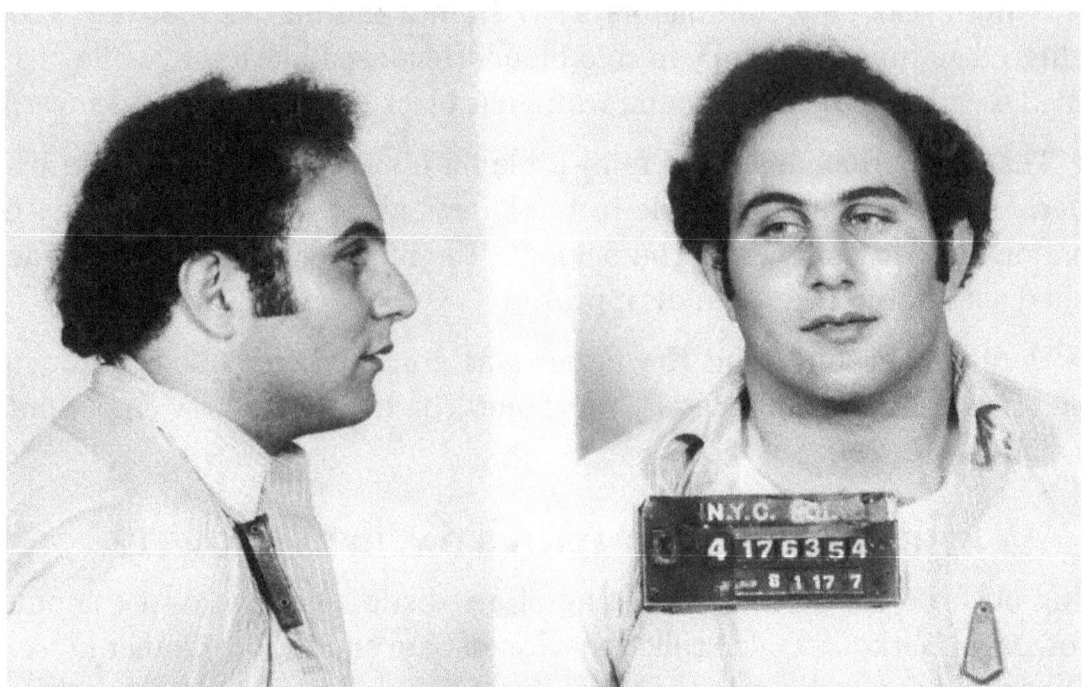

Did a noisome dog known as "the Son of Sam" make a killer out of David Berkowitz?

When he was arrested outside his Yonkers apartment building on August 10, 1977, Berkowitz initially claimed to have been obeying the orders of a demon manifested in the form of a dog named "Harvey," which belonged to his neighbor "Sam." Despite his explanation, he was found mentally competent to stand trial. He pleaded guilty to second-degree murder and was incarcerated in state prison.

"Berkowitz allegedly recanted his story of demonic possession," Bonn writes, "during a prison interview with the FBI in 1979. He reportedly said that he had invented the Son of Sam stories so that if he ever got caught he could plead insanity in court. The FBI claims that Berkowitz told them the real reason he killed was because he felt resentment toward his mother and other women who had rejected him. However, Berkowitz told me that the FBI's version of their 1979 encounter is inaccurate. Berkowitz maintains that at the time of the murders he believed he was being ordered to kill by Satan."

During the mid-1990s, Berkowitz amended his confession to claim that he had been a member of a violent satanic cult which orchestrated the incidents as ritual murder. A few law enforcement authorities have considered that his claim might be credible, but he remains the only person charged with the shootings. A new investigation of the murders began in 1996, but was suspended indefinitely after inconclusive findings.

Berkowitz became a born-again Christian after ten years in prison and today expresses a deep remorse for his crimes, as well as professing to being devoted to helping others and serving God from prison. While it is obvious that present day psychiatry would declare his "demons" to be a form of schizophrenic madness as opposed to a real and very evil spiritual presence, the question of what really drove Berkowitz to become a serial killer remains unanswered.

THE PITCHFORK MURDER

Was Berkowitz really a member of a secret satanic cult? Did the other members deserve to share his guilt? Murderous secret societies may be more commonplace than one might expect.

The prolific paranormal researcher and author, Nick Redfern, in his 2017 book **"Secret Societies: The Complete Guide to Histories, Rites and Rituals,"** discusses a still unsolved murder in rural England. It was a February day in 1945, and the killing bore all the hallmarks of death at the hands of a secret society. Some suggested a band of witches were the culprits and others said a secret sect of Druids.

"The victim was a farmworker," Redfern writes, "seventy-four-year-old Charles Walton, found dead with nothing less than a pitchfork sticking out of his chest. He was a resident of a small, picturesque village in Warwickshire, England, called Lower Quinton. Walton had lived in the village all his life, in a pleasant old cottage that stood across from the local church. It was a scene not unlike what one might expect to see on 'Downton Abbey' or in the pages of a Jane Austen novel. Until, that is, murder, mayhem and a secret cult came to Lower Quinton."

Walton was an affable but quiet person, and no one in the village had any sort of grudge against him, as much as it is possible to know. Intriguingly, he had the ability to entice wild birds to eat seeds from his hands and had the power to reduce a wild, aggressive dog to a man's best friend simply by talking to it. He was also an expert on local folklore and legend.

"Rumors suggest that perhaps Walton's uncanny powers had ensured him a place in a secret witchcraft cult," Redfern writes, "one that he ultimately fell out of favor with, and, as a result, paid the ultimate price – his life. What is known for sure is that on the day in question – the evening before Valentine's Day, no less –

Knife-Wielding Demons and Murderous Ghosts

Walton was busily trimming hedges on what was known as Hillground, a large field at the foot of the Meon Hill. His tools were a hook and a pitchfork.

"It was while he was working on the hedges," Redfern continues, "that someone stealthily intervened and took Walton's life – and in savage fashion. When his body was discovered by a shocked local, all hell broke loose in the small village. He was lying dead on the grassy ground, with the pitchfork pinning him to the ground, and the hook having pierced his throat in savage and violent fashion. On top of that, a large cross had been cut into his chest."

It should be noted that the Meon Hill area has for centuries been associated with supernatural activity, such as sightings of blazing-eyed black dogs – not unlike the terrible beast in Sir Arthur Conan Doyle's **"The Hound of the Baskervilles."** Satan himself is said to have kicked a large rock from the top of the hill to the bottom of it, with the intention of flattening Eveshame Abbey.

Such was the strange and sinister nature of Walton's death that the investigation wasn't left to just the local police. Scotland Yard stepped in and took over the investigation. The matter was never resolved to the satisfaction of the police and the mystery remained a mystery.

What occult forces were behind the pitchfork murder of Charles Walton?

Scotland Yard Detective Inspector Robert Fabian later said of his investigation: "One of my most memorable murder cases was at the village of Lower Quinton, near the stone Druid circle of the Whispering Knights. There a man had been killed by a reproduction of Druidical ceremony on St. Valentine's Eve.

"I advise anybody," Fabian added, "who is tempted at any time to venture into black magic, witchcraft, Shamanism – call it what you will – to remember Charles Walton, and to think of his death, which was clearly the ghastly climax of a pagan rite. There is no stronger argument for keeping as far away as possible from the villains with their swords, incense and mumbo-jumbo. It is prudence on which your future peace of mind and even your life could depend."

Even after many decades, the village folk are reluctant to speak about the murder. Tony Smith, the landlord of the village's College Arms pub, told the BBC, "I can't talk to you about that. After 17 years of running this place, I know there are some things we don't talk about. Talking about it would upset people, and there's no sense in alienating people in a small village like this. There are no relatives of Charles Walton left in the village and people that might have known what happened are all dead and gone."

A similar testimony came from a Mrs. Wakelon, who ran the village store and was equally reluctant to say much to the BBC.

"People don't talk about it," she said. "It's a closed subject. Those that know about it are gone, except one who's in hospital and another that's in a nursing home. All the others have gone or passed away."

Redfern concludes this section of "Secret Societies" with this summation: "Death by pitchfork, rumors of a witchcraft cult, and a village still living in uneasy and closed-mouth fashion: the memories of the murder of Charles Walton show no signs of fading away anytime soon."

WHEN EVIL BOLDLY INTRUDES

In a book called "***Demons, the Devil and Fallen Angels***," by Marie D. Jones and Larry Flaxman, some case histories are included in which an evil presence boldly intrudes into the homes of its prey.

There is the case of Pennie Brown, who says, "One night, when my eldest son was three months old, a tall, dark, black entity appeared in my house. I was in the living room with my son; it was about midnight and my husband was working the night shift."

Pennie says that she is no stranger to apparitions, having seen them all her life.

"But this one," she goes on, "was dark, blacker than black, and I got the distinct feeling it wanted my son."

She grabbed her son and ran into the bedroom, but the spirit came right through the door behind them.

"I really don't know if it was 'demonic,'" Pennie says, "but I knew in my heart it was 'death,' and it was wanting my baby. It kept floating to the ceiling and then back down again, moving from one side of the bed to the other and around the foot of the bed. I battled this tall dark shadow all night."

Finally, around 5 A.M., the spirit went through the wall and disappeared. She continued to sit holding her son for several hours, afraid the entity would return. To her relief, it did not give a repeat performance.

"I know it is tough for some people to believe in the paranormal," Pennie says, "but these things really do happen. I know firsthand. I don't know what this was; if it had or has a job to do that we can't fully understand or if it is something dark and evil. I pray it is not the latter.

Jacqui Codaro also shared her story with Jones and Flaxman. It all started for Jacqui when her father married her stepmother.

"From the moment she entered our lives until the day I moved away," Jacqui says, "there were unexplainable events. Everywhere we moved, any house we lived in, there was always a negative presence that followed."

The stepmother said she had experimented with spells and played with an Ouija board until she became possessed. She claimed to have undergone an exorcism, but it could be easy for her to be repossessed if she wasn't careful. The stepmother turned to religion to escape, attending church and reading her Bible continually.

"The more she clung to religion," Jacqui says, "the worse the incidences became."

In one particular house, shortly after the birth of Jacqui's brother, the activity escalated.

"The environment was heavy, negative and volatile," she says. "There was a constant presence that made everyone apprehensive; a feeling of being watched and not alone. We could hear walking throughout the house, as well as growling coming from nowhere. Our dog, Biscuit, died the first week we moved in, so we knew it was not him.

"My stepmother received many slaps and scratches," Jacqui continues. "One time, at dinner, she yelled. We saw three long scratches appear on her arm, as well as a handprint. Until that moment, we believed she self-inflicted the injuries. But to see it happen right before your eyes, without reasonable explanation, makes one reevaluate. We were horrified."

The stepmother's mental health deteriorated as she continued to be plagued by negative forces until she died in a house fire in 2012.

Jones and Flaxman also recount the tale of a ghost hunter named Jason Mansfield, who said that when visiting haunted locations, nothing really frightening would ever happen, even when he tried to summon entities out into the open.

"I got cocky," Jason says. "I got bold. I got challenging."

The psychic member of his ghost hunting team told him that a spirit had attached itself to Jason, but he "blew if off as BS." Then he began to suffer alarming symptoms.

"My moods got worse," Jason says. "My pain doubled. I became bitter, angry, almost to the point of violence, but I seemed to hold my ground and it was only verbal abuse, thank God. Visions of death, killing, silencing dumb asses filled my head. The weight of the world was on my shoulders and there were money issues."

On top of all that, Jason says he suffered a heart attack and literally died.

"I lay on a table for three hours," he says, "with no heartbeat, only a machine putting oxygen in my blood – and poorly at that. When I awoke, that weight was lifted. I no longer scoff at true paranormal dimensional shifting. Nothing is attached to me. I no longer fear death. I fear humanity.

"Was this something demonic that attached to me? I never saw its ugly face, only to once look in a mirror and freak out as the reflection was not of my own face. I thought someone was in the room and my face wasn't my face.

Whether it was demonic is a matter of interpretation, I guess. But I'll not let my guard down again, that's for sure."

The intruding spirits don't always carry out physical attacks or inflict real-world bodily injury. Many times their impact is felt in psychological or emotional terms. From David Berkowitz, who claimed to be led to kill by voices in his head, to the case of Jason Mansfield, who was nearly driven to violence by an evil spirit that had attached itself to him, there is some kind of negative spirit with the ability to cloud a person's rational thinking and implant the urge to murder somewhere deep in their victim's psyche.

If you are ever around Scotland's Crathes Castle, keep a watchful eye out for the Green Lady.

SUGGESTED READING

SECRET SOCIETIES: THE COMPLETE GUIDE TO HISTORIES, RITES AND RITUALS By Nick Redfern

THE *BELL WITCH PROJECT: POLTERGEIST, GHOSTS, EXORCISMS AND THE SUPERNATURAL IN AMERICAN HISTORY*

By Tim Beckley, Sean Casteel (and other contributors)

HOUNDS OF THE BASKERVILLES: FROM DEMON DOGS TO SHERLOCK HOLMES, THE TRUE STORY OF THE BEAST

THE OCCULT, WITCHCRAFT AND THE DEVIL'S FEAST IN OLD MOTHER RUSSIA

Knife-Wielding Demons and Murderous Ghosts

The Patasola is a female spirit that inhabits mountain ranges and virgin forests. At night, she appears as a beautiful woman to lure men to their death. She then uses her fangs to suck the blood from her victims. La Patasola is believed to possess only one leg, which terminates in a cloven-hoof.

Knife-Wielding Demons and Murderous Ghosts

TERROR-FILLED NIGHTS AND DISTURBING DAYS
By Adele Casales Rocha

EDITOR'S NOTE: Have you ever heard a voice calling your name in the middle of the night? Or seen a misty figure following you down a dark street? Almost everyone at some point in their lives has had a "paranormal" moment. Skeptics tend to dismiss these experiences as hoaxes or mistakes of perception...yet, who can tell? Our mainstream scientific understanding of human consciousness is by no means complete. There is still no consensus among researchers about what embodies "normal" and "abnormal" or "altered" states of consciousness. We might as well say that the paranormal exists as an intangible world that interacts with us.

Recently, on "Exploring the Bizarre" (KCOR Radio), our guest was Adele Casales Rocha, who agreed to appear with us to discuss her new book "***Portal: A Lifetime of Paranormal Experiences***," a compilation of eyewitness accounts and her own personal encounters with the unknown and terrifying. The material in this chapter is excerpted from Maria's book and those on the net can find the actual interview on our YouTube channel, "Mr. UFO's Secret Files," by going to the episode, "Evil Lurks In The Shadows"

www.youtube.com/watch?v=xYYUlqTY_M0&t=377s

Adele Casales Rocha has traveled extensively, visiting over 26 countries, and has compiled accounts of terrifying and uncanny experiences in both her native country of the Philippines and abroad.

Adele starred as "Elisa Simon" in episode two of the pilot, "*UFOs Over Earth*" while she was a field investigator for MUFON. Her personal experiences with the bizarre have led to a lifetime quest of investigating sightings and paranormal events through eyewitness reports.

Adele is also a screenwriter of science fiction and horror with over 11 screenplays which have placed in competitions in the United States. She has adapted for the screen books by Philip Mantle and Paul Stonehill, who are prominent investigators and authors in the field of UFOlogy.

Adele has been a guest on "UFO Topic," with Rick Scouler, "Arcane Radio," with Lon Strickler, "Paranormal UK Radio," with Chris Evers, "Night Dreams Talk Radio," with Gary Anderson.

Adele Casales Rocha is a trained therapist and amateur travel photographer. She can be reached by email at Cinegravitas@Yahoo.com.

www.StoryArtisan.wordpress.com

www.ImagesOnFilm.500px.com

* * * * * * * * *

THE HORROR OF LITTLE BAGUIO

From the book "*Portal: A Lifetime of Paranormal Experiences*,"
By Adele Casales Rocha

In the summer of 1959, a woman named Neala, a captivating young coed, married her college sweetheart, Ernest. The couple, both bent on careers in writing, settled in Little Baguio, a hamlet in the suburb of San Juan in the Philippines. They chose to rent in a newly-built townhouse complex perched at the edge of a creek. Neala had a degree in journalism and so did Ernest, but he sought a career as a freelance writer.

Both sides of the family disagreed with the marriage as Ernest was a sensitive young man who had suffered bouts of depression and Neala, his total opposite, was strong-willed, outspoken and wanted her way even as a young child. It was to be a new life for the young couple, just shy of a few months after college graduation. Young and idealistic, the new marriage was still in its first months when Neala learned she was with child.

The complex's first tenants were new families on both sides of Neala and Ernest's townhouse. As with the others, their unit was large, with a living room and TV room area spanning the entire front facing the common driveway. The back was the kitchen and dining room. A large window which spanned the kitchen and dining rooms in the back gave a view of the trees lining the creek just yards away. Sunlight filtered in through the trees and into the kitchen and dining area during the day. A view of the creek showed residences across the water which flowed clean and clear. The window was almost as high as the ceiling and as wide as the size of the wall. The large windows were the same size on the second floor, which spanned the breadth of the three bedrooms which sat side by side at the back of the townhouse. The proximity and size of these massive windows let in air and sunlight and will be important to remember later on.

Between the kitchen and dining area was a staircase underneath which the live-in maid slept. The stairs led up to the three bedrooms and a bath and closet opposite the hall. The center bedroom was the new nursery, right at the top of the stairs. To the right of the stairs was the first bedroom, which was used as Ernest's study where he did his writing. The last bedroom was the master bedroom.

In the early 1960s it was common for grown female children to live in or near their parents' home, until they married. Little Baguio was a mere 3-4 blocks from Neala's parental house. So convenient was the living arrangement that, despite a live-in maid, Neala still sought to arrange to have food delivered to the townhouse from her mother's house in San Juan. Still lovingly prepared by Adelaida her mother, dinner came with fresh rice, three main courses and the requisite medley of desserts now prepared by older sister Sonya, who was a home economics teacher at a local high school situated an hour away.

There are several haunted properties in Little Baguio. Guests are allowed to explore in this particular house, including this haunted staircase.

Knife-Wielding Demons and Murderous Ghosts

Neala spent most of her days with her infant, shopping with her friends and visiting with her sisters. However, this idyllic lifestyle was not to last; as the year drew to a close, the schism between Ernest and Neala became more pronounced – from child-rearing to finances, to time divided between in-laws. As Ernest's parents continued to lavish support for his writing and encourage him to visit an older brother's thriving bookstore, Ernest sank deeper into a depression. It was a depression made deeper by a force which appeared in the midst of the couple's growing discontent with each other.

In the early evening twilight, Ernest started reporting of a creature which he claimed "wanted to take his soul." It would manifest itself at the large window which spanned the breadth of the three bedrooms upstairs, once the sun began to set.

At the crib next door, Lisa, the couple's infant, was reportedly sensitive to the appearance of the creature, crying and screaming to herald its appearance. The nursery window connected to the window just next door – Ernest's office and den. The maid would anxiously check the infant's welfare and would dash upstairs as soon as she heard the child's cry. But as soon as she appeared at the door, the being would disappear – or so it's reported.

Neala, forever skeptical due to Ernest's history of depression, dismissed his growing fears. Ernest grew despondent and as the night progressed and the months moved to the rainy season, she found that he rarely slept. Neala addressed her concerns with her in-laws and Ernest's father, a bank executive, stepped in.

In the 60s, the advent of psychiatry came to the Philippines in the form of talk therapy, antidepressants and shock therapy. The mode of treatment at that time was invariably electroshock therapy, as medication was still novel and in development. Despite the psychiatrist and psychologist's "talk" to dissuade Ernest of his self-reports of this "creature", Ernest persisted in his accounts of the creature's visits.

The specialists, unable to relate to the paranormal nature of the case as they were trained in the manner of science, dismissed it as hallucination and the electroshock therapy began. Furthermore, they could not find anyone to corroborate Ernest's sightings, except his infant daughter Lisa, who, too young to speak, exuded terror at the creature's manifestation at the window.

www.girlchasingsunshine.com will be happy to take you on a haunted tour of Little Baguio.

Back at the town home, the creature's continued presence almost every twilight consumed Ernest's waking hours. His apprehensions of being "taken" by the creature, body and soul, started to show in his poetry. His poems, which were an outlet for his internal turmoil, turned even darker, drearier and more foreboding. His siblings, who read his opus, became concerned and from concern, became alarmed when he wrote one poem which began as "The bird that flies is false." Themes of death became prominent.

Ernest had a total of ten siblings of which he was in the middle. Among them were two sisters who approached Neala to intervene, as well as a brother who was close to Ernest as children and a younger brother who had looked up to him.

As Ernest's brothers and sisters attempted to seek evidence of the creature's existence, Neala responded by reluctantly reaching out to her mother. Unsure of what to do, her mother contacted Roberto, the patriarch and doctor in the family who had abandoned his wife and their growing children years before.

Neala's sense of betrayal by her father became complete: Roberto refused to intervene in the small family's growing problems and referred Ernest's issues back to his own parents. The rift between father and daughter would soon reveal itself again when Neala rejoined her family in the San Juan home a year later.

Knife-Wielding Demons and Murderous Ghosts

It was not long that the infant's cries which heralded the creature's appearance would save Ernest and win his credibility. One evening, as dinner was being prepared in the kitchen, Lisa, now a toddler, began her earnest screams of terror. Again, her cries brought the maid running up the stairs. But this time, she would reach Lisa at her crib in time to see the visitor outside the window.

Embracing the window, with a wingspan of more than 6 feet from tip to tip, was a bat taller than a man. Its leathery wings ended in a talon-like grasp at the edges of the window. Its yellow eyes were like a cow's, the semblance of horns protruded from its black head and it had a goatee at the end of its pointed chin. The face of a goat with the eyes of a cow – and a leathery body framed by the wings of a bat. The creature was glaring down at the toddler, who was poised to leap from the crib in abject terror.

The young maid, riveted to the eyes at the window, reached for the baby as she reached out to her with her tiny hands. Holding the terrified child, the maid bolted out of the nursery, sobbing in horror. The young maid's wails brought Neala to the room and for the first time, she beheld the massive being at the window. Neala described it as the devil himself. Emboldened to protect her baby and subdue the malevolence at the window, Neala reached for a large cross on an adjacent wall and dashed to the window with the cross in both hands. The being "folded" and effervesced from the window. It seemed, according to Neala, to cover its terrifying face with one wing as it drifted down and disappeared. Throughout the entire event, frogs, cicadas and the sounds of the night had completely silenced, only to be replaced by a "humming" sound.

As soon as the being disappeared, the sounds returned. Neala dashed outside and to the creek outside the window. There was nothing there. Sounds of rushing water and the chorus of frogs beheld her. The tree, where Ernest reported the creature would appear, stood silent and foreboding. There was no trace of animal prints or bat dung.

Back in San Juan, Neala's mother Adelaida did not know how to address the terrifying events that seem to be escalating in the townhome in Little Baguio. A devout Roman Catholic, she sought relief in the church and always hoped for an answer to every prayer request. She knew from her other children and the servant who delivered the prepared meals that Neala was on her way to tell her the events of the night before. Already convinced there was some type of paranormal infestation in the little home based on her own experiences, she believed it was only a matter of time before the hauntings progressed – and she did not know what to do.

Adelaida knew her daughter was not a staunch Catholic, so when talk of the monstrosity at Little Baguio had reached her, she had concerns about whether prayer and blessings would work, as Neala had a rebellious streak and did not welcome any input from her own mother. However, she was concerned for her first grandchild, a toddler that was now helpless to escape what Adelaida saw as an environment with a malevolent presence.

Neala might rebuff Adelaida's efforts to bring a priest to the home to perform a cleansing rite. Among the siblings, Neala rarely attended mass with the family, unlike the younger sisters who joined their mother at the local church every Sunday. In light of the past several months, Adelaida knew she had some persuading to do and may need the help of others. An optimist by nature, Adelaida however took a step back and saw the unfolding events as a possible way to get her daughter back to the church.

To Adelaida's surprise, Neala appeared, though it was minutes after the mass began. Adelaida hailed a taxi and Neala willingly accompanied her mother to the church just minutes away. There, Adelaida hoped the priest would have a solution, now that her daughter appeared receptive to intervention. It was a private matter with some urgency and she knew the respected parish priest would honor confidentiality, sensitive to their prominence in the community. Melissa, a younger sibling, was fortunately home for a visit and stayed to babysit Lisa.

There are many who believe that a crucifix or cross can fight off a demon.

Knife-Wielding Demons and Murderous Ghosts

Meanwhile, alone in the house with Ernesto, the maid sat alone in the kitchen, cleaning after the breakfast meal. She glanced up the ceiling above her with trepidation. Charged with staying in the house to watch Ernest and report anything unusual, the maid was ready to tender her resignation despite the financial needs of her own family in the far-off province of Leyte. Terrified of the being she encountered at the window the night before, she clutched a rosary and avoided looking out the window. She decided that if Neala didn't return by nightfall, she would call her sister and persuade her to keep her company until her return, or even perhaps step out briefly for some dinner. What could possibly happen in the few hours while she ate at a local restaurant nearby?

At the church, the parish priest eyed the two beautiful women. Their features betrayed their Spanish blood of Castilian origin, which made them stand out both in appearance and height from the rest of the congregation. He led them into the rectory as soon as the last parishioner had exited the vestibule, sensing the urgency of their visit. He recalled having met Neala once before when he conducted the wedding ceremony, but not since then.

He offered his condolences, then his intervention.

"I can come to bless the house."

"When can you do it, Father?"

"Next week?"

Adelaida glanced at her daughter with trepidation.

"It's Friday. We don't know if it can wait the weekend."

The priest frowned and looked at his appointment book.

"I have a few weddings this weekend. Monday?"

Neala stepped in. "Is that ALL you can do?!"

Taken aback by her vehemence, the priest turned to Adelaida for support.

Adelaida signaled her daughter to calm down and reluctantly agreed to wait the two days. She turned to her daughter as the priest left.

"Let's pray and light a candle on the way out."

Neala whispered en route to the side altar.

"Mama, I will make sure he's not alone over the weekend."

"Daughter, make SURE neither he nor the baby are alone."

Shadowy figures stalked the home of the author. Where do they come from? What do they want?

As the day grew old, the maid grew weary of her vigil. She reached for the phone in its cradle and called her sister. Upstairs, Ernest typed on his Smith-Corona, venting page after page a sordid composition of the being at the window, an oppressor which became an obsession.

He was nodding off, exhausted, but unable to allow himself to sleep. Still, the medication the most recent physician gave him would not allow him to sit. Finally giving in, he stood and retired to the master bedroom on the other end of the hall, passing the main bath on the way. He drew the curtains, closing off the only light in the room. His action, a feeble attempt at shutting out whatever may show at the window should he awaken at sundown.

A few blocks away, Neala, eager to get out of the dreary townhouse and the foreboding atmosphere, decided to take advantage of Melissa's visit to babysit. She departed the Lourdes Drive house in the company of older sister Sonya to shop downtown. Stores and boutiques in Manila and the suburbs were usually open late, sometimes until 10 p.m. It was also not unusual for people to dine as late as 9 p.m. At San Juan, Adelaida went about her daily business of running the large household and preparing for the weekend. It was an active household, as the younger children, boys now in their teens, brought friends to the house frequently, so Adelaida was policing their activities as the week drew to a close.

Night approached. A few hours earlier, the maid had ventured out of the townhouse to meet her sister at the bus stop to see a film downtown and have dinner. It was, after all, calm and uneventful. At approximately eight o'clock, Neala and oldest sister Sonya, now heavy with shopping bags, returned to San Juan. They were ready and eager to have dinner with their mother and siblings as well as to check on Lisa, her infant daughter. The weekend had begun and they were ready to attend some parties and had purchased some new dresses, the latest in fashion. After the shopping bags were divided up, the two sisters separated, Neala to pick up Ernest with the chauffeur so he could join them for dinner at her mother's house. The rest settled down at the parlor to catch up on the day's events with their mother and siblings while dinner was being prepared.

A few blocks away at Little Baguio, the lonely and dark townhouse had one sole occupant. Ernest awakened to a humming sound and a sense of menace. Growing fearful of being alone in the evening, he shot up from the bed and made for the hallway, yelling out the maid's name.

Ernest walked down the steps, turning the lights on in the kitchen and living room. Years later, his siblings and those who had visited always remarked how every room in the house was always lit which told them he was home. Tonight was no exception. As he walked, he pulled the curtains together to shield his sight from whatever could be at the window. Despondent, anxious and without appetite, he turned on the upstairs hall light and proceeded back up the steps in trepidation. Outside the baby's room, he paused and then entered to pull the curtains together. The hum had intensified, obliterating all other noises of the night.

He reentered his office. As he reached to close the window curtains, the tree outside the window seemed to come to life. His eyes opened wide as he backed away from the window. The humming increased.

Neala's watch on her slim wrist showed 8:30 p.m. The car slowed as she reached for her purse and to open the passenger rear door. The chauffeur sped away after leaving the shopping bags at the open gate of the compound. Neala made her way into the townhouse's front door, knocked and frowned when no one opened.

She unlocked the door with her key and sensed a complete feeling of isolation and menace. As she surveyed the dark living room, she realized to her consternation that the maid did not heed her direction to remain home while she was out. Neala switched the lights on, feeling a drop in temperature as she entered the home.

Knife-Wielding Demons and Murderous Ghosts

Up the stairs, Neala started yelling Ernest's name. No reply. As she ascended, the temperature, which would normally go up a few degrees on the second floor, plummeted even lower. She shivered with apprehension, having been raised in a haunted house. Since there was no air conditioning in the house, the chill in the air was unusual.

In the corner of her eye she spotted a foot within the open door of the bathroom. She stopped in her tracks and screamed. The maid had just returned and looked over Neala's shoulder to see the abattoir in the bathroom. She turned and bolted from the hall.

Roberto Junior, the fifth child from the oldest, poked his head out of the second floor window of the San Juan house upon seeing Neala's maid, white with fright and running down the street. He was by the window overlooking the street perusing "Katzenjammer Kids" comic books he had stashed in his father's army trunk, planning on a late, but quiet Friday night of fun reading after dinner. The teen sensed something very wrong as he saw her running and yelled "Mama" for Adelaida, who was downstairs in the family room waiting for the rest to sit down to dinner. Adelaida was watching a film after Melissa joined her, having placed the sleeping infant in the crib nearby.

Adelaida's youngest son Jose, still up, met up with the maid who was inconsolable and appeared terrified. Anxious to make out the facts amidst the maid's hysterical babbling, Adelaida sent Jose to run on foot to the home in Little Baguio as Roberto went to call his father. Adelaida was glad she had sent Neala home alone after both the maid and Ernest failed to answer the phone. She had a sinking feeling it was not the best time to send an infant home with her mother to a house that was infested.

Gifted with a sense of precognition, Adelaida knew in the depth of her heart that they needed a medical doctor, even if it meant fetching her estranged husband. It was to be one of the most traumatic events in Neala's life.

Dr. Alameda arrived shortly at the townhome, meeting with an ambulance crew who took Ernest from the home after Roberto pronounced his son-in-law dead. His sons, Jose and Roberto "Bobby" Jr., touched Ernest in disbelief, finding him already in rigor mortis. Ernest had given in to the malevolence at the window, freeing his spirit from torment by slashing his wrists.

He was only 24 years old.

Author Adele Casales Rocha

SUGGESTED READING BY ADELE CASALES ROCHA

www.StoryArtisan.wordpress.com
www.ImagesOnFilm.500px.com
www.twenty20.com/annamariaelisa.manalo
CineGravitas@yahoo.com

Adele Casales Rocha's book, "*Portal: A Lifetime of Paranormal Experiences*," shares stories from witnesses from all walks of life in the Philippines and their encounters with the unknown.

Original Art © Carol Ann Rodriguez

THE "EVIL WITCH" OF HAMPTON BEACH — GOODY COLE, NEW HAMPSHIRE'S TROUBLING POLTERGEIST
By Maria D'Andrea with Carol Ann Rodriguez

The billowing wind brought in salty brine as the sky began to cloud over and the waves offshore churned a bit higher and rougher. The heavens suddenly appeared very ominous; glowering over what a short while ago had been a bright, sunny afternoon in this beachside New England resort.

Not wanting to resort to pure melodrama, we are reluctant to mention that we heard the distinct clanging of the captain's bell perched on a pedestal nearby – though there was no one actually there ringing it. The heavy iron bell was "simply" reverberating of its own accord. The wind? Well, we would most likely have to assume so. Although we couldn't help but recall the many superstitions said to be associated with the sounding of bells at sea, which, for many who live their existences on the waterfront, often foretells a death. The ringing of a wine glass was such a sound, and had to be stopped before its reverberation ended. Ship's bells were exempted from this superstition, because they signaled time and the changing of watch duties. But if they rang of their own accord, as in an approaching storm, somebody was most likely going to meet an untimely fate.

We began to shiver. Not so much from this thought, perhaps, but from the misty spray that was beginning to pelt our faces as we passed along a block of side streets just off the boardwalk.

Perhaps it had something to do with the fact that both Tim and I fully realized that New England has its roots in the occult and the supernatural. The infamous Salem witch trials and subsequent hangings on gallows row still throw a murky shadow over America's colonial history.

Now I know that opinions vary and that most readers will already know what we are talking about, but for purposes of simplification let's start with a shortcut version of what a ghost is and what a poltergeist is most often thought of as being. To be clinical, there are various types of ghosts and spirits. Some are our loved ones or friends and these would be of a positive virtue. But we still need to account for the sinister spooks.

A ghost is a disembodied soul residing on the etheric plane. Of course, there are positive, helpful ghosts, such as those that give a warning of danger or aid us in various situations, like with finding lost objects or even a hidden treasure. However, those are not the ones we are talking about at the moment.

Sometimes ghosts are baffled about where they are or not aware that they are not in a physical body any longer. Some ghosts tend to haunt the place where they died; they are confused or recreating a situation that befell them in their lives. They may be grounded by intense emotions from when they passed on, dazed and puzzled, or they may be angry. These ghosts can be attached to an object, such as a favorite couch or a location that has some form of meaning to them. They can even be attracted to individuals or entire families, following them around from place to place (sort of a mobile haunting).

A poltergeist is one specific type of ghost or entity. Poltergeist is a German word meaning a "noisy, mischievous spirit" and for a good reason: They often partake in harmful acts and pranks. They display their presence by moving physical objects in a manner that defies gravity to let it be known that they are in the house. They can be perceived by some psychics clairvoyantly, clairaudiently or simply by clairsentience (knowing).

This leads us into the story of our experience in New Hampshire.

GOODY COLE, THE EVIL WITCH OF NEW HAMPSHIRE

My friend and publisher, Tim Beckley, and I set out on one of our many journeys together. We love to delve into the unexplained and the unknown. Our travels took us to Hampton Beach, a town that is directly on the shore. Tim had heard about the witch Goody Cole, and we were determined to see if we could connect with her. As we are all well aware, ghosts can be unpredictable.

The story we heard was about a 17th century woman named Eunice Goody Cole. Before we went to Goody's neighborhood, we made inquiries about this infamous figure. Tim and I were surprised that some of the people we spoke with didn't know much about their local witch. There are a few versions of the legend of Goody Cole, but eventually we settled upon one for the sake of our sanity.

Knife-Wielding Demons and Murderous Ghosts

The name "Goody" was considered short for the word "Goodwife," which at that time was a common term for the poorer wives in towns. It is obvious that we have already been handed a stereotype to deal with.

She was said to have married William Coules outside of London, England, around 1635. They sailed to America to have a better life and eventually ended up living in Hampton, where William was granted some land.

As soon as they arrived, their problems began with the neighbors and the magistrates. They didn't fit the mold of what was expected from a respectable young couple. They set their own rules, so they were in and out of court frequently. It was said that she was argumentative and annoying in several ways to the neighbors. I would think it was never a good move to act like that at a time when a strongly-held belief in witches prevailed. The belief in devil worshiping witches was carried over to the New World from England, where it was still a firm belief of many.

Goody's disagreeable nature antagonized everyone in the town and finally culminated in her being called names and attacked by the bigoted townsfolk who hit her with sharp-edged sticks. They blamed her for several deaths and community crises, all of which bolstered their allegations that she was a witch.

It is said that her husband tried to curtail her habits but that she took no heed. Her husband died and she became a shrew in the locals' eyes, giving the community more power to persecute the widow. She ended up in court for her perceived "attitude" and was physically punished and even whipped. She landed in jail several times, becoming increasing demented because of her ill treatment.

In her first trial there were 26 witnesses against her. They claimed, among other charges, that she was a miscreant and unruly. A further accusation involved "witch markings" being found on her body as she was being flogged. At this point, she was branded a full-fledged disciple of Lucifer.

The magistrates took her home and land, confiscating it under the guise of "justice" and "orthodox religion."

She was said to frequently stand gazing out at the water as if in a dark, brooding trance. They said she was furious at the town and, as a ship with many onboard sailed by, she had conjured watery demons and cursed the vessel. This caused a storm to come up and the boat sank into the depth of the waters. All the people onboard went to a watery grave screaming to be saved, but no one survived. Goody had reached the pinnacle of her bewitchment when the shipwreck was blamed on her.

At her death in 1680, the townspeople put a stake into the ground on her grave and some say they even added a horseshoe, a Pow Wow's symbol, to stabilize the curse.

Apparently, this symbolic ritual hasn't worked too well as she continues to be seen and to torment the community to this day.

THE APPARITION

Tim and I were at the Ashworth Hotel in Hampton Beach dining with our friend Sandra when we were told of the whereabouts of Goody's apparition on a nearby street. Goody was said to have lived in a house at the end of what is today a dead end street.

We have been ghost hunting, among other things, for so many years, it is second nature to us. We decided to go and have a look the very next day.

After locating the correct street, Tim got ready to write his notes and I tuned into the ethereal plane before we embarked on our walk toward the site. You can never be sure if you will connect with a spirit because it's not going to let you know its whereabouts in advance.

We were told that Goody was somewhere in that area. It was a nice, long, friendly looking street which ended at the last house. There was a large open field across from the last few homes. This was just one of the several locations where Goody was seen on this particular street.

As we were getting closer to the open field on the other side of the street, I started to feel an energy shift. There isn't any other way to describe the feeling that I was being overcome by.

I focused on calling Goody to come and let me connect to her. (I always do a method of psychic self-defense for protection before going into ghostly "battle.") As we walked closer to the field, from a little distance I saw Goody. I saw her at a younger age than when she died. She came in as if you were looking at a wispy grayish white tornado slowly building into her form.

She wasn't angry; she felt sad. It felt as though she was standing around where her home had once been. I felt from her that, in her lifetime, she was very much in love with her husband and sad about his dying before her. She felt to me as though she was simply thinking for herself and had strong opinions. To me she seemed like an independent thinker. She didn't feel confused; it was more that she was curious and didn't understand why people didn't accept her for who she was.

I asked if she'd like to move on. She wasn't ready to leave and chose to stay for now. She started to disappear and so we thanked her and said goodbye. It was really a sad feeling leaving as she dematerialized.

While we were on the street where she had once resided, we ran into people who lived there now and Tim and I asked them what they thought about Goody.

One gentleman had never heard of the story. Another older gentleman said that, as a child, he would hear noises and banging that others in the house didn't hear. The clamoring would stop when anyone else came into the room. The sounds didn't scare him, but he just didn't understand what was going on. As he grew up, he stopped hearing the noises in his house and hasn't heard anything since.

Another young gentleman lived right down the street from the field and didn't know about Goody either. We simply asked if he had any unusual experiences to report while living on his street. We said we were doing research and just picking people randomly. He told us that where he lived currently he would hear loud noises and had noticed that objects would move about the room and things would be flung around. Definite Poltergeist activity! He said he would sometimes pull the covers over his head because he thought this would make the commotion stop. Wrong!

He said he never told anybody about his experiences because he thought they would make fun of him and would think he was easily scared. He said that to this day, he doesn't like to go upstairs and still has an apprehensive feeling about that part of the house. He then asked us what made us ask him about unusual things happening. We then told him about Goody the witch and her incredible haunting. He repeated that he was not familiar with her apparition, but was happy that now at least he knew what the cause of the phenomena in his house was related to and it gave him a sense of peace and closure. However, he said that didn't mean he wanted to go upstairs. He did show a sense of humor about the ordeal. Sometimes you meet certain people for a reason. You can't make this stuff up.

Knife-Wielding Demons and Murderous Ghosts

The notorious Goody Cole tempts children with her spellbinding rituals.

Eunice Cole, maiden name unknown, was a woman from the coast of New Hampshire. Better known as "Goody Cole," she is the only woman convicted of witchcraft in New Hampshire.

Though no one can say for certain, it is believed that this is the house where Goody Cole lived while being persecuted by the townspeople because she was supposedly a witch thought responsible for numerous curses.

Those who point to her to this day say that Witch Goody was responsible for the sinking of at least one vessel as an act of revenge against the townspeople.

THE HAUNTING

Once I was called in to check on a house for a client who was very upset about things happening in her home that gave her the impression that there was a negative spirit residing with them.

I always do my self-defense before I work. You don't know what you are walking into. Many times, there is really nothing there. But you can never be certain.

When we spoke about the situation, the lady said they bought the house about two years prior. It was relatively new, with all the updated conveniences, so you normally wouldn't think there was a ghost afoot, as you would in an older dwelling.

She said that ever since she moved in with her husband and three children, they had nothing but bad luck. Now this could be just normal luck. However she went on to say that in one of the bedrooms, it always felt cold, even in the summer or with the heat up in the winter. It always had that cold spot only in that one room. They had the house checked for drafts or any physical issues, but there weren't any to be found.

First, her daughter stayed in that room. It felt scary for some reason and she wouldn't stay there. The parents were going to give this particular bedroom to their other daughter, who didn't want it because she liked her current bedroom more.

So it ended up with her son, who was the youngest. The lady said he always had good grades in Junior High School and he was never a problem. They were very proud of his achievements. She said he completely changed after he moved into the haunted room.

He always wore a sweater or jacket while in the room because of the cold feeling. He refused to move out of the room and would get angry when it was suggested. He spent most of his time in there. They would hear him talking to someone in the room when he was alone, as if in a conversation. They heard things moving and being thrown around, even when he wasn't home. His grades declined; he became despondent; he refused to come out of his room. Meanwhile, the noises escalated. He lost his appetite and lost weight – sort of a "ghostly" diet. They were truly worried and even had a priest come in. Nothing changed.

I checked out every room, the basement and outside the house to feel what was really going on. I'm a minister but I'm also a shaman. I went into the room and felt a presence that was angry. It felt like a man who was grounded there because he was upset someone was in his house. It seemed that this new house was built on the location of an older house. When this man passed, they tore down the house to rebuild anew. He was confused, upset and extremely angry.

Once he realized he was on the etheric plane now and the people living on "his ground" meant no harm (they weren't the ones tearing down his old house), he was ready to move on. Grudgingly, but ready.

I did a banishing ritual after explaining it to him and he gradually faded from view. A year later, I heard from the lady. She was very happy. Her older daughter was getting married, and the other one was moving out in a positive, happy way. Her son was back on track in school and in his social life. It was good to hear from her. I love when people are happy.

PRANKSTERS

Sometimes poltergeists are just pranksters. While it could sometimes be uncontrolled energy emanating from a person or child, in most cases spirits are the culprits. Some prankster spirits are the manifestations of children and oftentimes teenage energies.

I've had two teenage Native American prankster poltergeists with me for about 20 or so years. The "funny" thing about it is how I got them.

I had a friend who also connected to spirits. One day, we were talking about various experiences we've had. Joe told me about how he had these two pranksters and what their names were. He said they've been with him for a long time and he was tired of dealing with them. They were positive but always playing pranks. Sometimes that could be very annoying.

Joe was going to relocate and he told me he was giving me a personal gift. You guessed it! He passed the two pranksters on to me. Now, in the shamanic way, that is very personal, special and rare. But, they ARE prankster spirits.

They will move things to a different place. They will ring the doorbell and, when I answer it, nobody is there. As soon as I close the door, the doorbell rings again. We could play with that for hours if I was willing. I am not.

Both my sons have at some point opened the door at three or four in the morning and nobody was there. As soon as they went back to bed, it would ring again. They told me that they're MY "friends" and that if the doorbell rings, they are no longer going to answer at night and it's my problem.

Knife-Wielding Demons and Murderous Ghosts

Ship at port nautical bell was said to tell of a pending death if it rang by itself.

A memorial (right) stands as tribute to those who lost their lives at sea along the New England coast.

Shaman, clairvoyant, sensitive and seasoned paranormal researcher Maria D' Andrea (left) found herself fascinated by the urban legend of the witch known as "Goody Cole."

Unfortunately, many times I've answered in the daytime, because I don't automatically think it's one or both of the pranksters. I've learned that if I tell them in a serious tone of voice to stop doing that, they will. And so, instead of ringing the doorbell, they will start knocking on the door, kind of following my instructions in an offhanded sort of way.

Sometimes they aren't around for months. Then something will move, there will be a rapping on the door, wall or ceiling. Usually they like the doorbell the best – I guess it keeps them motivated.

As you can see, there are different types of poltergeist. They can be attached to a location, an object or a person. Hauntings are from the etheric realm and cannot be explained by physical means. Many people are sensitive and can see, feel or sense past our five senses. When we are speaking normally to others, our brainwave has been scientifically tested as operating on a Beta level. When we are psychically or intuitively tuned in to the other realms, our brainwaves are on an Alpha or Theta level or fluctuate between both. It is as though you are tuning into a radio station frequency.

Remember they are real. I always say it's like electricity – you don't see it, but you don't put your hand in the socket.

In this work, we even hear about how some poltergeists are a sort of energy force from another dimension which incorporates aliens and unknown creatures in their demographics. I have experienced contact with entities from other realms and do not discount this theory, though I operate on more of a spirit-based level in my own work. My book, *"Traveling the Waves of Time"* from the *"Yes You Can!"* series will give the reader the proper footing in this direction if one so desires.

Web Site: MariaDAndrea.com

SUGGESTED READING - BOOKS BY MARIA

HEAVEN SENT MONEY SPELLS

YOU CAN TAKE IT WITH YOU

POSITIVELY POSITIVE SPELL BOOK

SIMPLE SPELLS WITH PLAYING CARDS

Knife-Wielding Demons and Murderous Ghosts

Celebrity Sammy Davis Jr. believed in UFOs and also was known to fraternize with Anton LaVey as in this photo.

Self-proclaimed Satanist Anton LaVey set up his "black house of darkness" in San Francisco circa the 1960s.

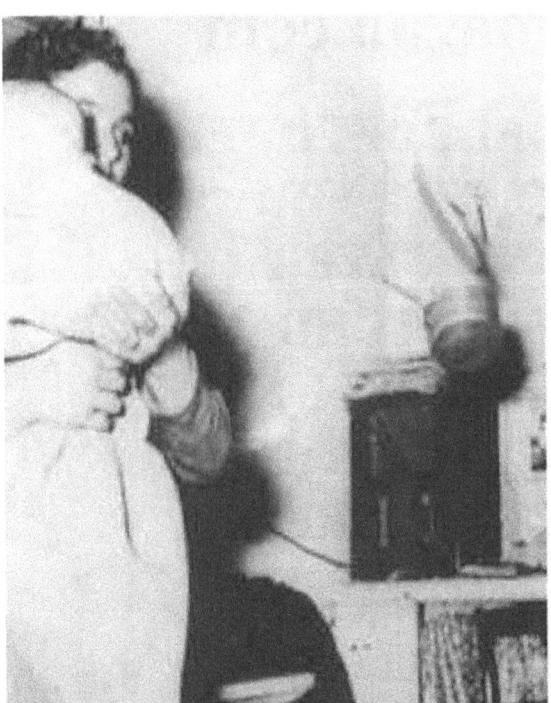

In many poltergeist cases, objects would fly across the room with no "human agents" having been responsible for throwing them around.

Parapsychologist Dr. Nandor Fodor took a more psychological approach to the poltergeist phenomena, associating it with a living, but troubled, person.

THE POLTERGEIST REVOLUTION OF THE 1960s – SO WERE THEY SMOKING WEED IN THE SPIRIT WORLD?

The 1960s were a pretty heavy duty time for poltergeists and the paranormal in general. Astrologers and "hippies" were telling us that we were entering the Age of Aquarius. Anton Lavey's Church of Satanism was considered a "hip attraction" in the Haight Ashbury section of San Francisco. His black-painted "dormitory" hosted all sorts of devilish festivities, including a nude altar girl. The Fillmore West and East were in full swing on both coasts with bands like Led Zeppelin espousing the occult philosophies of white witch Sybil Leek and Aleister Crowley, known foremost as "The Beast," I guess mostly because he liked to partake in orgies and drew pentagrams on the floor while performing mystical rituals.

Back in Manhattan, I had opened the doors to my New York School of Occult Arts and Sciences, presenting a variety of lectures and workshops on everything from out-of-body travel to learning to read the tarot cards. We had our own caster of love spells, witch Walli Emlark, who introduced me to David Bowie. But we weren't worshiping Satan, though I can't say for sure what was happening behind the sliding bookcases over at Herman Slater's Warlock Shop a few blocks away.

Genuine supernatural activity was also on the rise as "Poltergeists Just Want To Have Fun" seems to have been the order of the day. To testify to this, a number of magazines sprang up which chronicled the ongoing materializations and poundings and object throwing of whatever God-fearing spook was around. You could pick up *"Fate Magazine"* for two shiny quarters at your local mom and pop newsstand. Or, if you were a bit more "highbrow" in your psychic needs, there was always *"Tomorrow Magazine,"* which published pieces by noted parapsychologists like Dr. Nandor Fodor. Fodor held a bit more of a psychological view of the outbreak of demonic forces that were overtaking the land.

Knife-Wielding Demons and Murderous Ghosts

Hard rocking Led Zeppelin put a lot of faith in the controversial occultist Aleister Crowley, known as "the beast," presumably because of his liberal attitude on sex and drugs and worship. He is said to have conjured up a few poltergeist-like spirits during his trances.

Going through our endless files, we came across three such cases that "Tomorrow" thought were "legitimate" and worthy of scientific scrutiny.

I DON'T BELIEVE IT, BUT IT HAPPENED – CASE ONE

The year: 1960. The place: Guttenberg, Iowa. The conclusions: possible psychic events, but probably "the work of a mortal."

A tough, 265-pound ship's pilot, a scarred veteran of waterfront brawls, was all set to prove that the Guttenberg poltergeist was "a bunch of malarkey."

He changed his mind after it threw him out of bed.

"I'm a first-rate pilot; I'm no crackpot," said Pat Livingston, 38-year-old skipper of a Socony-Mobil Oil Co. tanker on the Great Lakes.

"I don't believe it, but it happened."

Reports of "mysterious disturbances" in a rambling old Iowa farmhouse attracted the attention not only of local authorities, the press and curious crowds, but of serious investigators from Northwestern University, State University of Iowa and Upper Iowa University. Translation of the term "poltergeist" into "noisy ghost" was unnecessary in this northwest Iowa hill country, Like the term itself, many of the people, including the owners of the disturbed house, are of German origin.

The disturbances themselves were not so easily translated into human terms. This was not a case of mere window rattling's or attic creaking's. This ghost, if it was a ghost, was a husky fellow, overturning a davenport, knocking over a refrigerator, tumbling that 265-pound man out of bed, in addition to smaller demonstrations.

The scene of this strenuous spooking was a northeast Iowa farm near the Mississippi river town of Guttenberg, at the end of a dead-end lane off Skip Level Road. The two-story frame farm-house, about 65 years old, is pocketed in a narrow creek valley. The hillsides rise abruptly behind the house. Stark outcroppings of sandstone punctuate the wooded, boulder-strewn terrain.

The house is owned, but no longer occupied, by Mr. and Mrs. William Meyer. The elderly couple – he's 83, she's 77 – moved last December 17th to a brother's home in Guttenberg.

"You'd have moved, too, the way things were flying around," the old man said. "And I won't go back. We've got stuff out there, but I won't go get it."

"It would frighten anybody," added Mrs. Meyer.

BLANKET OF DUST

It began last Thanksgiving Day. William Meyer, bedridden since July with a broken hip, his wife and their 16-year-old grandson, Gene Meyer, discovered that a blanket of soot or dust had fallen from ceilings or walls, although no holes or cracks existed for dust to seep through. Gene's father, Elmer, 53, came over from his house a few hundred yards away and placed an egg on a lamp chimney to test for vibration. The egg did not jiggle; the family claims it somehow flew across the room and smashed against a door.

Another time, Mrs. Meyer reported, a glass of water flew from a nightstand, landed on her head, shattering the glass and dousing her. As news of the strange happenings spread, curiosity grew and suggested explanations multiplied. For a time, even the Meyers' two cats came under suspicion. "They couldn't upset a refrigerator," Mrs. Meyer snapped. "It'd take two men just to lift it."

A glass bottle crashed to the floor on New Year's Day while Clayton County Sheriff Forrest M. Fischer, accompanied by several reporters, was investigating the house. Elmer Meyer said one reporter saw it rise from a box. The reporters accused each other of dropping the bottle, but none would admit it. Television cameramen reported that, on two separate days, films of the farmhouse were found to be completely blank after they had been developed.

Sheriff Fischer observed, "I'm satisfied in my own mind that this is all so much hocus pocus," but he joined in disparaging some of the suggested explanations. Shifting land under the home's sandstone foundation, it was suggested, might be causing the trouble. Sheriff Fischer said any shift strong enough to dump a refrigerator over surely would damage the house itself and no such damage was evident. The sheriff said someone had pointed out that the water table was at its highest level since 1954. Perhaps, then, a new spring was trying to erupt under the house. But could it toss a 265-pound man out of bed?

This man, ship's pilot Pat Livingston, whose home is in Guttenberg, came to the Meyer home the night of January 6. "I went down there to disprove everything," Livingston said. "I had made my mind up it was a bunch of malarkey."

Livingston said he lay down in one of the bedrooms about 9 or 10 o'clock while some companions went into the kitchen. First the chair near the bed moved. "The thing bobbled across the floor about eight feet and tipped over," he said. "I thought maybe some of the other people had tied a string on it and pulled it away, but they denied it."

So Livingston lay down again on the bed. "The next thing I knew I was lying on the floor," he said. "I'll take a lie detector test or anything. I woke up kind of groggy. I wouldn't have believed it for love or money."

Young Gene Meyer, who was with the group that night, said Livingston was on the bed only a few seconds before the others heard a loud crash as the hefty pilot was thrown to the floor. "Pat was going to make a big joke out of it," the Meyer boy said, "but he was the most surprised man I've ever seen." Livingston insisted that nothing human moved him and the mattress off the bed. None of those "present" was "big enough to do it," he said. There was also the factor of Livingston's rough-and-tumble reflexes.

The Meyer family found themselves the subject of media attention due to their poltergeist. Clipping from *The Des Moines Register*, Jan 10, 1960.

"When anyone grabs me, I grab back," he said. Only a quick look at this human bulldozer was necessary to convince a man of the complete folly of exchanging grabs with him.

"I haven't the intellect to explain it – and I still don't believe it – but it happened," said Livingston. "Let somebody else disprove it and I'll go along-with him."

CURIOUS CROWDS

During the weekend following the spectacular report of Livingston – the would-be debunker, who was himself literally debunked – curiosity seekers became a serious problem. The night of Friday, January 8, approximately 150 curiosity seekers from nearby towns roamed the grounds of the Meyer home. A back porch stud was torn loose and one of the "ghost hunters" poked out a kitchen window so he and his companions could get a better view. Some of the men used a ladder to the roof while others tried to batter their way through a basement door. They dispersed when Sheriff Fischer was called.

The following day authorities erected a road-block on the dead-end road to keep the crowds of the curious away. Despite these efforts, sightseers from Iowa, Illinois and Wisconsin continued to stream into the area. The Friday night crowd trying to enter the house was kept out of the building by eleven students and two professors.

Through Friday night (after the outside clamor subsided) and Saturday, the students applied themselves to their investigations. Phillip Lorenz, assistant professor of physics at Upper Iowa University, a private college at Fayette, and Charles Jones, assistant professor of chemistry at Upper Iowa, and Upper Iowa students majoring in physics conducted a fifteen-hour study.

Equipped with Geiger counters, oscilloscopes, an ionization chamber, and an electrometer, the Upper Iowa group took readings every 15 minutes. Five students from the State University of Iowa collected data for sociological and psychological studies.

Professor Lorenz reported that none of the instrument readings indicated abnormal conditions.

About 15 newsmen also were in the house that Friday night. Some of them took turns lying on the bed which had been so inhospitable to Livingston two nights before. Nothing happened while the newsmen were there.

There were suggestions that family difficulties might be at the root of the disturbances. Young Gene Meyer said his mother, Mrs. Elmer Meyer, and his grandmother "haven't talked together for years." Gene's mother, however, said she "gets along very well" with the elder Mrs. Meyer.

Elmer Meyer pointed out that no one claimed to have seen any of the supernatural acts. "They always happen just as soon as you'd turn your back," he said. "I thought at first that no human hands had anything to do with this, but I've changed my mind."

Elmer thus was leaning in the direction indicated later by investigations of two Northwestern University researchers.

PSYCHOLOGICAL INVESTIGATORS

Stanley Krippner and Arthur Hastings arrived at the Meyer home January tenth. Krippner is a graduate assistant in Northwestern University's Psycho-Educational Clinic and an associate member of the Para-Psychological

Association. Hastings is an assistant in the University's school of speech. Both are conducting doctoral research at Northwestern.

Krippner and Hastings examined the site, interviewed members of the Meyer family and analyzed the available data.

About the ship's pilot's experience, Krippner and Hastings noted that Livingston had had a few beers and suggested: "He could have stumbled out of bed and let his imagination get the better of him. Or he could have stumbled out of bed and told the story to 'save face' and add some general excitement to the proceedings."

In the instance of the bobbling chair, the investigators ventured a guess that "the spirits were probably inside Pat Livingston rather than inside the chair."

Livingston stoutly maintained that he was quite sober at the time he went into the bedroom. After he had been tumbled out of the bed by an unknown force, he downed several drinks with nervous deliberateness, he admitted.

Krippner and Hastings accepted the evidence of the earlier professors and students, ruling out geological causes of the disturbances. They also disposed of the hoax theory that the Meyer family made up the stories to gain attention. The attention had, after all, resulted in deposing the elder Mr. and Mrs. Meyer from the lifetime home in which they had planned to live out their years. It had also subjected the house to considerable physical damage.

Most plausible, to Krippner and Hastings, were the theories that someone inside or outside the family was playing jokes or that the events were caused by the paranormal power of a living person in the area.

In the light of the evidence and investigations of similar situations, they said, the existence of a genuine poltergeist seemed least plausible in the Meyer case.

"The only psychic explanation that deserves passing consideration," they said, "is the hypothesis that somebody in the area possesses a paranormal power over objects which they are consciously or unconsciously using."

Krippner and Hastings suggested that if some human beings actually have a psychokinetic power to mentally influence physical events, this could provide an unconscious outlet for the suppressed hostility toward parents which is not uncommon among adolescent boys.

"The high percentage of adolescents in poltergeist situations might be explained in terms of teenage pranks," the Krippner-Hastings report said. "But there is at least the possibility that some of these pranks – which seem explainable in no other way – may be the result of psychokinetic influence on household objects and parental possessions."

"PSYCHIC ABILITY?"

In the Guttenberg case, 16-year-old Gene Meyer was given restrictive responsibilities when his grandfather broke his hip, the investigators noted. Gene had to help with chores around his grandparents' house and spend considerable time there. The investigators stated that Gene had been in the area at the time of each disturbance.

"Slim though the possibility may be," their report said, "let us for a moment suppose that Gene does possess psychic ability, that he was hostile toward having to wait on his grandparents, that he could not express his aggressions openly.

"If he wanted to end his role as a houseboy and if he wanted an outlet for the rebellious feelings within him, an unconscious surge of psychic force could have caused strange noises, tipped over the refrigerator and sent his grandparents scurrying into town.

"The data, in fact, call for a theory allowing for motivation of the events. This is one of the outstanding conclusions we may make from the investigation. The disturbances show every sign of falling into a pattern, of being planned and carried out by an intelligent, purposive will...calculated to scare the Meyers.

"Those events which are not easily explainable by premeditated intervention of a human agent (such as Gene Meyer) may be assigned to a few other causes: expectation and psychological set (as in the case of Livingston falling out of bed); misinterpretation of natural mishaps (as the television films which developed blank); and impulse behavior on the part of human agents (as the bottle which broke in the' sheriff's presence)."

The Krippner-Hastings report concludes: "The Guttenberg disturbances, therefore, may be accounted for by a combination of natural causes. Some are easily explainable, some are not. These latter events we may never understand completely. And although we cannot rule out the possibility of psychic causes, the preponderance of evidence strongly suggests that most of the spoors of the

Guttenberg 'ghost' are merely the work of a mortal in disguise." – **Jack Magarrell**

* * * * * * * * *

DIAGNOSIS: MASS HYSTERIA – CASE TWO

The whole neighborhood was thrilled by the thumps and raps, while a young boy's mental health was seriously endangered.

Around midnight on Sunday, March 6, two doctors went to a terrace house in Salford, Lancs, England, and took a small boy to a hospital. Now certain people should feel ashamed, and some should feel disgraced, because of their superstition, ignorance and busybody tampering which for nearly three months kept this boy from medical help. And made him worse.

The boy is Alan Hill, aged twelve, who lives with his parents and his grandmother, and a budgerigar at No. 24, Tully Street, where for these three months, there were bumping and rapping in the night.

They were caused, according to the credulous people, by a poltergeist or "restless spirit." Most of them enjoyed their belief.

TYPICAL STORY

I am telling Alan's story, after investigating it for three weeks, because it is typical of other poltergeist stories which regularly make news and because the truth now may help expose much medieval and near-evil nonsense.

The story begins at Christmas when Mr. Jack Hill, machinist in his forties, and his wife Olive, thirty-eight, heard very loud noises, particularly the noise of a bouncing ball, coming from upstairs.

I heard this "bouncing ball." So did two doctors. It was like a heavy ball bouncing hard, and then fading. It has occurred in other "poltergeist" cases and has never, until now, been explained.

The noises occurred most nights between 11 P.M. (Alan's bedtime) and 1 AM. Neighbors heard them and even people across the street.

Mr. and Mrs. Hill were sleepless, distressed, and bewildered. They did not suspect Alan. True, the noises stopped when they rushed up to his room, but he always seemed asleep.

Knife-Wielding Demons and Murderous Ghosts

Then three groups of people came to help in their curious ways. The officials, the clergy, the psychical researchers, they all had one thing in common: good intentions.

First the officials. The police, the gas men, the water board men, the town hall people, two head masters, and a school inspector. They found-nothing and went away.

Some were content just to be puzzled, claiming "open minds." They talked of "a body of knowledge we do not yet understand." Others could not bear to be puzzled and preferred the supernatural. This, somehow, was more reassuring.

No one obeyed the first rule in investigating "poltergeists" – to look for a troubled child. No one thought that Alan, with his sensitiveness and his nervousness, might be a sick boy, needing help.

Then the Rev. Edward Diamon, thirty-three, rector of St. James's, of Salford, announced through the BBC that he believed the noises were made by a "restless spirit." And at around 11 P.M. on Monday, February 22, he and the Rev. Frederick Osborn, of St. Clement's, Manchester, arrived with cassocks and crucifixes and prayer books and faith to exorcise this "spirit"

The exorcism was thorough and awesome, but not a success, even though the priests advised with earthly insight that Alan should not be left alone. The noises went on (but only when, unavoidably, Alan was alone.)

These gentlemen now have to face that although they tried, in their way, to help this family, their ancient faith served only to make a sick boy more afraid.

Members of the Manchester Society for Psychical Research also tried to help, sincerely, in their way. But their sincerity was, in my view, dangerous; as sincerity sometimes is.

I first met Mr. David Cohen, the society's investigation officer, on the night of the exorcism service, though he had already been interested himself in the affair for some time.

Mr. Cohen, forty-five-year-old bachelor, is not typical of psychical researchers. The first step in a serious investigation would have been to make sure Alan could not make the noises himself. Mr. Cohen did not take this step, nor did anyone else.

Incredibly, no one ever had Alan provably in full view while the noises went on. Yet everyone agreed "it couldn't possibly be Alan."

Mr. Cohen based his investigation on, for me, unbelievable beliefs which, so far as I understood him, went something like this:

A "spirit" or "intelligence" on the "other side" was using Alan as a medium to get messages to Mrs. Freda Roberts (who lives next door).

This "spirit" was "Teddy Robert's," Mrs. Robert's father-in-law, who died four years ago, and Mr. Cohen, in order to receive the messages, had "educated" it in a tapping code. A – one tap; B – two taps; Z – 26 taps.

"There's no danger," Mr. Cohen assured me and everyone, "because the spirit entity will leave Alan alone once it has given its final message – the important one."

NEUROTIC EXCITEMENT

The "spirit" had already, during February, delivered some messages. It said Sheffield Wednesday would win the Cup. It said it didn't want any exorcism. It gave simple messages in bad German (which Alan is learning at school).

I asked Mr. Cohen how the tappings were produced if not by Alan and he suggested an "ecto-plasmic rod" which, he said, is "energy" projected from the body to some distant point.

One of the more macabre aspects of this whole affair was the neurotic excitement, the diseased delight, shown by many of the people concerned with it. Yet not all of them were unintelligent.

At this point my colleague, Raymond Hawkey, and I had heard enough and seen enough to call a doctor. We were afraid for the boy. The doctor came and was afraid for him, too, and arranged for him to be seen at a local hospital. Even then Mr. Cohen, not boasting but believing, said: "I've had 20 years' experience of this type of case, and I should know more than the doctors."

On February 29, the doctor asked Mr. Cohen to promise not to visit Alan for a week during the preliminary medical investigation. Mr. Cohen promised, and he gave me the same promise.

But on the night of March 1 the doctor visited Alan and found Mr. Cohen, with other psychical researchers, in full session, taking messages from "Teddy Roberts." The doctor and the hospital consultant withdrew from the case. They felt, rightly, that Mr. and Mrs. Hill had to choose between them and Mr. Cohen. Raymond Hawkey and I heard about this and returned to Tully Street on Sunday,

March 6, to find the situation greatly worsened. The mass hysteria, for long bad enough, was now dangerous.

One of the neighbors told me she had seen walking footprints on the carpet with no one there. Mrs. Hill said she had seen spoons flying and Alan said he had floated up to the ceiling. Mrs. Hill believed this because, she said, she saw him floating up to the ceiling and had only just managed to haul him down.

The noises stopped suddenly, after one wild night when the eager crowd in the living room – neighbors, researchers and all – heard, among other things, the noise of heavy furniture being dragged about.

But now worse was happening. Alan was going into trance-like states several times a day – in full view of everyone – and his parents and the neighbors took this to mean he was en route for the ceiling. So they were frightened and they struggled to hold him down and threw cold water in his face. And when they did this he got violent.

In cases such as the "Salford poltergeist," an exorcism is often attempted to rid a house of a troublesome haunting. Usually with little success.

TRANCE PHOTOGRAPH

Hawkey and I watched one of these trances. It lasted half an hour and we saw Alan, with extraordinary strength, drag furniture we could drag only with effort. So this accounted for one aspect of the "poltergeist."

We had this trance photographed to prove at last Alan was responsible for the noises and desperately needed medical care. And we gave the photographs to the doctors to help diagnosis.

Later this same evening of March 6, Mr. Cohen came because, since the trances, only he could get Alan to sleep. He had developed a friendship with the boy and he meant it kindly. But his friendship was bad for Alan.

Something had to be done quickly. Hawkey and I urged Mr. and Mrs. Hill to send Mr. Cohen away and call back the doctors. Mr. Cohen went and I think he was relieved to go (after asking Mrs. Hill to write a letter expressing gratitude for all he had done). By midnight Alan was in a hospital.

What is wrong with him? This intelligent boy, who for nearly three months was stuffed with terrifying nonsense, is emotionally sick and needs expert medical treatment.

And a doctor told me: "His experiences since Christmas have quite definitely made him worse."

Since he has been in a hospital he has admitted making the noises and he says he did it chiefly by banging a loose floorboard with the bouncy side of his outstretched hand.

REGRET AND PITY

Alan was aware of it all, in a shadowy way, as a person hypnotized is aware. He tapped out the messages, in the code taught him by Mr. Cohen, again in this trance-like state.

So this is the "Salford poltergeist" which would probably have gone down in psychical research history as a "classic case." Almost the only people who came out well are Alan and his parents, who trusted those they believed, must know better than they.

For most of these people now there will be only disappointment. They are cheated of their eager beliefs. No spirits, no messages, no ectoplasm.

Many will say: "It was only a sick child." They will say it, not with pity but with anger, and possibly no remorse at all. But for a few there will be real regret, and pity. Perhaps they may be pitied too. And forgiven. – **Merrick Winn**

* * * * * * * * * *

THE CASE OF THE NOISY INTRUDER – CASE THREE

Mysterious rappings and moving objects, part of psychic tradition, continue to occur in our own time. Recent poltergeist phenomena in various parts of the United States, narrated in other articles in this issue of "*Tomorrow,*" give current evidence. Another incident, strangely resembling an experience of our own, took place at Amherst, Nova Scotia, during the latter part of the nineteenth century (See: "**The Violent Ghost of Amherst**," pp. 37).

The occurrences I am about to report are unusual in that they did not come about spontaneously, but were nevertheless far from sought-after. As it happened, home experiments in extrasensory perception managed to get out of hand in a rather unique and frightening manner.

The incidents took place in 1934, in our home at Grand Rapids, Michigan. They involved my wife and several friends, who were experimenting with a method for testing telepathy, which had been described in an article by E. E. Free in the "*Scientific American*" of March, 1933.

The method suggested by Free offered a quantitative test which could be evaluated statistically. According to his technique, the telepathic sender, or agent, shook a single die in an opaque dice cup, concentrating upon the exposed face. The recipient attempted to guess which face was up. Two sets of records were kept: that of the sender, and that of the receiver. These were compared and tabulated later. We discovered that Mrs. Gibson and two of our friends were achieving averages in excess of chance.

One of our promising dice-guessing subjects was a friend whom I shall call Robert Larsen, a university student who experimented with us on weekends and during his vacation. He was as interested in the telepathic inquiry as we were. In some experiments we tried an Ouija board, to see if automatism might increase the result. We reduced the lighting in the room, to see whether telepathy averages would be affected. We discovered that when the Ouija board came into the experimental picture with certain percipients, occasional communications claiming to be from unknown personalities would then emerge. Our experiment would be ignored by these personalities, who wanted to communicate by writing.

In this manner, several of our experiments with telepathy were sabotaged by cryptic communications, which sometimes showed extrasensory powers of their own. They were especially good whenever Bob was operating the Ouija board in combination with another sitter.

Ouija Boards have been used in an attempt to contact the "spirits" believed responsible for poltergeist activity.

THUMPS FROM THE FLOOR

At 10 P.M., of May 9, 1934, we began experimenting, using the board as it lay on the dining room table between Bob and Mrs. Gibson. We reduced illumination to a single 50 watt ruby photographic bulb, hung overhead. At the table were also Miss Margaret Nelson (which is not her real name) and I. Soon after the planchette began to move, loud pounding seemed to come from the tabletop and from the floor. The "knocker" was noting certain letters, as the pointer swept over the alphabet. Changing the method, we moved the pointer slowly over the whole alphabet. The "knocker" pounded as we passed certain letters. These spelled out a message which we recorded.

The alleged discarnate communicator claimed to be from western Brazil. After some time the pounding grew louder, disregarding what we were doing. It pounded beneath each of the four sitters at request, and then wandered over the room. Our dog, Tag, nervous and uneasy, paced the floor and demanded to go out. I let him out. He refused to come in again when called. He lay on the front porch, in the light from a street lamp.

After we sat down again, the raps changed to muffled thumps, as though the floor were being struck from below by a heavy padded maul or sledge. Blows shook the whole floor. Next, the "knocker" struck the floor in a slow rhythm which built up to a crescendo. The room, and its floor and walls, shook and vibrated. Part of the time I lay on the floor below the table to see if anyone's feet contributed to the phenomenon.

We put our feet on the rungs of the chairs, out of contact with the floor. The pounding continued. Floor, table and chairs were shaking with great force! We put Bob's feet on pillows. The shaking built up with greater violence!

I was afraid that the house might be damaged and asked that the vibration cease. This had no effect. I turned on all the lights in the dining room. The pounding and shaking slowly diminished and ceased after fifteen or twenty seconds of bright light. The phenomenon continued in light of a possible intensity of 20 or 30 foot candles. I examined the cellar, the outside access to which was locked, and found no one.

"TAHMONAT"

Bob thereupon tried automatic writing, and the communication of the "knocker," who called himself "Tahmonat," continued in the automatism. Bob became facetious toward the personality and received this message:

"Fool you are, now but a mortal! I am greater; I can shake the floor from under you!"

Suddenly the muscles on Bob's forearm stood out, as a severe cramp struck his right arm and hand. He dropped his pencil, seized the arm which was giving him much pain, and rushed into the kitchen. He exposed his arm and hand to cold water from the tap for several minutes before the pain subsided. Bob then wanted to stop and our session broke up at 1 A.M.

Knife-Wielding Demons and Murderous Ghosts

On June 27, we tried the experiment, as Bob was in town again. We got the same group together and used the ruby light overhead. I had weighed the circular oak dining table and found that it weighed 147 pounds. Its diameter was fifty-four inches. It had four feet, radiating from a heavy pedestal.

Soon the table raised itself, until it pivoted upon one foot and caster. It then swung to left and right and moved laterally along the floor, bouncing on one caster. Bob and his chair, his feet upon the bottom rung ten inches from the floor, hitched and slid sideways along the floor about thirty inches. This performance was repeated. The light gave a good view as he moved out of the table's shadow.

Adjacent to us lived a family of Greek extraction who knew nothing of our experiments. They were unknown to Bob. Feeling that we might be victims of mass hallucination and noticing that they were up (it was about 1 A.M.), I went over and asked them if they would care to take part in an experiment. Mr. and Mrs. James Papageorgou returned with me. On their arrival, the board welcomed them by knocking, "Good Luck Greece." It then mentioned Ossa and Pelion. Mrs. Papageorgou exclaimed: "How astonishing! My home was between those mountains!" They witnessed the rappings, poundings, and liftings, saw the Ouija's pointer movements responded to by the thumpings in the floor, table, and walls. The phenomenon continued until 2:15 A.M.

On July 10, the family had gone to Lake Michigan. I was keeping house alone. Early in the evening, Bob, Vivian Carter, and I had planned to go swimming nearby. On reaching Vivian's house, we found that her mother had fallen, breaking her arm. We stayed at the house until the doctor came, and then left. Vivian remained with her mother. As it was too late to go swimming, Bob and I drove back to the house. On arriving, we met a friend of his, Louise Kerk. She joined us and we invited her in, explaining that we wanted to make an experiment.

It was 10 P.M. when we finally began our dice-guessing. Bob was the percipient and Louise was the sender. The results were most promising. At 11 P.M., Bob, Louise, and I sat on one side of the table, leaving the ruby light burning overhead and the Ouija board and pointer in the center. Louise sat between us, and we held hands, but Bob's right and my left hand were free.

Bob took notes. I pushed the planchette over the Ouija board alphabet with my left hand. Raps came from the underside of the tabletop and the floor, indicating the desired letter. Communications followed, which were recorded in part. The physical phenomena were our main focus of attention.

Knife-Wielding Demons and Murderous Ghosts

The raps sounded differently from any we could produce with our feet. They were heavier and more muffled. (In the early sitting I had put Bob's feet on a thick pillow. Then I put one hand across his feet and the other beneath the pillow, while I laid on the floor. I felt strong thuds coming from the floor and what seemed to be an electrical pulsation, without foot movement, coming from his feet. The raps came from below the floor.)

In the present sitting we sat on the west side of the table. I was at Louise's left. Bob was on her right. The table raised and lowered repeatedly, with or without our hands on its top. We turned off the ruby light overhead. The shades were up on the window and door behind us, and some light entered the room from the arch into the living room. In the living room, the shades were up. Light shone in from a nearby street lamp. The light was not bright, nor was it lacking.

I could see Bob's face and Louise's profile against the light. We still held her hands. No one moved. Suddenly there was a hissing explosion over her head. It sounded as if a toy balloon had burst. A book flew out of the hanging book rack behind her and struck the baby carriage behind Bob. Shortly after, a second book left the case in a similar fashion. There was the same hissing explosion. This book flew over Louise's head, across the room. We did not hear it land. It seemed to have disappeared.

Louise began to cry. I turned on the ruby light and then the white lamps which were in the fixture. Louise had had enough! She refused to let us begin again. The experiment was stopped. It was almost 3 A.M. The book which had left the case at the second explosion was not found immediately. It was a copy of Poe's "Tales..."

Two weeks later we noticed it lying across the top of other books in the case on the opposite wall. It had been kept in the hanging case on the west wall, and there was an empty space there at the close of the session where the two books had been.

NO CONSCIOUS METHOD

We had stopped this experiment on several occasions, meanwhile turning on the lights.

Later I tried to duplicate the book-throwing by means of a string, sitting where Bob had sat. (The phenomena had never occurred except in his presence.) I could not make a book fly across the room, nor could I throw one to the carriage. I battered up several old books in the attempt. I did succeed in dropping books on to the table and deposited several on the chair where Louise had been sitting. Such activity would have struck her in the back of the neck or head, but would not have produced the transit we witnessed. There was no explosive sound caused by the string-propelled book.

Later that summer, I tried to locate Bob and renew the experiments. He was out of the city. I tried to duplicate the table levitation by raising the table with toes and knees. The phenomena we had witnessed could not be duplicated, nor could the heavy table be held up, without extreme fatigue.

I could discover no method by which the heavy floor-pounding, wall-thumping, and floor vibration could be produced. Even if ten per cent of the phenomena we had witnessed could be produced normally with the existing precautions, I could not account for the remainder. The messages were quite unusual, but within the scope of the unconscious mind. Could the unconscious ac-count for the phenomena and the behavior of "Tahmonat"? I do not know.

Bob returned to Grand Rapids in mid-September. We tried to repeat the experiments of July, but little occurred. We heard some feeble raps, which could have been made by anyone. The table did not rise. The results were a total failure.

Later our experiments in extrasensory perception were resumed with some success. Occasionally we tried the Ouija with variable results. There was no reappearance of "Tahmonat." There was no recurrence of the physical phenomena, which had threatened the structure of the house. With the departure of Bob, the dog became a peaceful occupant, not a frightened dweller on our porch!

FAMILIAR PATTERN

Looking back, the events that startled us more than a quarter of a century ago seem to fit into a pattern that is familiar to psychic researchers. Levitation was the subject of a book, now rare, by an early British psychic investigator, Edward W. Cox, B Sergeant-at-Law and a writer on spiritualistic subjects. In his work **"What Am I?"** (London, 1873), he describes an incident of levitation which occur-red when he was alone with the famous British psychic, the Rev. William Stainton Moses.

Cox writes how, on a Tuesday, the Rev. Moses came to his home to "dress for a dinner party to which we were invited." Noting that Moses had "previously exhibited considerable power as a psychic," the author continues his account as follows:

"Having half an hour to spare, we went into the dining-room. It was just six o'clock, and of course broad daylight. I was opening letters; he was reading the Times. My dining table is of mahogany, very heavy, old fashioned, six feet wide, nine feet long. It stands on a Turkey carpet, which much increases the difficulty of moving it. A subsequent trial showed that the united efforts of two strong men standing were necessary to move it an inch. There was no cloth upon it and the light fell full under it. No person was in the room but my friend and myself.

"Suddenly as we were sitting thus, frequent and loud rappings came upon the table. My friend was then sitting holding the newspaper with both hands, one arm resting upon the table, the other on the back of the chair, and turned sideways from the table, so that his legs and feet were not under the table, but at the side of it. Presently the solid table quivered as if with an ague fit. Then it swayed to and fro so violently as almost to dislocate the big pillar-like legs, of which there are eight. Then it moved forward about three inches. I looked under it to be sure that it was not touched; but it still moved, and still the blows were loud upon it . . .

"I then suggested that it would be an invaluable opportunity, with so great a power in action, to make trial of 'motion without contact.' Accordingly we stood upright, he on one side of the table, I on the other side of it. We stood two feet from it, and held our hands eight inches above it. In one minute it rocked violently. Then it moved over the carpet a distance of seven inches. Then it rose three inches from the floor on the side on which my friend was standing. Then it rose equally on my side. Finally my friend held his hands four inches over the end of the table and asked that it would rise and touch his hand three times. It did so."

Stainton Moses describes a similar occurrence in his book **"Researches in Spiritualism"** as follows:

"Another singular instance occurred during a visit that I made to a gentleman interested in this subject. After some conversation, it was suggested that we should try the effect of placing our hands on a pillar work-table belonging to his wife. It danced about like a live thing: executed a series of gyrations, first on one foot and then on another; and finally lay down on the floor and jerked all its contents about the room."

Knife-Wielding Demons and Murderous Ghosts

What is the source of the energy which produces these strange events, historic and contemporary? Perhaps some energy is converted from the group of investigators, possibly by changing bodily heat into kinetic force. When our own phenomena occurred, the evenings were very warm. It seems possible that latent heat may have somehow been converted into supplementary kinetic energy. I have no idea how such conversions may be made. I was not aware of "cold spots," although I did experience spots of cold during sittings in which physical phenomena of minor nature were produced, with other experimenters.

Granted some means of converting heat into kinetic force, then heat plus considerable intelligence would seem to be the most likely source for the phenomena. The phenomena were directed by an intelligence which was in direct touch with us. Was it part of us? This poses the most difficult problem of all. – **Edward P. Gibson**

Rev. William Stainton Moses with Mrs Charlton Speer and an unidentified spirit figure.

There are vampiric spirits that seek to nourish themselves on the energy of their unwitting victims.

HERE THERE BE MONSTERS
By Tim R. Swartz

It is believed that we share our reality with unknown entities...spirits, jinn, shape-shifters, whatever name you want to give them. Sometimes, a person will inadvertently attract the attention of one, or more, of these "things." The result can lead to haunting, obsession, and possibly even possession. The incident in this chapter took place years ago, and yet, it still profoundly disturbs me. Even though this was not my first brush with the paranormal, this was my first contact with an entity that, for all intents and purposes, was clearly a spiritual predator. This demonstrated to me that the world beyond the physical is to be navigated carefully, because there are things other than kind guardian angels or ascended spiritual masters. In the other planes of reality, there also dwell the Stygian shapes of ultimate hunger and pitiless lust. They forever wait for that one innocent invitation to be allowed inside, as our naked fear and the putrefaction of our minds and spirit is their sustenance.

* * * * * * * * *

Back in 1982, I was a news videographer/reporter for a television station in Dayton, Ohio. Occasionally, I operated one of the "microwave trucks" which allowed for live news coverage around the area.

One of the engineers assigned to these trucks had a girlfriend that was experiencing some sort of unusual paranormal phenomenon. The engineer was an evangelical Christian and told me that he wanted nothing to do with the situation, but he also wanted to help his girlfriend with her problem. Since he knew that I investigated things such as ghosts and UFOs, he thought that maybe I could somehow help.

The girlfriend, Marilyn D., worked in Human Resources for a large company in Cincinnati. When I met her, I noticed right away that she looked thin, pale and ill. She reassured me that she felt fine and went right into her story.

A few years earlier, Marilyn had been a senior in college and one night, along with her roommate and other friends, conducted a séance just for the fun of it. For a half-hour or so, nothing happened, and just as the young women were ready to call it an evening, Marilyn's roommate suddenly went into what seemed to be a trance and began to address Marilyn directly.

"The voice that came out of the mouth of my roommate was totally different from her normal voice," Marilyn said. "The spirit was clearly a man as its voice was lower and gruff. It also spoke with an odd accent and occasionally used words no one could understand."

The entity identified itself as the spirit of Marilyn's lover from a past life. The spirit refused to give Marilyn his name, instead, it told her that in her previous life, she had spurned him for someone with more money and social class and he killed himself as a result of her betrayal.

Marilyn was shocked to hear the strange voice tell her that it still loved her and that she would eventually succumb to its seduction. At that point the spirit withdrew, leaving the roommate in a very confused and disoriented state.

SEEKING SEXUAL ENERGY

From that moment on, according to Marilyn, her spirit suitor never left her side. She could hear its voice in her ear, telling her how much it loved and needed her and they were destined to be together. Her apartment at night took on a life all of its own with strange raps and unearthly voices that whispered half-heard words in the shadows. As well, household items began to move about on their own. Marilyn's roommate finally moved out when she saw the door of a coat closet open and close as if by invisible hands.

Once Marilyn was alone, she began to see her ghostly beau whom she described as tall, dark skinned, and with eyes and mouth that seemed much too large for its thin face. She would awaken in the middle of the night to see it standing at the foot of her bed with a hungry grin on its face and its eyes seeming to radiate a light all of their own.

Marilyn explained to me that she tried moving several times, but the entity would follow her wherever she went. Even more disturbing, she said that it had started getting into bed with her, lying on top of her and biting her at various places on her body. It explained that because it had killed itself in its previous life, it had to drink her blood in order to stay in the material world. She showed me several small bruises on her arms and legs that she said were the places that it had last bit her.

I convinced Marilyn to let me stay in her apartment overnight to see if I could experience any of the poltergeist phenomena for myself. Marilyn's boyfriend also joined me, confessing that this was the first time he had stayed at her place overnight as his religious beliefs prohibited him from taking their relationship to a physical level before marriage.

I brought along my trusty SLR camera as well as a television video camera from work. However, the ¾ inch tape deck that went with the camera suffered from one mechanical problem after another. At first the deck refused to turn on. When it did finally power up, the tape cartridge became stuck to the point that I was afraid it would permanently damage the deck. Needless to say, it proved to be completely useless that night.

Marilyn stayed in her room, and we camped out in the living room of her small apartment. We kept a small light over the oven on so that we weren't in total darkness, and waited.

We didn't have to wait very long as odd noises soon began to emanate from various locations around the place. At times it would sound like a small animal scratching first in one corner, and then another. Then there would be strange knocks and raps on the walls and furniture. We tried to engage whatever was making the noises by asking questions and trying to get it to knock in response, but it ignored us and continued with its random noises.

At one point the scratching and raps got so loud and persistent that I wondered how the neighbors could stand the mad cacophony. (I later discovered that none of Marilyn's neighbors had ever heard a thing from her apartment, a fact that amazed me considering how loud the noises were when I was there.)

At 3:00 AM, I heard a strange whispering sound coming from Marilyn's room, so I peeked in. (She had left her door open.) I could see in the half darkness that Marilyn was obviously asleep, but was writhing on her bed as if in the throes of passion. It may have been the lighting, but it looked to me as if there was someone with Marilyn. Someone who was invisible to my eyes, but with a physical presence that was clearly making love to the young woman.

We left the next morning even more confused than when we had started. The photographs I had taken showed nothing extraordinary. And my video equipment worked perfectly once out of the apartment.

Marilyn called me a few days later and confessed that she had omitted to tell me everything about her relationship with the spirit. Starting several months earlier, she said it had been coming to her at night, making love to her as it bit and drank her blood. Marilyn said that her "Dracula," as she referred to it, was the best lover she had ever had and that she was addicted to its nightly visitations – despite the fact that she usually felt exhausted and weak the next day.

This case had taken a strange turn that I had not expected. In the past, Marilyn had a healthy sex life and enjoyed the company of a number of men. However, after she started dating her current boyfriend, who did not believe in sex before marriage, she began to feel depressed and frustrated from their lack of physical contact. It was at that point when her spirit friend began to push itself onto her sexually; something that she resisted at first, but soon relented when her resolve finally weakened.

I wish that I could say that this case had a satisfying resolution, but often with these types of cases, things do not always turn out happily. Not too long after my investigation, Marilyn broke up with her boyfriend and moved to another apartment.

As with myself, not too long afterwards I moved to another city and subsequently lost touch with her.

Several years later I found out that Marilyn had died of complications from anorexia, a condition that started with her shortly after she graduated from college. So I am left with a strange story of a girl who said that a spirit would make love to her and drink her blood, a girl that would later die of anorexia. I often wonder if her experiences were symptoms of her disease, or if her disease was a symptom of her experiences. I will never know for sure.

Tim R. Swartz is an Indiana native and Emmy-Award winning television producer/videographer, and is the author of a number of popular books including "*The Lost Journals of Nikola Tesla,*" "*America's Strange and Supernatural History,*" "*Time Travel: Fact Not Fiction!,*" "*Men of Mystery: Nikola Tesla and Otis T. Carr,*" "*Admiral Byrd's Secret Journey Beyond the Poles,*" and "*Gef The Talking Mongoose: The Eighth Wonder of the World.*"

Along with authors Hercules Invictus, Paul Dale Roberts, and Timothy Green Beckley, Tim R. Swartz examines the bizarre case of "Gef the Talking Mongoose" that took place on the Isle of Man in the 1930s. Was Gef a ghost, poltergeist, a house spirit, or as he put it: "An extra clever little mongoose?"

"*Gef The Talking Mongoose*" also includes the long out of print "*The Haunting of Cashen's Gap*" by Harry Price and R.S. Lambert.

Knife-Wielding Demons and Murderous Ghosts

96

THE MOOR
ANCIENT GREEK DAEMON OR VENGEFUL GHOST?
MUSINGS ON A FELL CREATURE FROM THE REALM OF DREAMS
By Hercules Invictus

EDITOR'S NOTE: Hercules Invictus is a Lemnian Greek, a proud descendant of Argonauts and Amazons. He is openly Olympian in his spirituality and worldview, dedicated to living the Mythic Life and has been exploring the fringes of our reality throughout his entire earthly sojourn. For over four decades he has been sharing his Olympian Odyssey with others.

Having relocated the heart of his Temenos to Northeastern New Jersey and the Greater New York Metropolitan Area, he is now establishing his unique niche locally and contributing to his community's overall quality of life. Hercules is also recruiting Argonauts to help him usher in a new Age of Heroes.

Hercules currently hosts **The Elysium Project**, **Pride of Olympus** and **Voice of Olympus** e-radio shows on the **Spiritual Unity Radio Network**. He writes for **The Magic Happens**, **Paranormal Magazine** and **Paranoia Magazine**, has published two e-books on Kindle, **Olympian Ice** and **The Antediluvial Scrolls**, and has been contributing regularly to Timothy Beckley's anthologies.

Hercules founded or co-founded **Mount Olympus LLP**, **Olympian Heroic Path**, **Olympian Shamanic Path**, **Cosmic Olympianism**, **Mythic Atlantis**, **Living Theurgy**, the **Order of the Golden Fleece**, the **Regional Folklore Society of Northeastern PA** and the **Center for the Study of Living Myth** in New Jersey. He also spearheaded many of the real-world Age of Heroes initiatives and the fictive Mythic Adventure tales.

For more information, please Friend him on Facebook or visit his website: www.herculesinvictus.net

Knife-Wielding Demons and Murderous Ghosts

Every night we are all unconsciously drawn into the Realm of Dreams to experience different realities, most of them unremembered by the time we wake up. To benefit from this process, one must first endeavor to recall, in detail, what transpired whilst one was there. The oft garbled fragments we manage to retain can be recorded upon awakening and reflected upon later in the day. This simple practice often rewards the practitioner with deep insights and panoramic perspectives that can significantly empower and transform their waking life. At times these captured nocturnal memories prove to have been prophetic, or to have accurately conveyed heretofore hidden information.

Dream Work is a very exciting and fulfilling discipline. I have joyously practiced it for most of my life. It is also highly entertaining, especially when some proficiency is gained with time-tested techniques for hypnotically seeding dream experiences or attaining lucidity.

There are actually many ways to approach or engage in Dream Work, and I recommend experimenting with as many systems as you possibly can before settling on the one that works best for you. You will find that dreams are very accommodating and will often communicate through whichever belief system you choose to embrace (or even temporarily entertain).

I've had great success with the Jungian, Transpersonal, Unariun, Edgar Cayce and Eckankar systems of Dream Work in the past and consider the time I spent experimenting with them as extremely productive and very much worth my while.

In Greek mythology, the Oneiroi were the dark-winged spirits of dreams.

My current explorations are guided and informed by Olympian Shamanic Path, a system I developed that is based on the heroic legends of old, mythic lore, folk tales, metaphysical speculations, superstitions and magickal practices of my Hellenic ancestors.

As Olympian Shamanism allows you to identify and effectively deal with entities from the Olympian Realm of Dreams, I will begin with some background info and useful lore before introducing you to the Moor, an enigmatic and sinister figure that destroyed the lives of many a dreaming Greek.

OLYMPIAN SHAMANISM

Shamanism is a hands-on and highly interactive way of exploring our inner and outer realities.

It has emerged in diverse cultures around our globe and throughout human history. The practice of Shamanism is remarkably consistent despite its many cultural manifestations. The mythos through which it emerges provides the maps that assist the Shaman in navigating that culture's psychic terrain and successfully interacting with the denizens encountered, some of whom can be deceptive or even extremely dangerous.

In most shamanic systems there is a mountain, pillar, personage or tree that serves as an Axis Mundi which connects the three primary levels of existence (Higher, Lower and In-Between) and their various Realms into a cohesive whole. Olympian Shamanism utilizes several representations of the central pillar including Mount Olympus, the Titan Atlas, the Omphalos and the Tree of Worlds. Unlike the Cosmic Trees of the Norse and the Hebrews, whose worlds are separate and clearly defined, the Realms of the Olympian Tree remain fluid and blend into one another, inviting continuous Shamanic exploration.

THE REALM OF DREAMS

The Realm of Dreams borders and blends into our waking world, the Underworld, Erebos and the Astral Realms. It must also (at least occasionally) touch upon the Realm of the Nature Spirits as I (and many others) have encountered and interacted with the Xotika (Exotics) in Dream's domain.

To consciously enter the Realm of Dreams one may venture (via Shamanic Journeying, Astral Projection, Active Imagination or any other preferred technique) through the Gates of Horn and Ivory. The Oneiroi (Dream Spirits) enter and exit our inner and outer landscapes through these Gates.

Below is an (incomplete but important) list of entities that may be encountered while exploring the Olympian Realm of Dreams.

Though all Dream personages must be approached and treated respectfully, the greatest caution must be exercised whilst encountering Phobetor and Epiales, as well as their many minions.

Hypons, the Greek god of sleep.

Hypnos (known to the Romans as Somnus) is the Olympian God of Sleep and Ruler of the Realm of Dreams. He often appears as a youthful man, nude and with wings sprouting from the sides of his head. He is the son of Nyx (Primordial Night) and the father (or brother) of Morpheus, Phobetor, Phantasos and Oneiros. He is married to Pasithea and his twin brother is Thanatos, the Titan of Death. Hypnos dwells in a cave near the Underworld which is surrounded by poppy plants.

Pasithea is the wife of Hypnos and the Queen of the Dream Realm. She is one of the Graces and sister to Aglaea, Efrosini and Thalia. She may also be a daughter of the Olympian Zeus and/or Hera.

Oneiros (Dream) is the son of Hypnos and Pasithea. He safeguards Hypnos' body and maintains the silence in Hypnos' cave while his Lord and father astrally wanders through his Realm. Oneiros (as the Oneiroi) is also the Shaper and Substance of the Realm of Dreams.

Oneiroi (Dream Spirits) are the native denizens of the Dream Realm. Collectively they are aspects of the cthonic Power Oneiros. They are often described as shadowy and winged in their natural state. The Oneiroi play the parts of everyone and everything in our dreams. If you become lucid and ask them nicely they will freely explain what they were trying to convey through their symbolic actions. Though helpful and friendly by nature, the Oneiroi can be manipulated by more powerful entities.

Epiales (the Melas Oneiros or Dark Dream) One of the Oneiroi and a daemon of Nightmares. On Lemnos he is known as Ephialtes. Please note that the term daemon denotes an entity which lives between our earth and the Realms Above and Below. An Angel (Messenger) is considered a daemon, as would one of the crude Kallikantzaroi who wanders the paths of the Greco-Roman Tree of Worlds.

Morpheus (Semblance) is a son or brother to Hypnos, the Archon of Dreams. He can assume any guise and influences the dreams of humans in all strata of society. He may be Sleep's Crown Prince as he has been recognized as royal and representing the Throne since our Middle Ages. In Neil Gaiman's ***Sandman*** universe Morpheus is the Ruler of Dream and the Lord of Stories. His vast library contains a complete copy of every book never written.

Phantasos (Fantasy) is also a son or brother of Hypnos. He, Morpheus and Phobetor are often grouped and mentioned together. Phantastos gifts us with surreal dreams and places inanimate items imbued with meaning in our path during our nocturnal wanderings.

Phobetor (Fear Inducer or Frightener) is often mentioned with Morpheus and Phantastor as a son of Hypnos but is sometimes introduced alone as a son of of Nyx and Erebos. He is the personification of Nightmares and enjoys assuming monstrous or animalistic guises.

Thanatos is the Titan of Death and twin brother of Hypnos, with whom he lives. As in antiquity he still escorts select souls to the Underworld. Sharing this task is Charos (aka Charon), formerly the ferryman to the Underworld, aka the Realm of Hades. A very large Raven sometimes heralds their approach to the family and friends of the soon to be deceased. I have heard many accounts on Lemnos of this giant Raven and the shadowy presence(s) that follow(s) his cry.

Shades are living humanoid shadows. They have thriving communities in the Realm of Dreams, live lives very much like ours and enjoy watching the living, whom they can observe unseen or interact with in Dream. The Shades seem to be connected with certain families, including my own.

Watchers are tall, thin shadowy presences that sometimes appear in the hypnogogic and hypnopompic states. If you notice them hovering around you and intently observing, one will calmly suggest that you go back to sleep. It sounds so reasonable that you will most likely do so without question.

Grazers are patches of hovering darkness with long tendrils. Though seemingly menacing, they are actually curious, cautiously friendly and playful. They seem to be animals that feed on the residue of stale, spent or cast-off energies. They are usually encountered during the hypnogogic portion of the sleep cycle.

Endymion is an ancient astronomer, hunter, shepherd, king or shepherd-king who resides in the Realm of Dreams, deeply asleep until joined by his lover the Moon Titaness Selene. He was granted immortality by Zeus (as long as he dwells in Dream and remains asleep whenever he is not with Selene.

Selene is the Titaness of the Moon. She visits her sleeping lover Endymion whenever she is not actively engaged with her assigned lunar duties.

Aletheia is the Goddess of Truth and is adored by all who sincerely seek her. She can sometimes be found at the Gate of Horn, through which True Dreams enter our consciousness.

There are many other Powers, personages, groups of sentient beings and creatures that live in or frequent the Dream Realms, but as including them will not contribute to this particular topic I will be speaking of them on another day. (Sorry Artemidorus)!

THE DEAD IN THE DREAM REALMS

The Realm of Dreams, as previously noted, borders Erebos and the Astral Realms.

The dead who have not yet crossed (or cannot now cross) into the Underworld usually reside on our side of Erebos. There they live in a society governed by Hekate. Residents of Erebos that live under Hekate's watchful eye generally cause few problems beyond occasionally making their presence felt in dreams or communicating through sudden variations in temperature or strong scents in our waking world. Though sometimes disturbing, most of these entities would not be considered dangerous unless controlled or overshadowed by a more powerful entity.

Some of the departed also choose to dwell in the Dream Realms as well as other Astral locations.

Erebus – Greek God of darkness and ruler of the underworld.

AND NOW: THE MOOR

In the days of my grandparent's generation (and in generations prior to that) people of means commonly hid their money in the ground at remote locations far from their village. They recited prayers, uttered spells and sometimes spilled blood (their own or that of a sacrifice) to energize their spell and attract (or bind) a guardian spirit to protect it. If the treasure was big enough a Drakos (Drake or huge snake) would be assigned this task.

The intent of these people was to keep their treasure hidden and safe until their dying day, upon which they would reveal the location (as well as any counter-spells) to their chosen heir(s). Alas, this plan hardly ever worked as the information, years later, was often forgotten, incorrectly recalled or the terrain had changed with the passage of time (the location of landmark trees and streams for instance).

Family members eventually moved away or died off, leaving behind caches of buried coins, gems or jewelry that they could never reclaim. Only the tales of lost treasure remained. The bound Guardian Spirits remained dormant as there was no one to release them and stirred only when someone strayed too close to the treasure they were protecting. They usually disoriented confused or frightened intruders away in ways that did not seem particularly odd whilst they occurred but were of high strangeness upon further reflection.

On Lemnos a merchant was said to have sacrificed his favorite slave, a Moor, to protect his family's vast (and soon to be buried) fortune. Though the merchant's name has been forgotten, he was said to be a fair man, though sometimes sullen and stubbornly set in his ways.

The soul of the Moor was to be assigned the task of guarding the treasure. Why? According to some accounts the merchant trusted the Moor, who had served him faithfully for many years. And the Moor personally knew all those whom his master mistrusted, and why he mistrusted them, making him the ideal guardian.

In Greek folklore, Black Guardians are dark and primordial shadow-giants who hang out on mountain tops and other difficult to reach places in rural Greece. They are said to gather together late at night to silently smoke long-stemmed pipes and enjoy each other's presence.

The Black Guardians guard hidden treasures and delight in tormenting (and sometimes killing) those who seek to steal it from them. Perhaps it was these tales that also inspired the merchant to choose the Moor.

Whatever the case may be, the Moor did not suspect that he was about to be slaughtered as he assisted his master with transporting the treasure and digging a deep hole. As this took place in Lemnos generations ago, I suspect that a donkey (or several donkeys) was present during this tragic event.

Knife-Wielding Demons and Murderous Ghosts

Without warning, the deed was done. The merchant's unexpected act, fueled by the Moor's spilled blood and sweetened by his fear, cries of alarm and extreme emotions sealed his sad fate.

No tale recounts what happened between then and the time the Moor re-emerged, about a generation later. His old master had predictably died without sharing his secret with his chosen heir and his family, unable to maintain his lands or run his household without him, slowly drifted away and sought their fortunes elsewhere.

A new family now owned and operated the land and, for a time, the Moor observed them. They had, of course, heard the lost treasure tale of the former owners and fantasized about accidentally finding it. Such things were known to occasionally happen on Lemnos and many hidden treasures have actually been unearthed while cultivating previously wild ground (this still happens, even today). Eventually the Moor entered the dreams of the pater familias and made him an offer: the location of the former family's treasure in exchange for a few drops of blood. The head of the household accepted the offer, dreamed of the location, awoke, immediately acted on the dream, found the treasure and cut his hand, offering his dripping blood and gratitude to the Moor.

He was now rich beyond his wildest dreams and lived in the grandest fashion with his family and select friends. The tale of the treasure-granting Moor was told and many wished that the Moor had come to them instead. But shortly thereafter the Patriarch sickened, then died. Then his family started getting sick and dying. Then their favored friends did the same.

As burying treasures small and large (and keeping the location secret) was a common practice in those days many family fortunes remain buried and unclaimed. On Lemnos pirates, raiders and bandits routinely did this as well. Plus there were all those whispered tales of Troy's lost treasury and the Drakos guarding it. The Moor, having much to offer, soon visited others in their dreams, at first those who wished for or fantasized about meeting him. The story always unfolded in the same way and the legend of the Moor grew.

Those who refused the offer, despite being tempted with images of soon having everything they ever desired, were left alone (though there are accounts of these individuals being revisited during times of extreme financial stress). Those who tried to cheat the Moor by not offering their blood when they dug up the treasure found themselves suddenly suffering from accidental cuts that spilled their blood into the ground. And the legend continues to grow.

Knife-Wielding Demons and Murderous Ghosts

Though seemingly not as active as he once was, I often heard tales of the Moor's most recent activities when visiting Greece during my formative years. In my studies I have come upon other folkloric Greek variations of the Moor, but the Lemnian tales I grew up with still impress me as being the most authentic.

ONCE OR NEVER HUMAN?

So, what exactly is the Moor? Is he an Ancient Greek Daemon in disguise or an actual human ghost hell-bent on exacting vengeance? For an Olympian Shaman, this will help determine the best course of action. Let's explore some of the possibilities and see where they lead us!

The Daemon Hypothesis: Some of the Moor's abilities hint at Daemonic influence.

Though Morpheus can assume any form and enter any dream, he is not reputed to be especially vengeful, murderous or a bringer or ruin.

Phobetor, though a personification of human Nightmares, likes to clothe himself in the forms of animals and monsters, not men.

Thanatos is the Titan of Death in Greek mythology.

Thanatos may be the Titan of Death but he seems content with escorting the dearly departed to the places that can best help them reach their soul's next destination.

The Moor, though dark of skin and a guardian of treasure, does not seem to be an actual Black Guardian as he is neither overly large nor brutish. The Moor operates alone and has never been observed sharing a smoke with other Moors (or anyone else for that matter).

Is the Moor a Shade? Shades are dark, shadowy and somewhat smoky beings, very difficult to confuse with living humans. Though they watch us unseen, their interest seems benign and is intergenerational.

Watchers usually hover around you and enigmatically watch you while you slumber. Aside from returning you to sleep when you stir, they show little interest in interacting with you. Although the Moor watches people unseen, his intention is to engage his chosen prey.

Is the Moor one of the Oneroi? Perhaps. Especially considering the existence of Epiales, a Nightmare daemon also called the Dark Dream.

Could the Moor actually be Epiales himself? Perhaps. This also seems plausible and definitely worth considering further. It must also be recalled that Epiales, as one of the Oneroi, can assume any guise he chooses.

The Ghost Hypothesis: As a human Ghost, the Moor's actions are understandable though very extreme. Despite their rarity and extremism, they also do not fall far beyond the known bounds of vengeful ghost behavior.

The departed dwell in, or wander through, many places that a ghost, even one bound to a buried treasure, can readily access. And there seem to be levels of Dream that can be accessed through sleeping in the Dream Realms proper. The once-human Endymion uses sleep as a mode of daily travel, as does the Dream Lord Hypnos.

As the Moor was not enslaved in a cauldron or other container and could have interacted with a variety of beings (some human and some not) from his remote location, it seems plausible that he encountered someone or something that helped him grow powerful enough to hatch and carry out his scheme.

My Conclusion: No tale survives of a human Magus ever having done such a thing, and it certainly would have if one had. Menandros and Kostas, both Magoi of my grandparent's generation (and members of my own family) left behind a handful of colorful legends that celebrated and preserved their boldest magical exploits. Had they met with or tackled the Moor, the encounter would most certainly have been immortalized in story form.

Based on the information at hand, as well as the results of my research and personal experiences, my best guess is that the Moor was once a person and that in the days of his soul's slavery he gained a Dark Oneiros, perhaps Epiales himself, as a Mentor. And let us not forget that the Moor operates in and draws his power from the Dream Realms.

I would also not rule out extensive interactions with Shades and Watchers as he routinely utilizes aspects of their modus operandi in his work.

Knife-Wielding Demons and Murderous Ghosts

Surprisingly I detected the subtle hand of Phantastor in the legends of the Moor. The treasures are inanimate objects imbued with symbolic meanings and the Moor's invitation can be construed as a twisted, though Mythic, Call to Adventure.

Besides exacting vengeance, the Moor also seems to be systematically freeing all the trapped and forgotten treasure Guardians. Perhaps the spilling of blood, which bound them to the site in the first place, was also instrumental in liberating them from their imposed task.

I also suspect that the Moor transcended his humanity and became a unique entity (an Exotic) during the course of his journey. I will be including him with all the Ancient Ones in future lists.

As to the after-death fate of all those who lost their lives due to the Moor's machinations – that still remains a mystery at present – but I'm on it!

WHAT TO DO IF YOU ENCOUNTER THE MOOR

Just say NO. You're now aware of the tales and know exactly what happens when you accept the offer and/or attempt to outwit this entity. If approached don't fall into the trap of elevating your excitement beyond your default "if I win the lottery" level.

Until Next Time, Joyous Journeys and Awesome Adventures!

-Hercules

Larger Than Life Living in the World Today

© Hercules Invictus

SUGGESTED READING - GLOBAL COMMUNICATIONS BOOKS TO WHICH HERCULES HAS CONTRIBUTED:

UFO HOSTILITIES AND THE EVIL ALIEN AGENDA

SCREWED BY THE ALIENS: TRUE SEXUAL ENCOUNTERS WITH ETS

WEIRD WINGED WONDERS

THE MATRIX CONTROL SYSTEM OF PHILIP K. DICK AND THE PARANORMAL SYNCHRONICITIES OF TIMOTHY GREEN BECKLEY

HIDDEN TREASURES OF THE KNIGHTS TEMPLAR

GEF THE TALKING MONGOOSE: THE "EIGHTH WONDER OF THE WORLD"

ALIEN STRONGHOLDS ON EARTH

Hercules Invictus

Knife-Wielding Demons and Murderous Ghosts

The Gaither Plantation

A MURDER/SUICIDE AND A CHILLING SOUTHERN HAUNTING
By Michele Lowe

These days, when you hear the word "poltergeist," most people of the younger generation will think of the movie directed by Steven Spielberg in which all sorts of activity happens – from a man's face changing shape in the mirror to items falling from out of the ceiling. One of the main characters, played by JoBeth Williams, turns her back for literally a second. Then the kitchen chairs move from their normal setting to suddenly being stacked neatly on each other on the table.

The word "poltergeist" is German and translates as "noisy ghost." People in the paranormal field also may refer to it as RSPK or "Recurrent Spontaneous Psychokinesis." Things considered to be poltergeist activity include large, heavy objects moving on their own accord or the opening and closing of doors or even disembodied voices, scratching sounds and beds shaking.

One recent popular theory holds that it is caused by a "human agent," usually an adolescent girl. There are several cases where that would apply, like the well-known and well-documented Enfield Poltergeist in Enfield, England, from 1977 to 1979. This involved a single mother with four children, two of them girls ages 11 and 13 years. The children claimed that furniture was moving on its own and that there were knocking sounds heard within the walls of the home. At the time of the activity it was widely covered by the British press. While the investigators on the case did consider the haunting genuine, other psychical researchers thought the case was "overrated," and many believed the girls had staged some of the incidents for the press.

Another very well-documented poltergeist case is that of the Bell Witch in Tennessee. A farmer named John Bell moved his family from North Carolina to

Knife-Wielding Demons and Murderous Ghosts

Robertson County, Tennessee, in 1804. They lived there peacefully for over a decade, and then that all changed in the summer of 1817, when some family members began seeing strange animals around the property. They also started hearing knocking on the doors and walls of the home and other strange noises they could not account for.

Although they initially kept the incidents to themselves, Mr. Bell confided their experiences to his neighbor, James Johnson. Mr. Johnson, after witnessing the activity himself for several days, suggested starting a committee to investigate.

As people started coming from miles around to witness some of the unexplained phenomena, including future president Andrew Jackson, the entity began to grow stronger and to speak! Though this entity gave many names, many believed it was the Bell's neighbor Kate Batts. It was believed that "Kate," or the "Bell Witch," wanted to kill John Bell for unknown reasons. Not only did she torment Mr. Bell, but his youngest daughter, Elizabeth "Betsy" Bell, was also the brunt of much of the torment, being pinched and having her hair pulled. Apparently Kate did not approve of Elizabeth's engagement to a Joshua Gardner. The engagement was eventually called off. Some even said it was Elizabeth who was the cause of all the activity, but Elizabeth demanded a retraction and threatened legal action. A public retraction was later published in the Saturday Evening Post.

"Kate" tormented the family for a full three years. When John Bell died from what people believed was poisoning, Kate took responsibility for it. Kate then left and said she would be back in seven years. True to her word, she returned on schedule for a few weeks, though people believe she has never left because the poltergeist activity continues.

Interestingly, both of the above stories did have a common factor of adolescent girls being involved. But I don't believe this is always the case.

My team of paranormal researchers and I were investigating a well-known plantation in Georgia, The Gaither Plantation (c. 1855). It has been used in movies and TV shows, such as *"The Vampire Diaries"* and *"Medea's Family Reunion,"* and is also known for its paranormal activity. Both of the casts had paranormal experiences while filming there. Both the cast and crew of *"The Vampire Diaries"* heard a piano playing upstairs and footsteps around the plantation while they were filming. During the filming of *"Medea's Family Reunion,"* the director had called for quiet on the set and had had the crew clear the upstairs. Right as they began to film they heard footsteps walking around upstairs. The director called for whoever was up there to come down. No one came, so he sent the crew up again only to find no one there. On the third try, after having the crew once again check for whoever was up there, the director yelled once again for everyone to come downstairs now, adding "And will the ghost of the house please cooperate!" After that, all was quiet, and the director got his shot.

Night photo of the haunted Gaither Plantation.

The property is huge, a sprawling 256 acres that at one time was 875 acres. In 1921, the Gaither family had to declare bankruptcy. Through the years, many families lived at the plantation, until Newton County acquired it and the surrounding property in 1996 as part of the Bear Creek Reservoir Project.

The property has a log smokehouse, a pole hay barn, the Gaither family cemetery and Gaither slave cemetery. Of note: there are several soldiers buried there also. Since then Newton County has also acquired several other historic buildings that are now located on the plantation property. Amongst the buildings is an old store, an old cabin and, most notably, a small church. This is where my story starts.

Our team has investigated Gaither Plantation several times through the years and it was on our last visit to the plantation that half the team had an experience they will not soon forget.

Dan, one of the team leads decided we would split up, with the guys on one team and the ladies on the other. So we set out to do our investigation. We girls decided to go out to the cemetery first. That was an interesting feat in itself; you see, to get to the cemetery we had to make our way through where they kept the horses. The horses were kept near the main house, and there were two fenced-off areas. One had several horses in it and the other area had just one horse in it. This horse was dark in color and quite beautiful. We wondered why they kept the one horse separate from the others and felt a bit sorry for it. But after spending some time with them all, we could see the dark horse, which I started calling the

Knife-Wielding Demons and Murderous Ghosts

Pooka, had issues with the other horses. The horses were only separated by one fence and could get close to each other, so, when it was time to hop the fence, we decided to go over to the one with several horses. It was a bit unnerving as they came up to us, but then we jumped yet another fence and made our way out several hundred yards to the cemetery.

It was very dark and the cemetery was covered in debris and brambles. We were recording audio and taking pictures when one of the girls captured what looked like ectoplasm which we could not recreate on camera. After spending some time in the cemetery, we decided it was time to head back toward the plantation, taking care not to step in the red ant hills that were out there in the fields in the pitch black. Once back to the fence we all freaked out, because the Pooka was standing right next to where we were going to have to hop the fence. After a bunch of laughing and quick maneuvering, we all made our way back over the fence without being bit by the Pooka.

After a break we headed to the other side of the property to investigate some of the buildings that had been added to the property. We decided we would go to the church first. The four of us girls made our way over to the church and looked inside before entering because we had been told the dark history of the church.

The church was established in 1822. It was originally located on Harris Springs Road, where it was an active church until 1985. When it was almost destroyed by fire in 1994, the building was relocated to Gaither Plantation, thus leaving behind the Harris Springs Cemetery. It's said that things got paranormally active once the church was moved to Gaither.

We were told of a murder/suicide that had taken place in the church when it was in its original location. The stories of the murder/suicide seem to vary regarding who shot who. We were told that the pastor of the church was having an affair and when his wife found out he killed her and then himself. Finding information on the murder/suicide has been difficult.

Some of the paranormal claims have to do with the sound of gunfire in the church, sightings of a woman pacing back and forth in the back of the church and the mysterious singing of an unseen choir.

Upon entering, there was a void-like feeling. We felt like we were trespassing. Quietly we walked around the church, looking about and trying to determine where the murder/suicide had taken place. It was not long before we felt a kind heaviness descend; we did not feel "alone." We made our way to the back pews of the church and sat down to do an EVP session. The team consisted of me, Cheryl and the two Cindy's, who we called "Isa" and "Iris."

We first did an EVP session at the front of the church in the front pews. We then made our way to the back of the church, where we were told the murder/suicide happened. Cheryl and "Isa" set up their equipment. Cheryl had a KII meter, used for checking electromagnetic field levels. "Isa" had a mel-meter, which is used for capturing electromagnetic fields also as well as ambient temperatures, on a display table. Both girls started getting strong activity on their meters in this area.

At first we seemed to be getting intelligent responses using the meters, but then the meters became more erratic. The energy of the "presence" seemed to be building and we could feel it in our bones as it seemed to be closing in on us. We then heard a loud bang coming from the front of the church and making us more on edge and uncomfortable. We then asked if the "presence" could make the loud bang noise again. There was nothing. Cheryl then said to the entity that, if it wanted us to leave, to make a loud bang noise again. And it did! It sounded as if something large and heavy hit upside the church! Between the intense feeling of not being welcome and the loud bangs, we decided to move to a different location. We collected our equipment and left the church.

Once outside we looked at the church where the loud bang had occurred and there was nothing to account for it. We then decided to make our way to the very small store that was right next door to the church. But then I saw a cabin about two hundred yards away. This was also one of the additions to the property. I said jokingly that we should head over to the "stabbin' cabin" instead. I had encountered that term previously when I investigated an extremely haunted house and had been amused by it. You can probably figure out what it meant.

Everyone agreed to head to the stabbin' cabin next and we all made our way over there. I don't know the specifics of the cabin as far as age or what is was used for, but you could tell it was old. I've yet to be able to find a history of this cabin.

When we entered the cabin it was, of course, dark since there was no electricity in any of the outer buildings. In the main area there were two old rundown beds on spring mattresses and a small table with a few chairs. There was a second room behind the main one. There was also some old wooden stairs that led to the attic/loft. We decided to go up there first.

Knife-Wielding Demons and Murderous Ghosts

Specters have been seen numerous times in the graveyard.

The minister's podium is said to vibrate if there is a poltergeist moving about in the church.

roswellparanormal.com

    Immediately "Isa's" mel-meter started going off in sync with Cheryl's KII meter. I had laid my rem-pod on a board of the floor, but it never responded. We did about a thirty minute EVP session while the meters were going off. Cheryl's back started hurting because she was standing the whole time and asked if we minded going downstairs. So we all agreed to head back downstairs.

    Once downstairs Cheryl and "Iris" sat down on the two chairs at the small table with Cheryl at the end of the table between the front door and the loft door; "Iris" was sitting to the right of Cheryl. "Isa" was sitting in a chair also in the middle of the room and closest to me. I was sitting on the bed furthest from the front door. "Iris" was asking EVP questions, and it was something to the effect of not being able to come down where we were now. All the KII and mel-meter activity had ceased once we were downstairs.

Knife-Wielding Demons and Murderous Ghosts

Michele Lowe
Board Member\Lead Investigator,
Roswell, Georgia Paranormal
Investigations

At that moment we heard a loud "swoosh" of the KII meter and then it flew about seven feet across the room! Cheryl said, "Holy shit," and I said something to the effect of "Are you serious?" As we sat there for a moment taking in what had just happened, Cheryl started feeling some faint nausea, though she had not mentioned it at that moment since it was happening so fast. It dawned on me that the instrument's flying had seemed hostile and I recommended we leave the cabin.

As we collected our things and started to leave the cabin, we felt it was urgent for us to get out of there. We quickly exited the building and started making our way back to the plantation. While we were walking away from the cabin, Cheryl started retching and almost threw up a few times. As we continued walking away, it felt like we were being followed by something or someone. That menacing feeling from the cabin followed us for a couple hundred yards until it finally dissipated. While we were heading back to the plantation we had radioed the guys to meet us on the path. It was when we were close to them that the feeling stopped.

We let the guys know what happened and they headed straight to the cabin. After a good bit they radioed to us that nothing was going on and asked if a couple of us girls would come back. Their thinking was that it may have had something to do with the fact that we were all girls. "Iris" and I went back to the cabin and there was no further activity.

What is interesting is, as I was shooting pictures with my full spectrum camera on our way to the cabin, I captured a giant orb-looking anomaly right behind "Isa." It was as if something was following us over to the stabbin' cabin.

It is my belief that something or someone followed us over to the cabin from the church. The negative feeling from the church and its intensity was the same as what ran us out of the cabin. Was this poltergeist activity coming from one of the people killed in the murder/suicide? Or had years of paranormal investigators investigating the church perhaps brought something there that was not there before?

Knife-Wielding Demons and Murderous Ghosts

The ghostly figure of a girl was photographed in 1992 on the Myrtles Plantation.

ALONE OVERNIGHT IN AMERICA'S MOST HAUNTED BEDROOM
By Joshua P. Warren

I am writing these words in the most haunted bedroom in the most haunted house in America. Honestly. Actually many people SAY it's the most haunted bedroom, but who knows? All I can tell you is that I experienced amazing stuff last night—things I will never forget—things that changed my life. I've been afforded the opportunity to pursue these kinds of places, and boy do I have a story for you . . .

You can learn a lot about Myrtle's Plantation in St. Francisville, Louisiana, on your own. I'm not a history teacher, so I won't bore you with the facts, names and figures you'll forget in two days. But just so you know where the heck I am and why this location is important, I'll hit the key points.

This place was built around 1796 by General David Bradford. In fact, I'm staying in the General David Bradford Suite. It's impressive; definitely looks "haunted." The ceilings in this bedroom are probably 15 feet high, dimly lit by crystal chandeliers, and the drapes are royal burgundy with gold trim. Those colors dominate this Victorian room, and the décor is of the period. It sucks in terms of modern accommodations. There are no telephones or a TV, and the bathroom faucet is all reversed, cold on the left, warm on the right, plus you turn the handles backward instead of forward to get the water flow. Lots of elements in this house are abnormal—the original owners installed all the keyholes upside down. They believed ghosts could slip in through them, and figured the spirits would be confused by the inversion. But I digress. I'm lucky my room has a shower. Many, if not all, of the other rooms simply have a bath tub. Long story short: If it weren't for the electricity and toilet, I could seriously be living in the 1700s.

Knife-Wielding Demons and Murderous Ghosts

When I arrived in Baton Rouge, Louisiana, rain was pouring, and the whole area was under a tornado watch. Bridges were flooded, detours were in place, and alligators were surely waiting to chomp me as I passed through foreboding swamps and ancient pools of quicksand. I'm lucky I even made it here. And mind you, I'm not some city slicker. I'm a guy who's used to rural living, but this made me nervous. Obviously, I made it ; so back to the story . . .

Why is Myrtles Plantation so haunted? I've heard some disturbing stuff through the grapevine. Rumor has it that in the 1790s, the Bradfords were looking for a new homestead. They were sick of mosquitoes and chose high land, a hill above the marshes. However once construction workers began digging around in the area, they discovered the property was an Indian burial ground. What did they do? They supposedly piled all the sacred bodies and burned them! No one knows if this is true, but that might set the stage for the events to come. In fact, the current owners of Myrtles don't even like to discuss that possibility, disgusted by the idea. We'll never know if this happened, but it adds to the mystery of the property. Whatever the case, it's clear the Bradfords were superstitious. Aside from the weird keyholes, there are crucifixes etched into much of the glass. They must have been afraid something was coming for them, right from the beginning.

Through the years, it's claimed at least 10 people died here. One of them, an owner named William Winter, took a shotgun blast on the front porch from a disgruntled neighbor. He supposedly staggered inside, his torso gaping and dragged himself up the main staircase. There he collapsed on step number 17 in a pool of blood, trying to keep his guts inside. His wife dashed to him from the floor above, and he died in her arms as she sobbed. Now when some "sensitive" people visit the house, they can't walk past step number 17, saying a terrible psychic force field stands there.

But the most famous ghost relates to a slave owned by the estate's second proprietor—Judge Clark Woodruff, a stern man as seen in his photo. Her name was Chloe (pronounced Cloe-eey). She was his house servant, and he made full use of her services, including a well-known sexual relationship. She wanted to maintain that relationship, since the alternative was breaking her back in the sweltering fields. Therefore you can imagine her upset, when Judge Woodruff began to fancy another young slave woman. Chloe was caught eavesdropping on the two, and the Judge sliced off her ear to teach her a lesson. Afterward she wore a green turban to conceal the horrible maiming.

Knife-Wielding Demons and Murderous Ghosts

After the ear incident, Chloe felt she'd surely be ordered outside. So she concocted a simple plan, extracting a poison from oils in the Oleander plant and spiking the meals of the Judge's wife and two children. Her intention was to merely make them sick, then tenderly nurse them back to health. Apparently she thought this would increase her value in the home, and help ensure her status. But things went awry.

Chloe put too much poison in the meals, and all three victims died. The mother only made it a day or so beyond the children. Both crushed and panic-stricken, she fled. But the other slaves captured her and brought her to Woodruff. They wanted to make sure no one pointed a dooming finger at them. The Judge hanged Chloe from a towering tree, and now, her dark, morose apparition is sometimes seen, meekly observing the grounds.

Over the years, every type of manifestation you can imagine has been reported. Objects fly off tables, voices, footsteps and crying are heard in empty rooms, a baby grand piano plays itself, cold blasts of air pass through hallways, handprints appear pressed into beds; you name it. There's an old portrait of an unknown man upstairs. The staff jokingly calls it the Gerald Ford painting, since the bald subject somewhat resembles the former president. His eyes are dark and penetrating. They literally follow you as you walk by, creepy to say the least. Furthermore guests have said his face shape-shifts, transforming into a monstrous visage. Others say he is sometimes wearing glasses, sometimes not. There is even a phantimal on the property, a ghost cat! He was put down a few years back, and the staff still feels his thick fur brushing by their legs.

Perhaps most well-known is a large mirror on the lower level. Prophets have gazed into mirrors and other reflective surfaces for years to attain psychic visions, usually called scrying. In the past, mirrors were sometimes thought to not only reflect light, but actually absorb the spirits of those who stared into them. When Chloe was executed, all the mirrors in the house were draped in a black cloth . . . except this one. And now, every year dozens of people say they see the figures of Chloe's victims in the mirror. Though the ornate frame is original to the period, the current glass was installed 16 years ago. Despite its relative youth, bizarre discolorations are strewn about its surface. Some look like streams of running blood, others like face-prints. Whether or not there is anything paranormal about those marks, it seems weird that glass would become so discolored in only 16 years.

Knife-Wielding Demons and Murderous Ghosts

In 1995, Jack Roth captured this photo of an apparition on the front steps of the plantation. Most believe it is Chloe.

A close-up of the figure in Jack Roth's photo.

Comparison: Joshua Warren reproduced the angle of Jack Roth's photo.

Knife-Wielding Demons and Murderous Ghosts

The Myrtle's Plantation at night.

FrontOfHouse
This shot gives you a better idea of where the phantom stood.

HesterFor Scale
Tour Guide Hester Eby stands in for the ghost. She is 5'5" and comes very close to the spot where the phantom's head is placed. The scale is correct for a woman.

Joshua Warren sits in "America's Most Haunted Bedroom."

Knife-Wielding Demons and Murderous Ghosts

When I arrived at Myrtles, it looked just like what I expected. The home is stately yet dreary, shrouded by huge trees, their crooked limbs reaching out as if they were skeletal fingers, moss dripping and hanging like long, rotting patches of corpse hair. The grounds are soggy, short stone cherubs sprinkled about the vegetation, standing eerie guard. Eight black cats roam the property like a silent pack of devils, always present, ever the familiars to whatever energy the home's solemn walls contain.

Out back is a lonesome fountain, illuminated crimson at night. Not far away, a small, muddy pond comes alive in the evening, a massive chorus of frogs chirping. After crossing a small bridge to the island gazebo in the middle, I was surrounded and enveloped by the high-pitched calls.

Also out back you'll find fine dining—Varnedoe's Carriage House Restaurant. The owner and head chef, Scott Varnedoe, is a highly-decorated professional who takes his "upscale down south" food seriously. I was able to sample four of his best dishes fresh from the kitchen, soft-shelled crab and roasted duck, and they were AMAZING. I wish that place was in my town. Not surprisingly, it's haunted, too. The bartender told me he was a complete cynic when he started working there. Therefore, he was perplexed to find the metal ceiling racks that hold the wine glasses and champagne flutes reversed, only allowing the glass to slide out from the back instead of the front. He was told it was to prevent glasses from inexplicably flying off and hitting the bartender or customers. He chuckled and thought it was ridiculous, until it occurred one night. "This glass flew off the rack backward, hit the mirror on the wall, bounced forward and exploded into a thousand pieces," he said. "I watched it happen and that's when I realized it wasn't a joke."

I have been to between 500 and 1000 supposedly haunted houses in my life, so I'm not easily impressed. But I had a feeling Myrtles might hold something special. I'd heard of the place for years. In fact, several years ago, I was contacted by the Make-A-Wish Foundation. A young girl with neurofibromatosis announced her last wish: to spend a night at Myrtles Plantation. She lived in my town, so the Foundation asked me to take her on a local ghost hunt then break the news that her wish had been granted. It's pretty outstanding that this would be a child's last wish, eh? And in September of 2007, I met paranormal photographer, Jack Roth, at a conference in Fredericksburg, Virginia. He took a famous photo of a cloaked apparition standing on the front porch of the house. It was about 5'5," according to my research and it's for sale in the gift shop as a

Knife-Wielding Demons and Murderous Ghosts

postcard. I reproduced Jack's photo angle with Hester the Director of Tours standing in for the eerie figure.

So now, at long last, here I was, ready to spend a night all alone in what might be America's most haunted bedroom.

Though I think everyone has the potential for a touch of ESP, I am not a psychic. When I walked into the General David Bradford Suite, I was immediately struck by a heavy sense of melancholy compression, despite the spacious rooms and high walls. Was it simply my mind playing a trick on me, fulfilling my expectations? Could be, but that's the way I felt regardless. Given the lack of TV, phone, internet access and other electronic distractions, it was the perfect place to sit quietly to focus on the room's environment. After taking some photos and video outside, I finally settled down for a night in this strange place.

I turned on my Sony Handycam with Night Shot. Though all digital cameras are somewhat sensitive to the otherwise invisible infrared realm, Night Shot is especially sensitive. And I was surprised at what I saw through the viewfinder.

The carpet in the room appeared normal to the naked eye. Yet when viewed with the greenish hue of IR, unsettling stains appeared, splashed about the room. One resembled a small footprint. Was this blood? I had no idea, but it certainly looked the part. I couldn't resist snagging a few fibers for later testing. I asked the Director of Tours, Hester Eby, about the stains. She had no explanation, and said that carpet had been in the room less than 10 years. Does that mean they were the product of a recent guest's mundane spill? Or is something more chilling at work? I know of several cases in which murder blood stains perpetually reappear at haunted sites, no matter how many times they are washed away. Perhaps something awful once occurred there, decades or centuries ago, and the phantasmal ooze inevitably rises to the surface. This was a good start to an unforgettable night.

I broke out a variety of scientific instruments: electromagnetic field detectors, electrostatic meters, Geiger Counters, anything I could use to measure the energy environment, perhaps revealing some hidden anomalies. All was calm until 11pm rolled around.

As I relaxed in the secluded, dim environment, I was overcome by a sense of calm, emphasized by a long, tiring day of travel from my home in Asheville, North Carolina. Suddenly, the stillness was shattered by a scream. Yes, that's right, a scream. Well, it was sort of a scream that morphed into a long, gravely, shrieking moan. It was a nerve-racking sound. I couldn't tell exactly where it came from, but I sprang to the door and opened it to see if a black cat was dying on my stoop. Nothing was there—just the raven, swaying trees and drips of remnant rain water softly plopping in the night. "What the &@* ! was that?" I asked myself. Fortunately my camcorder was running, capturing this unearthly cry for all time. I still don't know what it was, but the night was just starting to get really interesting.

I explored the room with a basic, mid-range, EMF meter. The fields in the room should have been consistent and predictable. As you walk toward electrical wiring, the field steadily increases. As you walk away, it steadily decreases. Yet, in this place, sudden, violent surges of energy would hit the device randomly. These erratic fields seemed to travel around the room, pulsating dynamically. I was thrilled to capture such kinetic jolts on camera, clearly demonstrating something unusual was growing, swelling, developing in the charged air. I turned out all the lights. There I was, standing alone, in complete blackness—a silence so complete that my breath was the only sound. I could only see through the green viewfinder of my IR video camera, and I sporadically snapped off 35mm shots with my 3-D still camera. At any moment I could turn to find a luminous form inches away. The thought alone was unnerving, and then, it happened:

"Bang! Bang! Bang!" A shot of adrenaline surged through my body when three sharp raps on the wall startled me. I swallowed and kept rolling. I spoke into the darkness.

"Is there someone here who would like to communicate with me?" I asked. "If so, please do that again."

"Knock! Knock!"

A chill ran down my spine. I must confess, there was an almost irrepressible urge to at least turn on the light, if not leave altogether to compose myself. No matter how many haunted houses you visit, true paranormal activity is so rare that no one can completely prepare for it. I am sometimes considered a "believer" by the layperson. That's actually not true. I don't believe or disbelieve in anything; I'm not a person of blind faith, but a person who simply addresses the evidence. And so my skeptical side persisted. I asked once again, "Okay if there is actually someone here, could you do that again?"

Immediately: "Knock! Knock!"

Knife-Wielding Demons and Murderous Ghosts

I was overcome by the realization I may truly be experiencing something wondrous and intimidating all at once, even historic for me, instant communication with something from beyond. And it was just the beginning. The rapping continued off and on. I couldn't tell exactly from where it came, but there were times when it sounded more like it emanated from a wall with nothing but vegetation on the other side. Could someone be out there knocking on the wood, playing a joke on me?

Without warning, I quickly and quietly slipped outside. Once again, there was nothing but the cool, moist Louisiana night. I returned to the Suite, the heaviness of the room stronger than ever. I measured and felt an electrostatic charge in the air. The hair of my neck stood on end, and a tingle touched my flesh.

The rest of the night, the banging and rapping on the walls continued sporadically. I tried to work out a primitive form of communication with a proposed entity—knock once for yes and twice for no. It didn't seem to work though. The percussion would often come at my request, but it was almost always the same: three distinct raps. All night I waited for a visual materialization. But alas, it never happened. I eventually dozed off and would awaken to the noise from time to time. Try sleeping by yourself in a completely dark room with a ghost tapping on the wall next to your head sometime. Ordinarily I would have stayed up all night, but I had to appear in a TV show shoot the next day. The last time I heard the knocking was around 8 in the morning. When I woke up for good, the entire setting had changed.

The energy environment was completely normal. Odd surges of electromagnetism and electrostatic charge were gone. That weight in the air had vanished. It was as if a window had been opened on an old, stagnant chamber, allowing the stale air to rush out, cleansing the space with thin, sweet freshness. Whatever had haunted my night was no more.

A gloomy, wet evening had been replaced by a bright sunny day. I went outside to take a better look at the grounds. There were no footprints outside my room, and I'm sure that slippery, muddy ground would have been disturbed. There was a small, young tree that touched the outside wall. I moved it around, pulling it back and letting it go like a spring to see if wind could have caused the sounds. No, it didn't come close. And besides, the rapping was almost always the same, consistent three hits. Nonetheless, a physical phenomenon like a bouncing tree would not cause the EMF anomalies I got, not to mention the nerve rattling scream.

The staff was not at all surprised by my experiences. In fact, they were surprised I hadn't heard more. Guests often report distinct voices, and sometimes the unmistakable shuffling of cards. According to them, activity seems to pick up when it's stormy and rainy, a fitting atmosphere indeed. And yes, they don't put it on brochures, but people do leave in the middle of the night. I can understand that now.

So here I am, lying on what might be the most haunted bed, in the most haunted room, in the most haunted house in America (at least some nights). I'll be here again tonight. Is it Chloe with a message? Will it come back? Are the stains on the floor really blood? Will my 3-D photos develop to yield a fantastic phantasm in glorious depth? We'll see. And by the time this is published (meaning RIGHT NOW, since you're reading it) you can see for yourself. I'll put an update, with pics, on my personal website for a while: www.JoshuaPWarren.com.

Come check it out while it's still there for free.

ShadowboxENT@gmail.com

www.JoshuaPWarren.com

Joshua P. Warren is a filmmaker, TV personality, and author of fourteen books, including Simon & Schuster's **"How to Hunt Ghosts."** He hosts the radio show, "SPEAKING OF STRANGE," and is the founder & president of L.E.M.U.R., one of the country's premier paranormal research teams. His museum and tours in Asheville, North Carolina, the oldest mountains in the nation, draw thousands each year.

Copyright© 2008-2019 by Joshua P. Warren

Knife-Wielding Demons and Murderous Ghosts

A crowd gathers in front of the small bungalow on Lindley Street, hoping to catch a glimpse of the poltergeist that was creating havoc inside.

MOST ASTONISHING POLTERGEIST CASES OF MODERN AMERICA
By Paul Eno

American history is full of poltergeists and nasty and vengeful spirits. We've written about the Bell Witch that frightened a U.S. President so badly that he fled in the early morning hours from a Tennessee homestead. Furthermore, this book contains the full story of the dreadful Amherst poltergeist, which is just as scary as any similar saga of evil you are likely to hear about from an historical perspective. This being said, I concentrate my work on cases of a more recent vintage that I have investigated firsthand.

As you can readily see, my attitude about such cases is a bit more "radical" than the views of other researchers, who tend to treat such poltergeist outbreaks as either restless spirits gone awry or put them in the general category of a purely psychological manifestation attributable to the witnesses' psychological state. I see such outbreaks more akin to a crossing of parallel dimensions by a variety of beings often mistaken for the undead – though they seem to have, in many instances, the same attributes as so called "aliens." Even cryptids from the darkest realms of our mind have recently been bought into the poltergeist equation.

THE BRIDGEPORT POLTERGEIST

With violent phenomena witnessed by almost 100 people over the course of a month in 1974, the Bridgeport, Connecticut, poltergeist outbreak, as I call it, is arguably the best-witnessed poltergeist event in history. And this doesn't include several thousand curiosity seekers gathered outside a tiny, backstreet house during the family's days-long ordeal.

Knife-Wielding Demons and Murderous Ghosts

The house was on Lindley Street, in a blue-collar neighborhood of Connecticut's largest city. The house was still there in 2016. People who go looking for it today are often astonished and skeptical that such dramatic events could occur before the eyes of trained observers, including police officers, firefighters and journalists, in such a tiny, three-room bungalow. But they did occur. I saw them, felt them and was hurt by them myself in the presence of multiple witnesses,

I was 21 years old and studying for the priesthood. Much to the displeasure of my seminary superiors, I was also studying the paranormal. I met the celebrated "grandparents of ghost hunting," Ed and Lorraine Warren, after Lorraine read something I wrote about ghosts in 1972 and invited me to their Monroe, Connecticut, home. I worked with them until 1978, as my school schedule allowed.

On Sunday, November 24, 1974, home from the seminary for Thanksgiving vacation, I found myself chugging down Interstate 84 in my 1968 Ford Fairlane in response to a dinner invitation from Ed and Lorraine. As soon as I pulled up to the Warren home, Lorraine came hurtling out the front door.

"Are you in a high spiritual state right now?" she cried.

I wasn't.

"Yes!" I replied.

Within an hour, I found myself at the house on Lindley Street, with Ed, Lorraine, Fr. William "Fr. Bill" Charbonneau, an indeterminate number of police and reporters (they kept coming and going) and a very frightened little family. The latter consisted of Gerard Goodin and his adopted daughter and only child, Marcia (pronounced Mar-SEE-a). Shortly mom (Laura Goodin) returned from the St. Vincent's Hospital Emergency Room with her right big toe bandaged. It had been broken by a flying television set.

The house itself was a mess. "The thing" as Laura called it, had been tearing pictures, especially religious objects, off the wall all morning. A priest had come to bless the house, apparently to no avail. Marcia's toy baby carriage had been commandeered by unseen hands that had filled it with clothing from bedroom drawers. The carriage sat in the living room as I arrived.

Here are the highlights of what I witnessed in the Goodin house:

Knife-Wielding Demons and Murderous Ghosts

- I stood in the kitchen with three firefighters on one side of me and three police officers on the other and watched the refrigerator float off the floor, turn right, turn back, then settle gently back to the floor.

- Late in the evening of that first day, I was sitting at the kitchen table with Lorraine. Also in the kitchen was a huge police officer, Ed Warren and a reporter from WNAB Radio. Lorraine suddenly let out a yelp. I watched as a second-degree burn, with its trademark white blister, appeared on Lorraine's left hand, between thumb and forefinger. This was all caught on the radio reporter's tape, which still exists. You can hear a youthful me stating, "There's a blister forming!"

- Later that night, I was in the kitchen again, standing between Marcia, on my right, and a large, floor-model television set. The TV suddenly tipped over with a crash, slamming me in the leg and knocking the child and me across the room.

Feeling the force of the crash, I was astonished that the television was undamaged. The screen should have been in smithereens all over the kitchen floor. But my leg sported a minor gash for several weeks, a battle scar from my bout with the Bridgeport poltergeist.

- For me, the most dramatic event came on Monday evening, November 25th. The Warrens had left to be on some broadcast, leaving the Goodins and me in the house. Marcia and I began to play Monopoly®. Suddenly an acrid smell, like ozone mixed with sulfur, came from the kitchen. Instantly Gerard Goodin was up, dashed into the kitchen and started chanting in Latin!

My skin tingled with an electrical charge that I now associate with the electromagnetic "branes," as physicists call them, presumably the boundaries between parallel worlds.

A whitish, gauzy cloud began to form in the kitchen, and Goodin was back in the living room at once. I immediately sat everyone down and took out a Russian Orthodox prayer book I had with me, starting to chant the first thing I came upon. This happened to be an ancient "akathist" or hymn in praise of Jesus Christ. Marcia joined me.

I was convinced that four entities were "arriving" in the kitchen from Marcia's adjacent bedroom. They weren't entirely invisible, and there were four indistinct shapes coming from the kitchen in a line. They were each about four and a half feet high and had rounded tops, with no discernable head or shoulders.

Goodin saw these figures also, and he followed one as it moved from the kitchen. As they entered the living room one by one, Laura Goodin started to cry, while Marcia clung to me.

I put the child behind me on a stool next to the front door. One of the almost-invisible things approached me and stopped. That's when I made my mistake: I began to feel angry toward this thing, which at the time I thought was a demon in the classic, theological sense. I was angry because it was obviously trying to get to this child. The whatever-it-was simply fed on the negative energy I was releasing and grew stronger.

Poltergeist victim Marcia gives her pet a big hug while trying to put the events of the past out of her mind.

What happened next was the biggest shock I'd experienced in paranormal work up to that time. As the entity moved to get around me and at the girl, I instinctively pushed toward it. It resisted as though it was entirely material. In fact, I felt flesh and bone structure as if this were a solid being.

These "demons" were supposed to be spirits! In fact, it took me many years to come to grips with this experience, let alone explain it in terms of parallel worlds. I never even reported it to the Warrens, and it was decades before I could write or speak about it.

While I stood there dazed, the entity got around me and threw Marcia across the living room. She ran back to me, crying. Finally, as the gauzy cloud inundated the whole interior of the house and as I tired from, I would say today, being drained by this powerful parasite, I ordered everyone outside.

Luckily, the police had cleared away the crowds and cordoned off both ends of Lindley Street. There were still thousands of onlookers, gawking from each end of the block.

I could hear a voice in the crowd preaching something about this all being a "sign of the end." These being the days long before cell phones, I had to use a neighbor's phone to call the Warrens. It took them an hour to get back into the

Knife-Wielding Demons and Murderous Ghosts

city because of all the traffic caused by this paranormal circus. When they finally arrived at about 9:15 p.m., we all reentered the house. Things were quiet.

When we turned on the radio, a newscaster was speculating about why we had left the house.

• There was the case of the talking cat, a major sideshow in the whole Lindley Street affair. In fact, "Sam" was featured in many a headline and newscast that week.

It was perfectly clear to me that Marcia would sometimes hold Sam close to her neck and do some rather decent ventriloquism. This was one patient feline. Still, Gerard Goodin insisted that the cat had vocal abilities far beyond the usual "choir practice" on the back fence at night. According to him, Sam had been in the veterinary clinic for an operation several months before. When he returned to Lindley Street, the Goodins, and even some of their neighbors, insisted that Sam could talk. While at the clinic, Goodin told Paul, "the damn thing must have swallowed a myna bird!" He swore that Sam would come to the top of the cellar stairs and demand in colorful language to be let out. Sometimes he "swore like a sailor," Gerry asserted. At other times, Sam would somehow pound on the door and shout, "Open this door, you dirty Frenchman, you dirty rat!"

All I know is that Sam became famous, thanks to the media. I'll never forget the sight of reporters from ABC, CBS and NBC, who came in from New York, standing around Sam with microphones that Monday, begging him to say something.

So why the Goodin Family? And why Lindley Street? It was, in my opinion, a classic poltergeist pattern. But if I knew then what I think I know now, neither demonic spirits nor exorcism had anything to do with it. Neither did RSPK as caused by Marcia as the "agent."

What I encountered in that house were four very non-human beings I could only describe as "alien" in a very broad sense of the term. I believe they were quite physical parasites whom Nature has adapted to move between parallel worlds to feed, in this case on the fear and anger in the Goodin house. They had such a feast that they were strong enough to cross the "brane" into our world in quite a dramatic manner. It was a classic pattern I've seen in many poltergeist cases.

Here are some of the factors that rang the dinner bell and set the Goodin family aside as a hot lunch.

- The Goodins were very introverted and held to a devout, but fear-based and negative, variety of Roman Catholic spirituality.

- The couple smothered Marcia with overprotectiveness, not letting her have any real friends.

- Relatives, neighbors and friends of the family said Marcia was sneaky and manipulative.

- There was a great deal of pent-up frustration and other negative energy in the house.

Meanwhile, throughout Monday, November 25th, and the early part of Tuesday, November 26th, we all stood around waiting for the Roman Catholic Bishop of Bridgeport to grant permission for an exorcism of the house. That wasn't as easy as it sounds. Unlike most other religions, Roman Catholics have highly ritualized and official forms of exorcism. A Roman Catholic priest can find himself in big trouble with the local bishop if he uses these rituals without permission, especially in a highly public situation.

Permission never came.

We left the house in the wee hours of Tuesday just to get some sleep.

"How can we ever thank you?" Laura Goodin said as she hugged the Warrens and me. As if to say farewell, the coffee table jumped across the living room as we walked out the front door.

After another few hours on the Warrens' living-room couch, I headed back to my home in East Hartford to shower and talk with my priest. The Warrens had to go to Hartford on business. We agreed to meet back at the Goodin house at 2 p.m.

As I headed back up Interstate 84, I turned on WCBS Radio, New York. The newscaster was saying that Bridgeport police had declared the poltergeist a hoax perpetrated by Marcia! Every station I could get said the same thing. I returned to Lindley Street at 2:30 p.m. and stood aghast on the front steps as Laura Goodin ordered a policeman to throw me off the property. I finally met the Warrens back at their home at about 5 p.m.

This is the story I heard: The city was tied up in knots because of this paranormal ruckus, so the police entered the Goodin house within minutes of our departure that morning. An officer had seen Marcia kick a piece of furniture, and that was all that top minds at headquarters needed. Veteran police interrogators grilled Marcia. Ultimately, according to police reports, she "confessed" to being the culprit. Police Superintendent Joseph A. Walsh announced Tuesday morning that the Bridgeport "poltergeist" was a child's hoax.

All kinds of crazy rumors flew back and forth across the media. The Warrens' phone didn't stop ringing all that evening. At 7 p.m., Ed and I were guests on the three-hour Tiny Markel Show, a call-in program on WNAB Radio. Virtually all callers agreed that the sudden police declaration of a hoax was hard to swallow, no matter what the explanation for the Lindley Street happenings might be.

Accusations were hurled at us from Lindley Street and police headquarters during the rest of November and early December. Believe it or not, these included:

- Candy I had bought and brought back to the house on Monday afternoon was drugged and somehow caused the phenomena or caused Marcia to cause the phenomena.

- Ed Warren caused the events from his own home by witchcraft.

- All the witnesses were put under some sort of spell.

How any of these goofy charges were easier to believe than the truth is beyond me to this day.

Fr. Charbonneau became so famous that fan mail addressed simply to "Fr. Bill, Bridgeport, Conn." was forwarded to him by the Bridgeport Post Office without problem. To the best of my knowledge, not one witness, including the police officers who were there, ever retracted a story.

However the poltergeist was far from banished. According to a number of reliable sources, the ordeal continued. Laura told a friend that her husband had to plant their Christmas tree in concrete because it kept moving. Reportedly some of the furniture had to be wired down.

By January 1975, an investigative team from what was then the Duke University Parapsychology Laboratory worked out a deal with the family and the police to go to the house and conduct a thorough investigation of its own. The team included Jerry Solfvin and Keith Harary, along with Boyce Batey, a lecturer and Connecticut resident affiliated with the Spiritual Frontiers Fellowship. Dr. Solfvin later told me that the Goodins vehemently denied any hoax and insisted that Marcia had nothing to do with the events.

Late in January 1975, the Goodins appeared on a local radio show, where they also nixed the hoax allegation. They also said that paranormal events continued in the house. In early February, a "For Sale" sign appeared out front. It took time, but the place finally sold, and the Goodin family vanished from the public eye. As far as I could determine at the time, nothing weird happened at the address after the Goodins left.

Both Gerard and Laura Goodin died within a decade, and Marcia passed in 2015.

For the full story of this case, I recommend "The World's Most Haunted House" by William J. Hall (New Page Books, 2014) and "Behind the Paranormal: Everything You Know is Wrong" by Paul Eno and Ben Eno (Schiffer Publishing, 2016).

COMBATING THE SPACE-TIME BEAST OF NEW HAVEN

Ironically, the worst poltergeist I ever faced was the easiest to get rid of. It was March 1979 when a frantic call came from Steve Cargill, a friend of mine in New Haven, Connecticut.

"Even you won't believe this one!" Steve was yelling. I could hear banging and shouts in the background.

"What?" I shouted back, alarmed.

"The craziest poltergeist you ever saw! I'm there now!"

Fortunately, I was still living in East Hartford, about thirty-five miles to the north, so I wasn't far away. I dropped everything and headed for New Haven. Following Steve's hasty directions, I soon found myself at the back door of a good-sized, "mom and pop" convenience store not far from the city line. There was a big "closed" sign at the front door, and the store windows all were curtained. I'd been told to slink around to the rear door as invisibly as I could. I knocked, and I jumped back when the door opened immediately.

"Are you Paul?" asked a big, forty-something woman.

"Yes, ma'am," I responded.

Without another word, her arm shot out, grabbed my sleeve and pulled me in. She looked exhausted, but her strength was alarming! The door slammed with the nervous rustle of Venetian blinds. Before she hustled me through another door and up a flight of stairs, I had enough time to see that the darkened store was a shambles. Everything that should have been on the shelves seemed to be on the floor. There was an unpleasant smell, and I could have sworn that I saw a bottle of soda suspended high in the air over the middle aisle.

"Up this way. This is where it's worst." My apparent hostess pointed up the stairs, which were littered with articles of clothing. At the top, a spacious apartment opened out. The place would have been beautiful had it not been an absolute catastrophe. The floor was covered with debris, there were black scrawls of "death," "die" and a few less mentionable things on the walls, and the place reeked of sulfur. The electrical field was so powerful that it felt like bugs crawling all over my skin.

"This is my home! Do you believe this? Ahhhhh!!" She shrieked, and my head quickly swung around to look where she was looking. We both ducked just in time as a huge armchair whizzed over our heads and crashed against the opposite wall!

"What now?" came a shout from the bathroom, and Steve stumbled out, still fastening his pants. "Oh, you're here!" He picked his way across the room to shake my hand. Somehow, I felt free to skip my usual "Is this really paranormal?"

"All right!" I stated with a glance over each shoulder. "What's the story?"

At once something started to pound on the floors right beneath our feet. I had just turned to run back down the stairs to see what it was when the woman, whose name turned out to be Liz Centracci, shouted over the din: "Don't bother. It's the ghost."

Well, it seems that "the ghost" had been raising the devil at this scene off and on for over a year.

"A year?" I blurted in amazement.

It's unusual for a poltergeist to last more than three months at a stretch. The longest documented case I'm aware of was at Kuokkaniemi in Finland, and that went on for a little less than three years, beginning in 1900. It's also unusual, in my experience anyway, for a poltergeist to keep going flat-out when I arrive. Usually things calm down for a while, seemingly until it gets "used" to me and my own electrical field is introduced into its "mix."

The thing was quiet long enough for me to hear the whole tale.

Liz had been a widow for about five years. Her husband had left her the prosperous little store beneath our feet and a decent chunk of money. That was good, because Liz had their little girl to bring up. Things had gone pretty well until early 1978, when pounding had started on the floor of the apartment, seeming to move rapidly around underneath. In the store below, the pounding was on the ceiling, of course, and Liz would tell customers hastily that she was having some repair work done.

On the sly, she had the place checked for mice, rats, termites and every other physical pest known to man. She sought help from utility companies and even consulted a seismologist from nearby Yale University, all to no avail. The phenomena kept getting worse and, within six months, Liz had to close the store – after something started throwing bottles of soda at customers one day. That's how she had met Steve.

"I happened to be in the store about six months ago, and I got beaned by a bottle of ginger ale!" he recalled. "There was nobody else in the store, and Liz seemed real nervous. I 'put two and two together' and told her I knew a guy who worked with 'weird stuff.' I left her my phone number."

Meanwhile, Liz told customers that she was closing the store to start a major remodeling project. She even had her brother-in-law, a contractor, park one of his trucks outside a few days a week. But if anybody was going to do some remodeling, it was the space-time beast inside.

By mid-1978, voices had joined the pounding. Liz and her fourteen-year-old daughter, Anna, would hear each other speaking even when both parties weren't present. Not long after that, apparitions began, getting more terrifying by the week: faces bobbing in the air, black shadows creeping across the floor and through the air, both in the store and the apartment, and red eyes seen peering from beneath furniture.

That's when Liz packed the frazzled Anna off to her sister-in-law's in nearby East Haven. But Liz, a sort of Annie Oakley of the paranormal, was determined to fight it out. She would take "breathers" from time to time, staying with Anna and her sister-in-law for a few days just to get her strength back. Courageous and cavalier as Liz was, things only got worse when she went back to the apartment and the parasite started sucking her energy again.

After a while, Liz wasn't able to sleep in the apartment at all, and she moved in with her sister-in-law and daughter. But nearly every morning, Liz would be back in her domain to keep watch and battle the poltergeist, almost as though she were going to work. Of course, all she was doing was feeding the thing. Liz told me that it would take the beast a good hour to get revved up after she arrived in the morning. In fact, she was a sort of human cup of coffee for it.

Down in the shuttered store, what was left of the stock wouldn't stay on the shelves, and Liz finally gave up trying to keep it there. About two months before I showed up, the black scrawls had started appearing on walls and ceilings in the apartment, and the poltergeist began literally punching holes in the walls.

The real trouble here was that Liz had done everything wrong from day one, right down to the last detail. She and a friend had been playing with a Ouija board for weeks before the trouble began. Obviously, something unpleasant came through. Later, when phenomena got worse, Liz became convinced that it was a ghost and organized a séance with a local medium and a few trusted friends. This just took what the Ouija board had done and made it worse. I later met two of Liz's friends who had attended, and they confirmed that "the voice of an angry young woman" had come through the medium, claiming she had been murdered in a house on that spot in 1820 and wanted revenge. It was the usual nonsense parasites dish out to get their victims stirred up. The spot had been the middle of a cornfield in 1820, at least in our corner of quantum reality.

The haunted Bridgeport house (in reality a small bungalow) as photographed by Wm Hall.

Ben and Paul Eno interview Tim Beckley on Behind The Paranormal broadcast Sunday's live over station WOON in Woonsocket, RI. (www.BehindTheParanormal.com)

The medium never came back.

Liz's solution had been to alternately shout at the poltergeist, then ignore it. She sprinkled holy water or salt, burned incense and otherwise called upon every folk remedy she could find in books at the local branch of the New Haven Free Public Library.

It's not that these methods don't work, but they work much better when done with faith and a positive spirit than with fear and superstition. That's because they're tools. They have little power in themselves, but they can concentrate and energize the power of our own minds to positively take control of our own environment. But the tools must fit the user. Crosses rarely work for non-Christians, for example, but I've seen teddy bears work as protective tools for children. It really does depend on the person. Liz was using her chosen tools in fear and anger.

All this hullabaloo provided more energy for the original parasite and attracted some of its buddies. In my initial investigation, when I wasn't dodging flying furniture, I felt strongly that there were at least six parasites having a field day, not only in the apartment but also in the store below.

In a situation that would have sent most people packing long before, Liz had gotten more and more determined. But as her anger grew, it, too, fed the parasites. And as she continued to live off her savings, without income from the store, she got more and more worried, and that fed the parasites.

I've seen this circle-the-wagons mentality many times, though not for so long a period. Homeowners and even renters have a certain primal instinct to defend their homes. I've often seen people stick it out even on the rare occasions I've advised them to move. Of course, phenomena at Liz's weren't constant. Poltergeists tend to be active for a few days or a week, then re-energize before getting active again. So Liz did have a period of relative quiet every week or so. But nothing she could do seemed to bring the trouble to an end.

Liz struck me as not only strong but also scrupulously honest. For example, she was a Roman Catholic, but she hadn't called her priest, because she was afraid he'd be upset about her using Ouija boards and doing séances. The idea of simply not telling him the truth evidently hadn't occurred to her. Actually it probably was just as well that she didn't call in clergy. People often are shocked when I say that few clergy are educated about the paranormal, but it's true. At times, they can do more harm than good.

Knife-Wielding Demons and Murderous Ghosts

A real miracle of this case was that Liz managed to keep the information lid on the situation for as long as she did. I found all sorts of rumors flying around the neighborhood, what with the store closing, Anna leaving and all sorts of odd noises. The general belief was that Liz had gone a little batty and was holed up above the store. The fact that nobody who had seen anything in the store or apartment had talked about it, probably for fear of sounding crazy, was a minor miracle in itself.

It was a good thing for all concerned that the media never got hold of this. With the Bridgeport poltergeist outbreak (Faces at the Window, New River Press, 1998) only a few years before, reporters would have loved it! If Liz had called the police, one of the first things most poltergeist victims do, the media would have found out for sure.

It was a good thing, too, that poltergeists don't last forever. Sooner or later, they get all the energy they can from their victim and they start to weaken. This rat pack got weaker, I'm convinced, simply because even the gallant Liz was starting to wear down. By the time I took over the case, these "noisy spirits" were near the end of their electromagnetic ropes anyway.

I suggested calling in a priest I knew to at least bless the house, but none was available. Since I realized the parasites were playing themselves out and because I already was starting to form my "out with the bad air, in with the good" theory, I was convinced that Liz, Steve and I could get rid of them ourselves.

So that evening, after we'd gotten Liz out of the apartment for a decent meal, we marched straight back in. All was quiet as we stood in the middle of the floor and held hands. We said the Lord's Prayer, and I announced calmly to the parasites that we had their number, that the game was up, and that Liz wasn't going to be their meal ticket anymore or words to that effect.

There was a thump under our feet that shook the floor, but I had told everyone to remain calm at all cost. That night, I convinced Liz to stay with her sister until we had pacified the situation. The next day and the next, Steve, Liz and I were back. We did everything positive we could think of. We read from the happier parts of the Bible, we shared stories about our families and our happy memories, and we even had a great evening reading from a joke book and singing songs. On the last evening, we had Anna with us, and she seemed completely renewed afterward.

That really did it. I checked with Liz often over the next two months, and Steve stopped by frequently. She and Anna, who moved back home, had cleaned up the apartment within the week and had repairs done. Within a month, the store was open again, and it didn't take long for things to get back to normal.

As far as I know, Liz never had trouble again. The key was that she kept that positive spirit and broke her link in the chain of factors that can permit paranormal phenomena of this kind to take place. With the love of her daughter and her home, she won the victory that anger never could.

BOOKS BY PAUL ENO

Behind The Paranormal: Everything You Know Is Wrong

Footsteps In The Attic

Faces At The Window

The Bell Witch Project

Spooky Treasure Troves

Author William J. Hall investigated a case that has gone down in poltergeist history.

THE GRIPPING BRIDGEPORT STORY CONTINUES

WHAT EVER BECAME OF MARCIA?

She died at an inappropriate relatively young age without any fanfare and with no one at her side. If it were not for paranormal researcher and author William J Hall who penned the book "**The Most Haunted House In America**" about this legendary poltergeist case no one probably would have missed her.

Hall, who maintains an active website at: *worldsmosthauntedhouse.com* filed the following report.

2015 UPDATE: November 12, 2015

They say the most striking news hits suddenly in the middle of an otherwise ordinary day. That is just how this important story began. On Friday, March 20, 2015, at 4:58 P.M., I received an email from a reader that alerted me to a short notice she had run across in a recent edition of the Mansfield News Journal:

"The Richland County Coroner's Office is requesting the public's help in finding next of kin for Marsha Godin, 51, who died Feb. 10 at Ohio Health Med Central Shelby Hospital. Godin died of natural causes, according to the coroner's office.

Anyone with information is asked to call [phone number] so Godin may have a proper burial."

And there it was staring at me a new mystery of sorts. Could this be, in fact, the Marcia Goodin who played a central role in **"The World's Most Haunted House"**? There are many Godins and her first name was officially Marcia, not Marsha. Her last name was Goodin, not Godin. Godin was, however, the proper family name. Jerry, Marcie's father, left the mistake on his birth certificate and the name carried on to Marcia.

I anxiously dialed the number and offered my story. The man who answered wasn't handling that case, so he took my information and promised he would have the proper person - Bob - call me back. He did. Bob was appreciative that I had taken time to contact him. I provided several pieces of information: her prior name, her date of birth, ancestry, and the belief that she was in Canada. After I divulged those facts, he said we were definitely considering the same person. He confided in me that, "Instantly, I had a very eerie feeling when I walked into her hospital room. And it wasn't that she was dead. Heck, I have seen so many unusual deaths so it had nothing to do with that. I even commented to the nurse about it."

The story unfolded in the following way: About six years before, Marcie came back to the United States from Ontario, Canada - alone - settling in Shelby, Ohio. (She previously lived in Tiffon Ohio from 1998-2002.) There, she lived with a man who was much older than she. When interviewed by the authorities, he disclosed he didn't know much about her. He explained that he met her in a diner and helped her out because there was a lot that she could not do for herself. He needed a place to stay and ended up moving in with her. It appeared their relationship was a friendship. Presently, he won't speak to the coroner. Bob thinks it is because he is afraid he will have to pay.

The man was in a nursing home when Marcie died. Bob said they found a letter from her brother from Canada in with her personal belongings and he would try to retrieve it for me. A stepmother was mentioned, but I told him I had no information about that. Canada wouldn't release any of her records or information to him. (Their policy of not releasing records is what kept me from finding her when I did my initial research.)

Bob related to me that her hospital records noted she suffered from remitting and relapsing MS and epilepsy and has had seizures since 1993. She had four to five seizures that would result in her "spacing out." There appears to be a correlation in poltergeist cases with epilepsy in particular, but the sample size is naturally small, so we cannot say it is a correlation with causation as opposed to just a coincidence. Evidence, however, does start to point to that as being a factor in the amount of cases that we obtain information on at least.

Bob related to me that she had MS and had been on some heavy narcotics for pain management. He felt her death might have been related to that. The neighbors were unaware Marcie lived there because she kept to herself and was never seen coming or going.

Bob's dilemma was that he could not find any next of kin to sign off on the paperwork so she could be given a proper burial. Furthermore, he couldn't issue a death certificate in Ohio without knowing the names of her parents. I provided him with a copy of the book and the information he needed on Jerry and Laura and explained the couple had adopted her.

Since I knew several members of the Godin family, I was able to get in touch with one who was willing to sign the proper documents so Marcie could be given a proper burial. It turns out the letter from her brother was not available or kept and therefore we do not have access to that information. But the story is not over yet.

On July 10, 2015, I received a message sent from my website from Marcie's biological sister from Canada! We spoke by phone and I learned the following addition information about the family:

- Her half-sisters called her "Jean," not Marcia. The siblings only met once but Marcie saw her half-sister in Ohio more often (but not regularly). I did interview that half sister and Lindley Street was never mentioned but Marcie said that Laura was very mean to her. At one point, Laura took all of her possessions and destroyed them (Actually, some were given away as detailed in the book). Her comment was "They were too old to have children." She never said a bad word about Jerry.

- Marcie was described as normal, quiet, very nice, and a lover of animals (especially dogs and Rottweilers in particular). She never married but had several long term relationships. She was a cheerleader and played softball in high school. She did graduate college, focusing on technical writing and earlier, computer engineering. She never lived in Canada. She was in the states her whole life. Marcie was Jewish.

- She confided in the sisters that when she was a teenager, she was sexually abused by her uncle.

- Marcie hid from people in her past by using different emails and changing her name enough to remain difficult to locate. You won't be surprised to know she hated the media.

- She worked in retail most of her life. Overall, the sense I got was that she didn't have a horrible adulthood until the sickness became very debilitating in the last five or six years of her life.

- Both Marcia and her biological mother died at the age of 51.

- The biological sisters found out about both of their deaths on the same day, July 7th.

- Marcia was one of six biological children from the same mother, all girls and one boy.

- The brother died before any of them were able to meet him. No one knew their father.

- Marcie was not the only child given up for adoption. Three of the children were, since they were all the result of teenage pregnancies from different fathers.

At the same time, I received an inquiry from the daughter of Robert Roberts, brother of Laura Goodin! Her father is still alive but is not fond of his sisters and has not spoken to them for many years. She wrote me and relayed that her dad lost contact with his sister and niece when they moved out of state. She did visit Laura Goodin (her aunt) at the house when she was about five years old; before the Goodins had adopted Marcia.

They received news that Laura Goodin died in a car crash from a family living in Connecticut but had no news about Marcie. She thought the accident was strange because it was a nice sunny day so she is not sure what happened. (Marcie told her half-sister that Jerry was the driver in that accident.)

I returned the conversation back to probe about why her dad didn't like Laura. He said Laura fought all the time with her mother and was not a nice person. Robert was quite surprised to learn she was religious at all! And the last comment that solidified so many of the rumors for me was when I told them of the rumor that Laura was said to have locked her mother in the bathroom and they would go out. The words I heard next sent a shiver through me, "That doesn't surprise me. That sounds like Laura."

Her biological half-sisters learned of the book and I spoke to two of them. Marcie's ashes were sent to them and they got together as a family to bury her ashes on a piece of land where her grandfather had a home - close to where Marcie's biological mother is buried. Her sister told me that "It's a real peaceful place."

Although the revelation provides some closure, there is an element of the sadness that characterized her life, which seemed to follow her to her grave. None of the after-stories associated with Lindley Street seem to have been anything but sad, if not tragic. They still resonate in our hearts and minds as we remember, the Roswell of Haunted Houses, known to the world as "Lindley Street" or "The Bridgeport Poltergeist."

William J. Hall's book is available through his website or Amazon.com

Haunted House On The Edge Of Forever.
©Carol Ann Rodriguez.

HOBGOBLINS AND UNFRIENDLY REALMS
By Maria D'Andrea

EDITOR'S NOTE: Maria D' Andrea is an internationally known professional psychic from Budapest, Hungary. Since early childhood she has demonstrated high spiritual awareness and psychic ability. Over her lifetime and as a Spiritual Leader, she has provided excellent psychic guidance and enlightenment to many people, assisting them on their own personal path of spiritual self-discovery. Many occultists and psychics specialize in only one area, for example Tarot card reading or Psychometry. Many have said that when you work with Maria, you can rest assured that she will be able to use the best method to achieve the best results for your particular circumstance in outlining your needs and destiny. Maria is known for a unique form of divination called "Rune Casting." This method was used by Vikings and Europeans to unlock information about the past, present and future by tapping into the Universal Mind. Maria's occult philosophy is: "The responsibility of a selection of paths is yours after you have been made aware of the underlying factors and forces at work."

* * * * * * * * *

Not all ghosts are satisfied just going "BOO!"

GHOSTOLOGY – FINDING UNSEEN FORCES

Ghostology has been with us for ages, although not necessarily known by that term. It is the study of spirits, phantoms, humans – like apparitions, shadow forms and any other denizens of the unseen. Most people are not aware, but that also includes various forms of receiving information from different realms.

Psychic Maria d' Andrea with devices that could chop off a good head or two.

One such form is the sense of smell. Certain odors may be detected in the area of the spirit's vicinity, such as a rose or a perfume the spirit may have worn in life. It may be one that is a scent that is negative to the senses. People who are sensitive in this area or psychics may pick up this spirit smell.

Others, who are sensitive in varied forms, will pick up the spirit ghost differently, such as the "feeling" that someone is in the room. There isn't a way to explain it; you just know. You may also sense if the ghost is male or female; positive or negative; tall or short; old or young or any information which comes through.

Many times, the information will aid in helping the ghost in some way, or help identify it and thus release it from that particular location.

Ghostology is a study of many forms, to help us understand and to work with the levels not seen or known to most of us.

Sensitive people will in some form be tuned in to the vibrational forces and will comprehend them. However, that does not always mean that they can explain this to others.

We need to simply trust our own instincts and learn to listen with our sensitivity, not just our ears.

If you give yourself a few moments, look back in your life and notice how many times you "thought" you sensed something, only to logically talk yourself out of it. Now, some, if not all, of that time, you can see that your "abandoned" thought least was really correct.

Spend some time really letting yourself feel and smell and touch and sense what is around you. Close your eyes and really "know" your environment. You may be surprised at what you discover to be really true.

Ghostology has been widely accepted and basically understood by the general population.

HOBGOBLINS

They can be a force to be reckoned with.

Goblin Market (The Devil) - Victorian Fairy Tarot.

Many people have heard of the hobgoblins and some as children listened to negative stories about them. Children's stories used to keep them in line, told for fun, but nonetheless scary. Myths, tales and stories passed down through generations, retold so often and in such varied ways that at times it is forgotten that there was ever a truth that they were based upon.

Hobgoblins are nature spirits. They are also known as goblins on a more familiar level and are able to be seen by some people, such as psychics or people who are sensitive to the non-physical realms. There are times you may be more open to your psychic levels.

These nature spirits are really fairies. However, fairies have numerous categories. The name "goblin" is given to the spirits which are more mischievous.

These nature spirits are on a lower mentality level and thus are also unreasonable. If one is in your home area and you make contact, this is not a spirit you could explain your situation to and ask it to leave. You would need to give it a command for it to have any effect.

Hobgoblins like to make contact and be seen when possible. (This would be on a psychic/clairvoyant level.) This is due to the mischievous attitude of the spirit, having fun and delighting in causing surprise, unsettlement or chaos.

Sometimes these spirits are also known as shape-shifters. Thus, they can appear on and off as animals or thieves, among other forms. These nature spirits are also known for their small, heavy-set bodies and rough-looking countenance or scary looks.

Although at times these hobgoblins manifest extremely negative aspects, they can also just be minor troublemakers.

Knife-Wielding Demons and Murderous Ghosts

All spirit is under our control. Being in the physical body, we all have free will over spirit. Thus, any spirit that you may come into contact with and do NOT want around, you can command to leave. Say it as a command that the spirit has to leave NOW. State that you are commanding this through the Power of God. (Say the name of whoever to you is Divine Power.)

Keep repeating this on and off until the spirit leaves. And it will, since it does not have the control. YOU do.

When you hear myths or legends, you can look into them in-depth and find the basic cause or truth behind them.

There are numerous nature spirits and hobgoblins are only one type. Think of them as "mischievous" fairies.

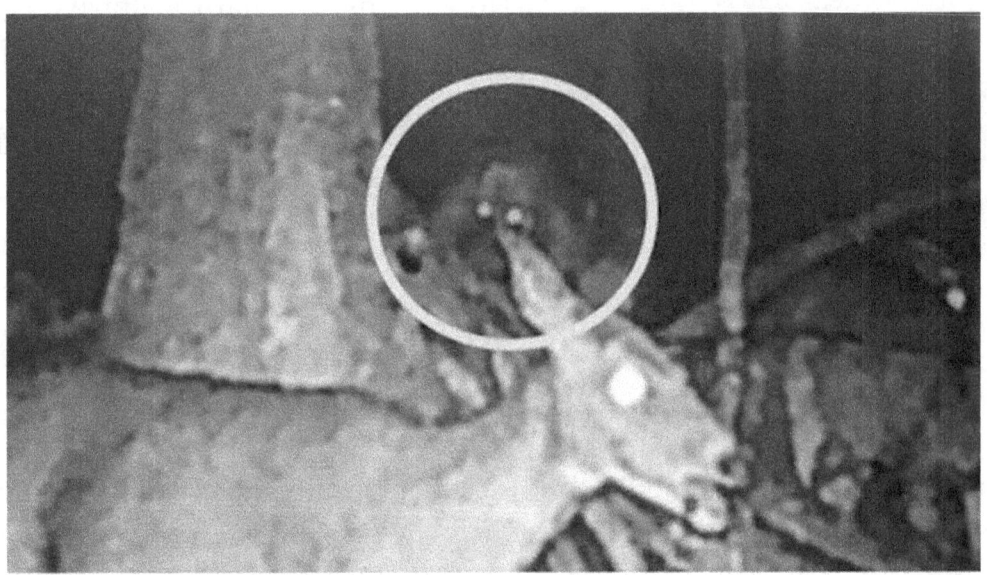

They are in "hiding" all around us. Hobgoblins often take refuge in wooded areas.

PSYCHIC SELF-DEFENSE

Any time you work with spirit, you need to know how to protect yourself. You always use a shield before you start dealing with anything on a psychic level. You are too open otherwise. You need psychic defense for various reasons. A psychic attack is the conscious or unintentional sending of negative vibrations or thoughts from one or more persons to another. Also this includes any beings on the inter-dimensional plane sending negativity.

Some who will be helped by this are: mystics, psychics, occultists, shamans, business people (from rivals), nurses, homemakers (from pushy sales people), and so on.

You need to fortify your aura, the energy shield which surrounds your physical and astral body.

I developed this system over many years and it will help you in unlimited ways.

To put up your strongest shield, you need to do the following:

You should relax physically. Picture yourself in the center of a solid white egg shape. Visualize it as starting a foot below your feet up to a foot above your head. Now say:

"I am putting up God's shield of the white light of love, truth and protection. Nothing negative or harmful can get in, only what is positive and good."

You are now protected from negativity but you are open to positive opportunity. This will shield you from negative spirit and tone down negativity from other people. The white light will flow through your body and its vibration will strengthen your aura. You need to know this light will always be with you.

Visualize this for a few minutes. After a while you will be able to put it up extremely fast. Notice how at peace you feel within this light. You can always have this feeling any time or place. You only need to practice.

BATTLE AT THE CEMETERY

One cold and dreary night, I was doing some spiritual blessings at a cemetery at the request of a client to help his recently passed away relative through the transition from one reality to the next.

As I walked through the grounds looking for the gravestone, I thought I heard a strange sound. As I tried to listen more, I realized it sounded like arguing, but in a language I didn't know. I ignored it, thinking it had nothing to do with me, and kept walking in search of the gravestone.

I found the spot I was looking for, did the blessing and started back to my car.

Soon, it sounded like the arguing was closer, then it sounded far away, then again closer, like they were moving around everywhere in the cemetery.

I was still thinking it didn't concern me. But I became curious as to what was going on, so I started to walk toward the sounds. Yes, I knew it wasn't my smartest move.

Knife-Wielding Demons and Murderous Ghosts

As I headed in the direction of the sounds, I heard what sounded like metal hitting metal. I rounded a bend and there were two etheric soldiers fighting. There were swords clashing and making a terrible clanking sound. One was a confederate soldier and the other a union soldier. Apparently they didn't know the War Between the States was over.

They seemed out of control, vengeful as though they were in a whirlwind and couldn't stop.

I heard a few words although not the whole sentence, and I wasn't paying attention to their meaning. They said the following words: ambush, conscript and a few more, but those are the ones I remember. After all, I was more focused on the deadly fight.

They were both covered in blood; some blood looked dark, with an eerie glow, while some looked like the blood was dripping off various body parts. It looked gruesome.

As I stood there transfixed, at a distance, all of a sudden they both turned their heads and looked at me. First I thought they were looking at something else. Why would they notice and see me?

They both started running toward me waving their swords. Initially I thought that, since they were spirit and non-physical, that they wouldn't harm me. I was wrong.

As they ran toward me, one of them threw his sword toward me, and I heard it as it splintered part of the tree near me. So it could harm me physically. It didn't occur to me previously that anyone would throw a sword.

I turned and ran toward my car. I know when to retreat. I kept thinking as I headed toward the parking lot, "I hope they don't realize they're spirit because they would be able to gain quicker ground not being limited by physical laws." I didn't even look back, since I still heard them yelling and they sounded like they were getting nearer.

I heard the second sword hit a stone near me, but by then I was at my car. It seems they were attached to the cemetery because they didn't follow when I got to the parking lot.

Some days it doesn't pay to be curious. Hopefully nobody else will see them because if you don't see them, they might not be aware of you either.

THE ATTACKING HEAD

The head of a decapitated ghost screams for its body.

In my many years of astral traveling to the etheric other side, I've run across positive and wondrous beings, but I've also run across dangerous, scary and deathly beings.

I've learned, through time, to always use some form of psychic protection before putting an etheric toe on the other side.

One such time, after making sure I was safe, I went out-of-body and was meandering down a dark path with darkness all around me. I felt safe but curious.

Everything felt like open space surrounding me. I felt I was not alone and started to feel edgy. Usually with a positive being around, you notice the energy but feel calm.

This was different and I thought about trying to feel where this entity was located. I knew it was near. I felt heat all of a sudden, like a furnace being turned up. I could hear the sparks from the fire and started to see the flames all around me. I knew I was safe as long as I stayed on the path.

Next, I heard grinding sounds, like stone grinding on stone. It kept getting louder and became deafening. First I tried to put my hands over my ears, and I realized I didn't physically have ears when I reached to do so. That was honestly unnerving.

All of a sudden, I knew I was being attacked and saw this gigantic, ugly head coming toward me. It was dark brown in color, completely furry, and had big white glowing eyes. I thought it was snarling, but I wasn't sure since I was busy planning a defense. I knew it had a body but all I saw was this menacing head.

On the etheric realm, the moment you have a focused thought, it happens. I remember forming a spear with the staff being solid and made of a pink color and

Knife-Wielding Demons and Murderous Ghosts

the tip being solid white glowing light. The pink is an occult color with healing and love vibrations, and the white light is all positive energy and force.

Negative entities are repelled by love. It is the opposite energy from them. And the white light does the same.

As it came toward me, I focused all my will power on charging the spear to illuminate brighter, but that thing kept coming toward me. As I kept increasing the light, I mentally directed it toward the being. I said it that way, so no matter what direction it changed to, I would always be aiming toward the being.

It actually circled for a while, and the heat kept getting more intense. I knew I couldn't just go back to my physical body, because it would follow me and I had more control being on the same plane.

In these situations, you always have to remember you're in control, and not to let your guard down. By the way, it's not that easy to remember while the event is happening.

It seemed like it started to run toward me, but it was in midair. I can't really describe it fully. As it got closer, I kept the spear up toward it, whichever way it went to attack.

I started saying a banishing spell. As I did so, it stopped in midair and seemed confused. It started howling. There's no other word for it, like it was wounded and very angry.

Then it attacked. The strange thing, which I still can see clearly to this day, was that, as it got closer, it started to get smaller and smaller. It realized this and stopped, howled, stayed still for what seemed forever, looking surprised. Then, with a vengeful look, it turned and disappeared back into the darkness.

I waited for a while, standing on guard, but it didn't come back. I no longer felt a presence so I came back to the physical realm, into my body.

Time being different in those realms, it seemed a very long time.

When I came back, I put protection around my home, just in case. I already knew it wasn't needed, but extra protection can't hurt.

It took a while for me to sojourn out again, but those who know me understand that that's just me.

Knife-Wielding Demons and Murderous Ghosts

POLTERGEIST – THE NOISE MAKERS

Poltergeists are noisy, playful spirits from the etheric plane. These spirits can manipulate the physical objects in our world to cause havoc, be playful or to be harmful. They are trying to make their presence felt. They are much like small children saying "Here I am. Notice me." They can be kind or destructive.

They can sometimes be perceived by psychics and other sensitive people.

They should be banished as soon as possible since they gain more power at each demonstration of their feats. They need a focus point, usually a psychic person whose energy they can tap into.

Of course, there is more to this subject, but you should know they can move objects for helpful reasons or destructive ones.

I was called to a house one day by a family who had recently moved to this new home. They were very happy at first. It was a beautiful home with a serene looking garden and pond in the backyard. The inside of the house was modern with a feeling of warmth.

The couple had three children. One boy was thirteen, the other college age, and the girl was in high school. They all got along well.

The teenage boy was happy in his room at first. Over time, he started to tell his parents he wanted to change rooms because his room felt cold in a corner where his desk was located. When they changed his room around to calm him, the coldness moved with his desk. The coldness eventually engulfed his whole room. After a while anyone who entered his room would feel the cold and become uncomfortable.

The parents, although baffled, didn't have another room to put him in and told him to ignore it.

He told them how things moved in his room at times, scaring him. They floated, at first not bothering him. Later, small objects started flying toward him. They didn't hit him, but he didn't know if they would or not. The parents didn't see this and dismissed what he was saying.

The other children also said they wouldn't go into the room because it felt bad. They couldn't explain what exactly they meant, but kept saying nobody should be in that room.

Knife-Wielding Demons and Murderous Ghosts

The boy went from being scared to be in his room to not wanting to leave it. When noises were heard from the room, like things being thrown, the parents just thought it was the boy doing it.

As time passed, the boy became sullen, angry and very distant. His shoulders drooped and he looked drawn.

The parents took him to a psychiatrist. Although the psychiatrist tried, he wasn't able to help him.

I think parents and people in general need to really learn to listen to each other. If they listened to their children, much of what happened could have been avoided.

The boy was going on a downward spiral. They tried everything, but couldn't find a way to stop it.

I was probably their last resort. In fact, when the parents called me to check things out, they told me they didn't believe in any people in my field (psychic/paranormal). They just wanted to feel they had exhausted all resources to help their son.

Before I went to their house, I explained to both of them what I do and how it will work. I didn't know it was a poltergeist before I arrived; just that it was something negative in the house.

As soon as I walked in, the whole main floor of the house became cold. Only one parent was there, due to her husband being at his job. She was surprised at the coldness. It only lasted a minute but seemed longer.

I walked throughout the house and the teenager's room was the only one freezing. He was in there and wouldn't come out. You could hear things being thrown, objects banging against each other and a low whistling type of sound, much like the sound the old radiators made.

I told her she has to tell him to come out. She said she didn't want to force him out of his room and upset him. As though he wasn't already upset? Sometimes I just don't understand some people.

So I went in and gently pulled him out by his arm. Since he didn't know me, he didn't resist. (I wasn't a parent.) While in the room, objects were hurled at us until we were out and the door closed behind us.

To the mothers' surprise, you could hear objects still moving, banging and making noise within the empty room. Her son and her other children were telling her for months about it, but she and her husband didn't listen until her son became ill-looking and depressed.

As I started a banishing ritual, the noise got louder and the objects were thrown more violently. I'm a European shaman and a minister, and this type of situation doesn't come up often, but it unfortunately does come up at times.

All of a sudden, it got very quiet. The mother thought it was all over, but the poltergeist had just moved to a different part of the house temporarily. They can be tricky things.

We had to walk through the whole house, one room at a time, including a basement, to keep the spirit moving from room to room until it had nowhere to go but out. It put up a good fight since it had nowhere to go. It took hours but it finally left.

I went back days later to make sure it didn't come back, but everything was clear.

The mother told me that they bought the house at a very low price and just thought they were very lucky. Upon looking into it more, they found out the previous owners felt very uncomfortable in the house but didn't know why. It was such a strong feeling, they just left one day and hired people to go to the house, pack their things and move everything out. Thus, they avoided all the issues. You need to always listen to your instinct.

As you can see, there really are things that go bump in the night.

Some people are so busy looking for logical reasons that they don't work on a situation to make it better until it's almost too late.

There are positive entities and beings in various realms, but don't be fooled by trickster beings that are also disincarnate. The negative spirits are also out there. Be on your guard. Don't take everything at face value. Put up your psychic shield of protection and stay positive. Know that you are safe and moving forward in your life. Your Source wants you to be happy and do well. Whatever obstacles come up in life, you can be safe, win and be successful. Yes You Can.

Banishing By Sacred Power
By Maria D'Andrea MsD, D.D., DRH

By the Power of three times three,

The Power of the earth now comes to me,

The Powers of sky and fire too,

Of water flowing straight and true.

Fire blaze and burn away ,

Negativity now cannot stay.

Earth rise up and sandstorm whirl,

Let all danger now unfurl.

Water flow against the beast,

Darkness drowns in waters deep.

Air and wind now do prevail,

Banish this beast to a lower scale.

Light above and light below,

Light from all directions flow ,

Brightness glows and darkness shrivels,

Per the ancient Sibyl.

And so it is.

Love and Light,

Maria

SUGGESTED READING

A highly respected author, D' Andrea – through her publisher Tim Beckley, Inner Light Publications – has penned such works as:

WITCHCRAFT, THE OCCULT AND HOW TO SELECT A FAMILIAR

SEXY MEDIUMS LOVE AND LUST SPELLS

100% POSITIVE SPELLS FOR ALADDIN'S MAGICK LAMP (ABOUT THE DJINN)

HEAVEN SENT MONEY SPELLS

HOW TO ELIMINATE STRESS AND ANXIETY THROUGH THE OCCULT

MIRACLE CANDLE SPELLS

POSITIVELY POSITIVE SPELL BOOK

SECRET MAGIC ELIXIRS OF LIFE

SUPERNATURAL WORDS OF POWER

COMPLETE MAGICAL SPIRITUAL OCCULT OILS WORK BOOK

SECRET OCCULT GALLERY

Above: The Lee family home located in the Black Forest area outside Colorado Springs.

Below: Photographs taken in the house often had strange streaks of light running through them.

THE POLTERGEIST EFFECT!
By Sean Casteel

The case of Steve Lee and his family is a long and complicated one, but it serves to reinforce the connection between aliens and paranormal phenomena. Some dare call it the "Poltergeist Effect"!

The Lee family's case received a great deal of media attention in the 1990s, including three visits to the Lees' home from the groundbreaking FOX Network series "Sightings." Several well-known psychics were brought in to examine the home for the presence of spirits, all of whom sensed a brooding presence that jealously guarded what it thought of as "its" home.

In the midst of the media circus that surrounded the Lees I interviewed Steve, the head of the household, on a couple of occasions myself.

"Colorado resident Steve Lee does a daily battle with extremely strange happenings around his house," I wrote at the time. "Everything from laser-like shafts of light that shine through the walls and then tie themselves in knots to ghostly faces that peer back at him from his mirrors are part of everyday life for Lee and his family."

Lee said the whole business began when he and his wife and children returned from a ten day hunting trip. They discovered that their expensive log cabin in the exclusive Black Forest area outside Colorado Springs had been trifled with.

"When we came back," Lee told me, "we noticed the furniture wasn't in the same place. The dishes and the carpets were different."

But there was more amiss than just the household fixtures.

If one didn't know better, it would seem that Lee and his family were suffering some sort of psychic attack. If not a poltergeist, then something damn well close. Readers should mentally compare the Lee's chaotic episode with that of the "Crawling Lights" incident described elsewhere in this book by Tim Beckley.

"It's a whole new ballgame regarding what we have come to think of as 'poltergeist phenomena,'" the well-known publisher commented as we went about the editing process for this book. "No longer can we think of poltergeists as simply unfriendly – unharnessed – spirits of the dead. Nor can it always be a matter of repressed hostility coming to the surface from an individual undergoing unbridled mental instability, which often manifests itself in progressively harmful phenomena."

This pattern of progressive escalation of strange events is also operative in the case of the Lee family.

"We started seeing lights," Lee said, "laser light-looking beams. Then shortly after that we started hearing voices in the house that shouldn't be there. During this time period, I was taking photos of the kids around the house – I take a lot of pictures – and things started showing up in them."

Longtime paranormal writer Dennis William Hauck has also covered the Lee family's ordeal. In an online posting called *The Black Forest Haunting*, Hauck writes: "Lee noticed that photographs and videotape taken in certain locations on the property had strange light streaks running through them, and sometimes translucent faces even appeared on the film. Film emulsion is sensitive to a wider range of the electromagnetic spectrum beyond visible light, which is why the fleeting events can be caught in photographs. Three parts of the Lee house seemed especially prone to these unusual photographic effects: the outside wall next to their satellite dish, the living room and the upstairs master bedroom."

Lee felt, at first, that the problem must be with his film or camera equipment.

"But no matter what type of camera or film he used," Hauck writes, "he captured evidence of unexplainable light phenomena that included brilliant beams, floating balls of light and glowing outlines of humans and animals. Sometimes the mysterious lights could be seen with the naked eye, though most often they lasted just a split second and showed up only on film."

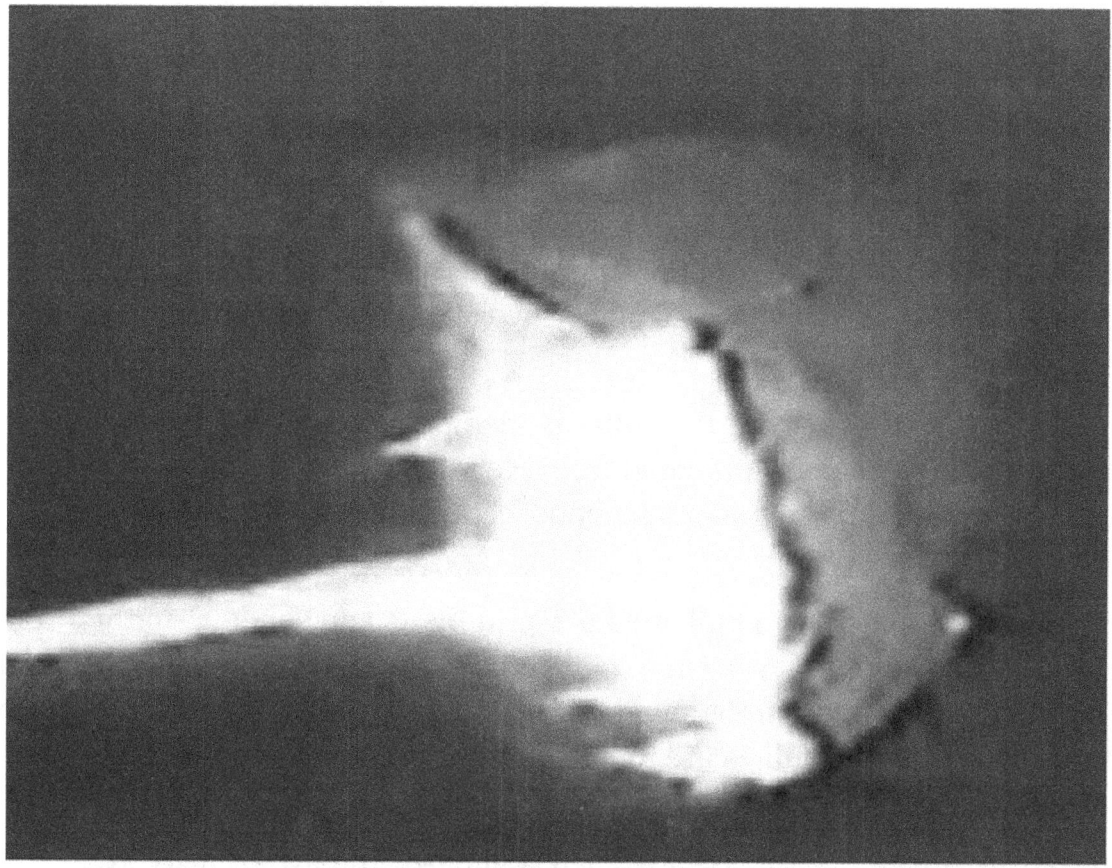
One of the numerous strange lights caught on film by Steve Lee.

It is here, in this description of the various lights captured on film that we have an aspect of poltergeist manifestation that perhaps can be seen to directly correspond to similar factors in the alien abduction phenomenon. Abductees often report mysterious lights as part of their encounter. Brilliant beams of light that shine in through their bedroom window from a waiting ship outside are a regular part of the abduction experience, as well as the balls of light some abductees see floating through their living room in the aftermath of their abduction.

The lights often roam about the walls of a dwelling as if they are under intelligent control, the product of some independent source. No one can really pinpoint their origin or determine what sort of intelligence they might represent. Objects often seem to vanish in the property being visited and things do go bump in the night – as if a tried and true poltergeist of your garden variety were responsible.

UNEXPLAINED SOUNDS AND LIGHTS

Lee's wife, Beth, also provided Hauck with some info on the mysterious lights and some equally mysterious sounds.

"One day we came home," she said, "and it was like the Fourth of July in our living room and in our bedroom. We had all kinds of lights flashing through, and it sounded like people stomping across the roof. We would lie in bed at night and hear chains rattling. One night we woke up and heard orchestra music. Strange things were happening every day."

Naturally, the question is – what is the nature of the beast and from what dimension did it arise? Did it come from Hell or from some other place that we might not even want to theorize about because of its aggressively negative nature?

The Lees' sons also complained of weird lights and shadows in their rooms, while lights and appliances started going on and off by themselves. Untraceable chemical odors burned family members' eyes and throats. Steve firmly believed that someone was trying to "scare them out of their home," Hauck writes.

But, as every journalist who covers the Lee family's story soon learns, Steve preferred to stay and fight. He installed a state-of-the-art security system with video surveillance cameras and motion detectors. In spite of the high-tech equipment, however, they still suffered more than 60 unexplainable "break-ins." The El Paso County Sheriff's Department was called to the scene on numerous occasions but could never find any evidence of a "crime." They eventually stopped responding to the Lee's calls for help. So the Lees hired private investigators, again to no avail. Meanwhile, the mounting cost of security equipment, etc. soon reached into the many thousands of dollars. The otherworldly entities were seemingly batting a thousand regardless of whom they represented.

The Lees finally acknowledged that the events happening around their home might indeed be paranormal and decided to send some of their photos and videos to the aforementioned "Sightings" television program. The producers showed the material to Hollywood special effects technician Edson Williams, who examined the Lee films and concluded that most of the light images would be hard to reproduce and some seemed to defy the laws of optics entirely.

"Sightings" immediately dispatched a film crew to the Black Forest, and the crew was able to document some of the bizarre phenomena that the Lees had been struggling with. The film crew also brought along Minneapolis ghostbuster

Echo Bodine, who, according to Hauk's posting, "quickly identified a threatening male spirit in the living room. A sophisticated thermal imaging camera showed the presence of the ghost, who, Bodine said, was 'responsible for things happening here and considers this to be his place.' Bodine determined the presence of at least 20 more spirits and judged the level of poltergeist activity in the house as 'monumental.' She felt especially uncomfortable in the upstairs bedroom, which she said was 'full of spirits; not a restful room.'"

During the filming of a discussion between Bodine and Beth Lee at the kitchen table, Beth "suddenly felt like someone was holding her down and complained of difficulty breathing. She asked to halt the interview and staggered from the table, obviously distraught. Then Sherry, a member of the film crew, felt 'something go into her,' as her chest, arms and legs became numb. She fell into a chair and started crying uncontrollably, in abject terror, as some unseen force seemed to possess her. She had to be escorted off the set and did not recover fully until she was off the property."

UNUSUAL ELECTROMAGNETIC INTERFERENCE

The film crew recorded unusual electromagnetic interference in the room throughout the above emotional outbursts. When some film that Steve had shot around the time of the film crew's visit came back from the developer, one photo showed a white dagger pointed directly at his forehead.

"The next day, he awoke with a painful, golf ball-sized welt on his forehead," Hauck writes. "He was rushed to an emergency room in Colorado Springs, but a CAT scan of his head could reveal no cause for the disfiguring lump, and all the doctors could do was try to treat his excruciating pain."

This was not the only time that the mysterious presence caused an actual medical problem, however. In my own reporting on the Lee family's experiences, I wrote about a strange disease/malaise that seemed to infect many people in the upscale community of the Black Forest.

"There's a lot of other people out here who are getting sick," Lee told me, "and having illnesses that no one can explain. We've got something going around and we've all had it. I have it a lot. You kind of feel lightheaded all the time and dizzy – like you're going to pass out or are on the verge of passing out. There's six people in the hospital from the Black Forest right now, and they can't figure out what the hell's wrong with them."

Knife-Wielding Demons and Murderous Ghosts

The Lee home with bizarre light forms in the foreground.

Lee claimed that the Centers for Disease Control out of Atlanta, Georgia, was brought in to assess the situation and could not pinpoint the origin of the malady.

"They couldn't find anything in the victims' blood or anything else," he said.

I tried to get confirmation for Lee's report and contacted the Centers for Disease Control, the Colorado State Health Department and the El Paso County Health Department, in whose jurisdiction Black Forest is located. At the national, state and local levels, officials maintained that they had no knowledge of the alleged outbreak.

Although the sickness had spread to Lee's neighbors, most remained unwilling to discuss the matter. Lee said he placed an ad in the local newspaper asking if others in the area were suffering similar problems. He received several calls in response to the ad, but even those people were hesitant to talk about what was happening, as though they feared some kind of repercussions for speaking out.

There is a half-mile stretch of road near Lee's home that seemed to cause motorists in the area to experience similar strange symptoms.

"People will be driving down that damn thing," he told me, "and they almost pass out. They think they're going to have a heart attack. Their heart starts beating real fast."

There are other locations such as this where similar things have happened. Noted researcher of Hispanic UFO studies Scott Corrales says that "UFOs' powerful lights have caused highway accidents in the Yucatan. One of them occurred five years ago on the Tizimín-Calotmul highway. "A driver from Merida claims that after seeing a UFO," Scott continues, "with a powerful beam of light in front of him, he was blinded and forced to skid off the road. He told journalist Mr. Héctor Garrido Poot: 'At the time I traveled once a week to the eastern part of the state to sell cleaning products. I remember well that it was a Tuesday, around nine o'clock at night. I was on my way to Calotmul when I suddenly saw a powerful light coming toward me in the distance. I thought it was a trailer. However, it was on me in a minute. It was so bright that I made a hard turn off the road. All I remember is that it rose into the air as it approached, making no noise whatsoever,' he said. 'Fortunately, I didn't fall into a ditch and nothing happened to my car, since I was driving slowly.'"

Returning to the Black Forest and the Lees, beyond the medical anomalies that took place, there is also the constant attack from the mysterious disembodied voices that afflict Lee and his neighbors as well.

"As soon as I get into the car," he said, "I hear, 'We're going to kill you. We're going to kill your kids.' It just goes on and on."

Lee told me that he knew of two members of area families who were confined to a mental institution after hearing these same voices. He also recounted the story of an unfortunate Vietnam veteran who was pronounced mentally ill after talking to someone about intruders he had repeatedly sighted near his home.

"This guy kept seeing these two men in military fatigues on his property," Lee said. "I've seen these same two guys on my property as well. I've shot at them, and the bullets go right through them, so I know they're holograms. Anyway, this guy had served in Vietnam, so they said, 'Oh, well, there you go. He's having flashbacks.' And they put him away, too. Whoever is behind that one, I think that's pretty low."

Lee said that he had been out on his porch smoking one winter evening and saw three men in snow-camouflage about 50 yards in front of his house pointing rifles at him. He went inside and got his own rifle, and his wife joined him outside, camera in hand. He told her to start taking pictures as he approached the two interlopers. He was looking through the rifle scope, prepared to shoot, when one of them said, "Easy does it, buddy." Then the two men instantly vanished. There was fresh snow on the ground, but there were no telltale footprints or tracks left behind.

Apparently a situation which only a poltergeist could get behind. Some poltergeists, in fact, could be what the Native American tribes call "shapeshifters." These are entities that can cleverly disguise themselves and alter their forms at will so that you never know precisely what they look like.

Another incident, also involving disappearing soldiers, happened a short time later. This time, there were more witnesses than just Steve and Beth.

"I had some friends over one night," Lee said, "who worked at Martin-Marietta, the space engineers. They'd been trying to figure out what was really happening for a long time. So we started looking with infrared binoculars over towards a nearby house."

The inquisitive group next saw twelve men in camouflage go into the neighbor's doghouse.

"After about the third one," Lee recounted, "one guy said, 'Hey, that many people can't fit into a doghouse.' So we walked right over to the fence. His doghouse was about ten feet on the other side of the fence. And these guys continued to walk in there, and there's a guy standing on the outside, guarding it. They're acting like we're not even there. We're talking to them and they won't even look at us. So afterward I was wondering, 'Did we really see that stuff or was it a hologram?'"

Tim Beckley says when he first met paranormalist John A. Keel in the late 1960s, the author of "**Jadoo**" and "**The Mothman Prophecies**" claimed entities were coming into his apartment in the Kips Bay area of Manhattan near the East River and disappearing inside a cupboard underneath his kitchen sink.

Meanwhile, there is a subset of experiences found within the overall alien abduction phenomenon in which human-looking soldiers or military "doctors" seem to be cooperating with the familiar grays in whatever procedure the abductee is being subjected to. This kind of abduction is sometimes called a "MILAB," an acronym for "military abduction." While it is not nearly as frequent as the more typical "aliens only" encounter, it turns up often enough to have an accepted place in the literature.

Do Steve Lee's seeming incursions with ghostly "soldiers" fit into the overall matrix of a MILAB alien abduction? In fact, are we dealing with aliens as the real culprits who have laid siege to the Lee household, manifesting as the standard poltergeists with strange lights and threatening voices but also afflicting the family and others in the neighborhood with a frightening and un-diagnosable epidemic?

Steve Lee himself believes it can be explained as some kind of mind control effort of the government, that only human agents are involved in the events that have so long plagued him and his family. He has fought long and hard to get some kind of official response to his complaints, even conducting a letter writing campaign to the Attorney General's office in Washington.

A mirror in the Lee home with yet another mysterious light display captured in the photo.

Knife-Wielding Demons and Murderous Ghosts

But perhaps there something more like an "alien/poltergeist" entity afoot here, an entity or entities who can cross the borderline between both phenomena and form a continuum of interaction with humans that we label as "ghostly" on the one hand and "alien" on the other. The supernatural comes to us in many different forms, but does it all ultimately originate in the same place?

NOTE: The Lee's log cabin was one of 509 homes destroyed in the 2013 Black Forest fire. This fire was El Paso County's second devastating blaze in two years and is Colorado's most destructive fire ever.

SUGGESTED READING

BOOKS BY OR CO-AUTHORED BY SEAN CASTEEL

UFOS, PROPHECY AND THE END OF TIME

SIGNS AND SYMBOLS OF THE SECOND COMING

THE EXCLUDED BOOKS OF THE BIBLE

OUR ALIEN PLANET, THIS EERIE EARTH (With Tim Beckley)

SUGGESTED VIEWING ON YOUTUBE *BLACK FOREST HAUNTING UPDATE*

www.youtube.com/watch?v=wkahvz0ZZT0

Sean Casteel

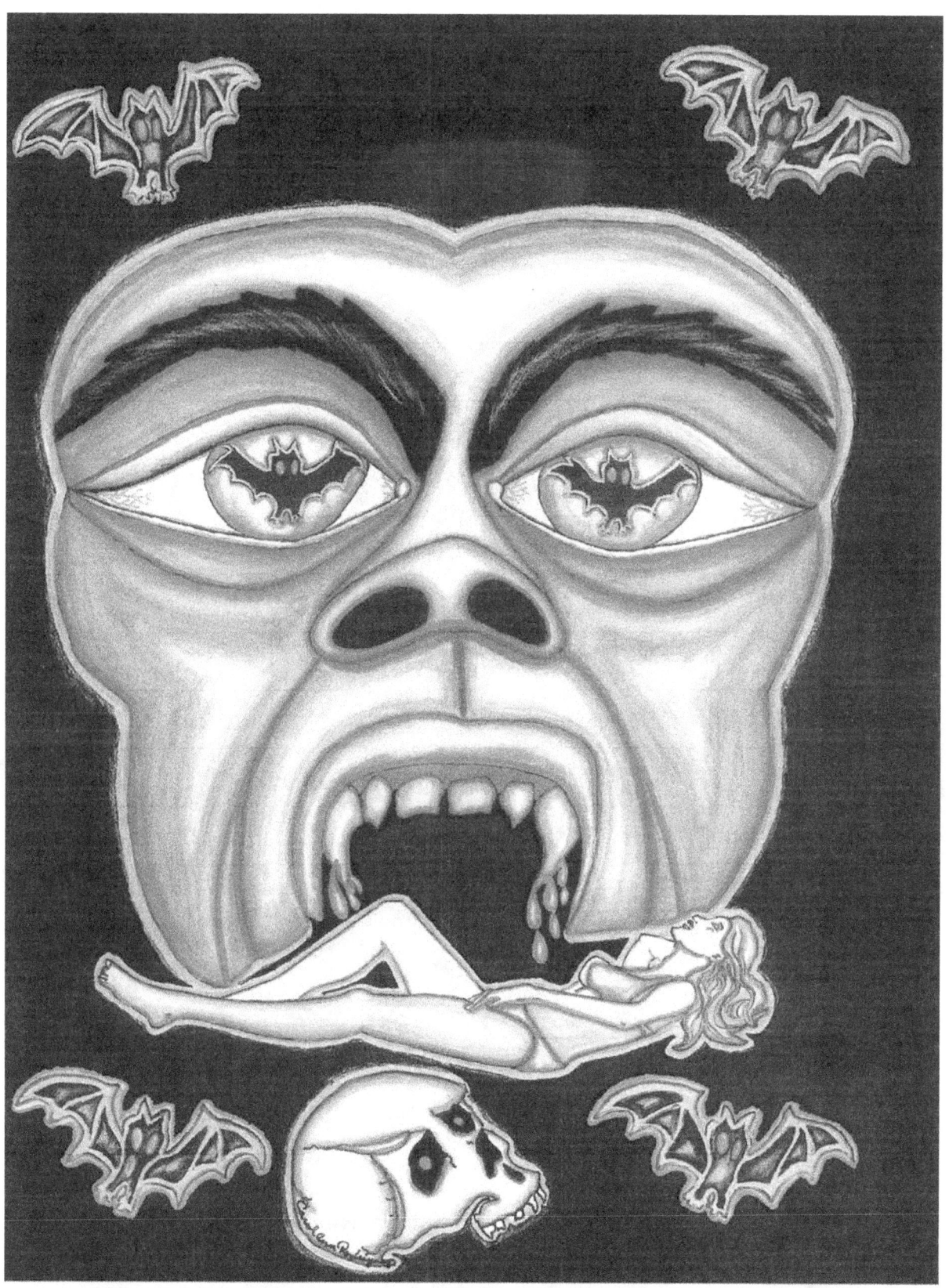

Some ghouls come to feast on human flesh and blood.
Art © Carol Ann Rodriguez.

Knife-Wielding Demons and Murderous Ghosts

This bizarre part-dog/human looking creature was spotted walking on two legs, but dropped down to all four just as the photo was taken.

CRYPTIDS – A NEW WAVE OF "HAUNTINGS"
By Timothy Green Beckley

To those who think we pretty much have pulled out all the stops in our relentless search for the truth about the soulless creatures we identify as poltergeists, often for lack of a better term, please be advised that you ain't seen nothing yet – for we have at least one more corner to turn in our paranormal phenomena researchers' "game."

A former law enforcement official, Butch Witkowski has acted as a state director for MUFON and today heads the UFO Research Center of Pennsylvania. Tim Swartz and I have had Butch on several times as a guest on our *Exploring The Bizarre* show, aired over KCORradio.com and archived at Mr. UFO's Secret Files on YouTube.

Butch has been an independent researcher since 1989 when, along with four other people, he witnessed a UFO of unbelievable size quietly hover above a mountain in Tucson, Arizona. It moved slowly up and down, then rose upwards, moved forward and vanished at lightning speed. Calls to the Sheriff's Department, the news media and the local Air Force base yielded no confirmatory sighting reports. He began his own investigation into the UFO phenomenon on that day.

The first time we had Butch on the program he laid out the specifics involving the case of a young man who was found deceased, hanging from the upper branches of a tree without having any way of climbing that high. Though there was no definitive proof that UFOs were involved, there are some who speculated that this might have been an abduction gone awry.

But I think the thing that stunned Tim Swartz and I the most was Butch's revelations about a strange creature from the dark domain of cryptozoology known as the Dogman, which had appeared as if out of nowhere invading the

Knife-Wielding Demons and Murderous Ghosts

woods of Pennsylvania and frightening local hunters. The "animals" stand upright, have the face of a pit bull and the body of a young Arnold Schwarzenegger.

Reports were coming in at a rapid clip and some of the eyewitnesses were both perplexed and frightened. It was if they had seen a ghost – and maybe they had seen an upright poltergeist of sorts. Tim Swartz writes later in this book that some poltergeists develop the ability to talk. Taking that into consideration…if a poltergeist can talk, it most definitely could shapeshift!

And there is a definite tie-in with UFOs in some cases, giving us even more to ponder. Butch works in alliance with Lon Strickler, who has written up some of the cases reported to him in his daily blog *"Phantoms and Monsters"* as well as going into depth on his podcast Arcane Radio.

PARANORMAL EVENT
NORTHERN LANCASTER COUNTY, PENNSYLVANIA

I'm stuck and unsure on what to do. About a month ago I took some pictures of what appeared to be UFOs and a UFO hovering above my car. About two weeks later I told my wife that I woke up in the middle of the night and for a split second I could see them (aliens) standing over me and shooting a red light into my forehead. Then about a week later I woke up in the middle of the night and found them standing in the corner of the room. I proceeded to wake my wife and was able get the entire encounter on film with her cell phone. We have been visited every night since and we are at a loss in terms of understanding what is even going on anymore. I feel so helpless and don't know what to do, where to turn, or how to make it stop. We have a year-and-a-half old baby at the house and I'm so scared they are going to hurt him. There is so much more that I want to share, but I can't . . . please, if there is anybody that could help or could lead me in the right direction, please contact me.

We are antique dealers and collect Satanic and religious artifacts. We have a number of strange things going on in the home with areas we will not go into no matter what. A closet door that opens on its own, buzzing and humming in the basement and shadows in the attic with a circle that appears on the floor and moves around. Could it be a portal? We need help with this.

Investigation opened 12.27.16

UNKNOWN CANINE VIEWED BY HUNTER IN CENTRAL PENNSYLVANIA

Witness was deer hunting in Central Pennsylvania State Forest. This was on Saturday, December third. He has a tree stand on the edge of a large field owned by a friend. He has been hunting there for almost 20 years and has bagged several deer at this location. He saw something that early morning and is not sure how to explain. It was about 7:10 A.M. and just turning light. He noticed a few deer in the distance running towards the state forest. He looked through his scope and saw what he thought were two coyotes following the deer. But these coyotes didn't look quite right. They were larger, almost like wolves. About 15 minutes later, he was watching a buck about 600 yards south in the open field when it bolted towards the trees. Then he saw a large dog-like animal. It was slowly walking or stalking, he's "not sure which," but it was heading in his direction. He was upwind from it, and it soon noticed him in the tree stand. It stopped and looked at him for a few seconds, then started walking towards him again. It was about 100 yards or so from the witness, and he heard it growling. "This was not a dog or coyote or a wolf. It reminded me of a wolf, but the back was arched and the head was huge. The fur was very dark and the legs were oddly shaped with sparse hair. I thought about shooting it, but something told me not to. I was shaking as well. This animal really terrified me."It once again stopped moving and looked at me for a few seconds. The face was that of a wolf, but the snout was shorter than any wolf I've ever seen. It had 'steely' eyes, almost like those of a human. Really weird."Something caught its attention and it ran off towards the south. The witness stayed on the stand for another hour and didn't see anything during that time. When he did leave the stand, he was very cautious. He had no idea if it was still in the area. He reached his car and left."I talked to a game commission officer later and reported the animal. He said that there had been a few reports of large dogs, but that they were most likely coyotes. I told him that this was NOT a coyote, but he didn't seem to care."Rec'd 12.5.16

Investigation and area research started 12.6.16

Unknown Canine Viewed by Hunter in Central Pennsylvania

Notes For Tim Beckley From Paul Eno

Publishers Note: When Paul heard I was going to include an update on the possible role cryptid creatures play in the investigation of the paranormal and the appearance of poltergeists, he sent me the following notes describing his own experiences of a "weird nature" in a flap area he and an associate had discovered in a remote part of Pennsylvania. The events reported there included everything from Bigfoot to UFOs to hauntings to mysterious figures in a military-type van which could not be photographed. He filed his report thusly:

POLTERGEISTS AND 'FLAP' AREAS

There is far more to poltergeist phenomena than just broken dishes and frayed wits. This is vividly manifested in what my son and co-researcher, Ben, and I refer to as "flap areas." These are regions of intense paranormal activity of many kinds: UFOs, cryptids, ghosts, time slips and, of course, poltergeists.

For those who believe in the old, classic theories – that ghosts are spirits of the dead, that UFOs are necessarily spaceships, and that poltergeists are evil spirits at worst or, at best, "recurrent spontaneous psychokinesis" (RSPK) caused by some sort of "agent" – the phenomena that occur in flap areas are unrelated.

It's been a very long time since I believed that. In our opinion, flap areas are places where there are multiple intersects and over-washes between multiple parallel worlds with different laws of physics and many different kinds of inhabitants, some of whom feed on the others – including us.

Take, for example, the flap area that, as of this writing, we have been investigating most recently: the western Pennsylvania triangle. Since our first expedition to this rural farming area in May 2016, we and our colleague, Shane Sirois, have had firsthand encounters with Bigfoot, UFOs both in the sky and close to the ground, "shadow people" and (so far) minor poltergeist activity.

So have all the people in the area. Some 20 people turned up at a neighborhood meeting Shane and I organized in September 2016. All of them had some experiences to report, and one reported hearing what I believe was a Bigfoot I myself saw the night before.

On that occasion, the bright, moonlit night of Friday, September 16, 2016, I was parked at the edge of a field in my truck, expecting to see strange lights, such as we had photographed in May. It was chilly, so only the driver-side window was open. Suddenly, something to the right caught my eye. It was a large, brown, hairy, bipedal creature in the moonlight, its head bowed as if looking for something in the tall grass.

For a moment, I felt an inexplicable sense of peace! Then I hurriedly snapped a photo, with an infrared camera, through the cold, passenger-side window of my truck. Naturally, there was no heat signature, so I got nothing.

Knife-Wielding Demons and Murderous Ghosts

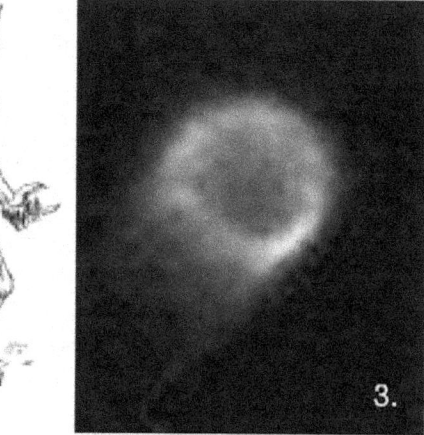

1. Butch Witkowski has been collecting reports of cryptid creatures in Pennsylvania.

2. A humanoid known as the "Dogman," which stands 8 feet tall and has the face of a pit bull and the body of a young Arnold Schwarzenegger, has been terrifying hunters while Butch continues to investigate.

3. As in Paul Eno's investigation, red and orange balls of light known as "orbs" have been known to appear mysteriously in the vicinity where Butch's group is speaking with witnesses.

4. Did Paul photograph a strange creature hiding in the woods behind some trees?

5. In the daytime this secluded Pennsylvania landscape looks as serene and as peaceful as can be. As the sun sets there is a chance that anything can happen.

Knife-Wielding Demons and Murderous Ghosts

Left: Something "not quite human" may have left an impression in the ground.

Below: While no one can swear that they are "spacecraft," mysterious orb-like objects did materialize in the area of their parked vehicle.

Knife-Wielding Demons and Murderous Ghosts

To add insult to injury, I got out of the truck as quietly as I could. And as I did so, the Shire theme from the "*Lord of the Rings*" movies – my ring tone – went blasting over the field.

It was my wife! And it was the closest I ever came to divorce. Needless to say, whatever it was was long gone. The next day, Shane and I found a path through the tall grass, made by something big that had approached the center of the field, then turned back toward the woods.

We have only spent about five days in this region so far, but we expect to find two more things: poltergeists and the military.

As explained previously, we don't accept the standard, for-lack-of-any-better-narrow-minded-explanation, that poltergeists are effects produced by tormented human minds. From what I've seen, poltergeists are inter-world parasites, perfectly physical life forms, not spirits, that feed on the energy of other life forms – including us - sometimes in more than one parallel world at the same time.

And the military – or what seems like the military? We run into them in every flap area we investigate, and we fully expect to do so in the Pennsylvania Triangle on our next expedition. People at that neighborhood meeting gave us an earful about where they might be based. We did photograph a strange van but when we went to examine the photos there was nothing there. A UFO hovered over a nearby row of trees. Something did show up – a rather brightly lit object we couldn't explain. And we thought we could make not the image of a Bigfoot hiding in the shrubs.

Why would the military be interested in flap areas? Well, wouldn't we just love to weapon-ize the paranormal, to manipulate parallel worlds and to appear to control space and time?

If we don't get arrested or shot, look for more from Ben and me on this topic in the future. If there is a future.

Those anxious to keep abreast of activities in the Pennsylvania Triangle are invited to check out the archives of "Exploring The Bizarre," which can be found on KCORradio.com or on YouTube on our *Mr. UFO's Secret Files page*. Paul's own weekly show can be found on the net at: *BehindTheParanormal.com*. Other websites to check out: *www.ufocop.com* and *www.phantomsandmonsters.com*.

Knife-Wielding Demons and Murderous Ghosts

Some UFO reports just don't seem to fit into any existing mold and thus do not even correspond with other existing reports...no matter how strange or bizarre those other reports might be.

DOING BATTLE WITH ULTRA-TERRESTRIALS
ATTACK OF THE ALIEN POLTERGEIST
By Timothy Green Beckley

We live on a strange planet in a very bizarre universe.

All is NOT what it seems and, as I've long ago discovered, it's best not to take anything for granted – speculating can get you into a deep load of doo doo, though it always seems that readers of a particular book want the author to pigeonhole him or herself and tightly close up the case for or against a theory by the end of the closing chapter. In the case of this book, we have several authors within these pages and we have several theories as to what poltergeists might be or might not be or could possibly be. Personally, I think you can take at least one theory from each contributor and blend them all together for a legitimate outcome.

Many millions of words have been written about ghosts and their noisy counterparts the poltergeist. Last time I looked, I think there were 23,000 books on the subject available on Amazon. That's a hell of a lot of reading about a hell of a subject inspired by a group of entities some good Christian folks think reside in hell. That's a concept, of course, fostered by a growing number of terrifying, Hollywood-produced epics dealing with the supernatural in general and exorcism specifically. Who can't remember Linda Blair projectile vomiting a thick stream of pea soup across the room and telling the priest that his mother does something really nasty in hell?

This book – at least to some degree – has ushered in a new paradigm for what a poltergeist might be. Not all "angry spirits" need necessarily be earthbound souls anxious to pound the bejesus out of the occupants of a particular dwelling and take advantage of its womenfolk.

Knife-Wielding Demons and Murderous Ghosts

Friend and colleague Paul Eno, host of the popular "Behind The Paranormal" broadcast, started out in the ministerial field and attended a Jesuit seminary school. He wound up joining forces with famed poltergeist researchers Ed and Loraine Warren and set out to battle demonic devils – the kind that toss your TV onto the floor and spit on grandma (who today would probably spit right back!).

Paul speaks about how at least some poltergeists may be dimensional, shapeshifting "aliens" who pop in and out of our environment without a second thought, causing a mixture of mayhem and havoc in our homes. People believe that they are ghosts because this is what they have been conditioned to believe by a multitude of cinematic and media portrayals.

I have gone through my expansive files and culled a number of cases where the poltergeist being confronted could easily be misidentified as the garden variety goblin. But the witnesses experienced the events from a slightly different prospective, which put Mr. Poltergeist at the helm of what we would more easily identify as a UFO. Readers are welcome to draw their own conclusions.

THE STRANGEST UFO 'POLTERGEIST' EVER ENCOUNTERED

The following report has all the earmarks of a traveling poltergeist circus, one which takes place over a number of states as two young woman try desperately to make it to their destination.

Some UFO reports just don't seem to fit into any existing mold and thus do not even correspond with other existing reports . . . no matter how strange or bizarre those other reports might be.

The hallucination or "Oz Effect" (a term coined by British UFOlogist Jenny Randles) is well illustrated in this account, which I personally investigated, meeting with the witnesses several times.

Mickie Eckert's experience is totally unique in the annals of flying saucerdom. Her story does not seem to mesh with any preexisting patterns, and yet the sincerity shows on her pretty face as she relates a bizarre tale that defies explanation.

Looking at me with bewildered eyes, it was obvious that Mickie, a young woman in her mid-twenties, was seeking answers. She was confused about what had happened and was anxious to find out the reasons she was selected to have a close encounter that goes beyond anything previously recorded.

Knife-Wielding Demons and Murderous Ghosts

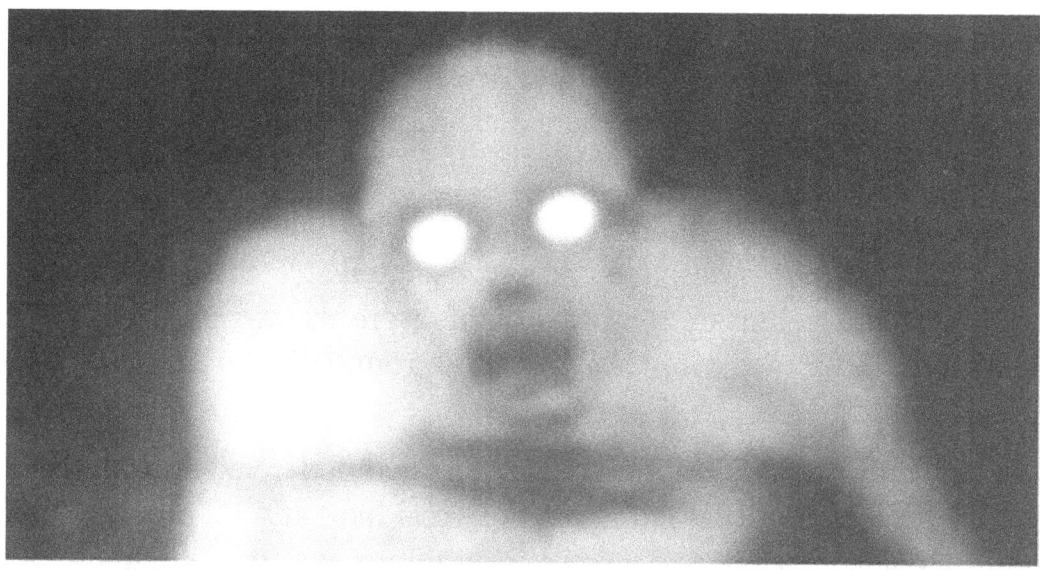

Above: Alien visitors today take on many of the same characteristics as old-fashioned poltergeists. They could be part of the same negative energy being released inside a home or attaching itself to specific individuals who normally have no idea what is transpiring. Some, like this purported authentic Ultra-terrestrial, even take on a ghostly quality.

It was July 22, 1978. Mickie, along with her best friend, Kathy Echard, was driving along Interstate 80 East. They were headed towards Nebraska, near the Wyoming border, when they saw what they thought was an accident on the side of the road.

"We turned to get a better look and saw these white lights bobbing up and down. In order to get a better look, we pulled over to the shoulder of the road and aimed our car headlights in the direction of the crash."

It was apparent that Mickie very much wanted to talk about what transpired that night. We were seated around a large table in a private conference room at the Royal Quality Inn in San Diego, California. Mickie had come to the privately-sponsored UFO conference (promoted by veteran newsman Hal Starr) mainly because she wanted desperately to talk with some of the top names in the field who are supposed to be trained in the handling of such matters. At the podium that day were such leading UFO luminaries as Jim and Coral Lorenzen from APRO (since deceased), Walter Andrus, then-director of the Mutual UFO Network, and Dr. James A. Harder, Associate Professor of Engineering at the University of California (Berkeley).

Maybe it was because of their tight speaking schedule, but none of those present seemed to be able to find the necessary time to speak with Mickie Eckert.

Knife-Wielding Demons and Murderous Ghosts

It was only after she was introduced to me by John DeHerrera (a practicing hypnotist who has been involved in the investigation of several contactee cases, most notably that of Brian Scott) that Mickie found someone who would listen intelligently to what she had to offer,

Going back to the evening in question, Mickie maintains that the sun had just set as they drove on a desolate and very isolated stretch of road eighty miles north of Wheelock, Nebraska. "Our headlights were trained on what we thought to be a mishap, but all we could see was three round circles hovering a few feet above the ground."

At the time, neither of the two young women realized that they were headed for a journey to a Twilight Zone more real than any TV program about the supernatural could ever hope to be. "In front of our eyes these lights turned into two sports cars that were coming toward us." One moment they had been confronted by the mysterious presence of airborne lights and the next thing they were aware of were two automobiles speeding in their direction. To say the least, they didn't know what to make of this transformation.

"We wanted no part of what was happening, so we took off in the opposite direction. As we turned the car around to leave, in back of us we saw this whole bunch of lights. We backed up on the Interstate and now there were two trucks that had appeared out of thin air. On the trucks were teeny little lights. The trucks were following us, of this I'm sure."

The two tractor-trailers kept a steady pace on the highway in back of the girls. It was as if unseen eyes were watching their every movement, perhaps seeking an ideal spot to overtake them for some fiendish purpose.

"For some reason, Kathy asked me to stop and she got out of the auto and stood in front of the car. It was then that we saw all these other cars parked along the side of the road. They were just stopped there. When Kathy got back into our vehicle she wanted to drive and so I let her take the steering wheel. To her it felt as if something – some force – were trying to take control of our car. She got scared and eventually turned the driving back over to me and I too felt this strange pulling."

Putting as many miles behind them as possible, the two girls sped on through the night, anxious to get back to their home in California. "As we were passing through Salt Lake City, we stopped off at a Safeway store to get some gum and cigarettes." Mickie makes no bones about the fact that they were still shaken but says they were trying to pull themselves back together again, not having seen anything unusual on the road for quite some time now.

"As we were about to leave the Safeway supermarket, I noticed a reflection on one of the large windows coming from either inside or outside. Initially, I just assumed the reflection was caused by either the store lights themselves or from some street light nearby.

"Out in the parking area I discovered this was not at all the case, for directly across the lot was this little light about the size of a basketball just sitting near the ground."

There seemed to be so much that Mickie had to say that the words wouldn't come out fast enough. Several times I had to slow her down so as not to miss any part of her narrative.

Totally freaked out by what was transpiring all around them, Mickie's friend was anxious to push on as quickly as possible. "As we entered Wyoming we stopped again to get some bottled water. We were in a pretty good-sized town called Evansville, and it was still pretty early, but there wasn't a light on in the entire city. Everything was closed. None of the houses had lights on either. I looked out of the window on the driver's side of the car and there were these two ships hanging there. One was orange, the other yellowish-white. We continued on toward Green River and the objects passed through the trees on the side of the road. At this juncture in time we lost control of the car once more. No matter how hard we put our foot down on the gas pedal the car refused to accelerate past a certain speed."

In the middle of nowhere, the car died completely. With this, a light came into the auto passing right through an open window. The light touched Kathy Echard and, for no explainable reason, Mickie began talking to that light. "Come on, little light, why don't you touch me, too?" she remarked, despite the fact that everything up until this point had frightened her.

Looking over my notes, which I hadn't referred to in a while, I felt like I was reading through the original script to Steven Spielberg's made-for-television thriller "Duel," in which a rampaging truck driver terrorizes an innocent motorist over an isolated stretch of highway somewhere way out West.

No sooner had it appeared than the light inside the car vanished. "All of a sudden we didn't see the ship anymore, but we started seeing trucks. Northwestern, American and other big-named rigs. They were traveling in both directions, up and down the northbound and southbound lanes. The only way I can describe it is as a caravan of big lights going back and forth. This one particular truck stopped directly in front of us and we knew something was wrong. It was freaky—the trucks were now ships; dome-shaped, 3-sided ships about the same size as a compact automobile, and they were no longer on the road, but traveling about six feet off the ground." Mickie admits that she was too bewildered to be an excellent observer. She finds it hard to estimate the number of trucks or dome-shaped ships but she does know that the car they were in got pushed forward about 20 feet as if it had been lifted by a terrific force from underneath.

Despite their accelerated heartbeats, the girls decided to get out of their car to have a look, to see if anything might have gotten caught underneath their wheels which might account for the sudden tug forward. There was nothing there that would offer a solution to the puzzle, and so they climbed back into the relative safety of their vehicle.

"Soon there was this other car that pulled up directly in back of us and Kathy said she wanted to get out and see who was driving it." It was quite apparent from Mickie's comments that the girls were anxious to seek help from any other companion of the road they might find driving so late at night.

"When Kathy got back into the car I was anxious to know what she had said to the individuals in the car behind us. She just looked me straight in the eye and said, 'Turn around and tell me what you would have said to them.' There was this black dog, tail curved up and two red eyes blazing, just outside our car door."

It should be noted, and it is dealt with in more detail further along in this work, that the appearance of huge black dogs – often with blazing eyes – and other creatures from unknown domains, mostly referred to as "Cryptids," have become part and parcel of the paranormal, being seen in conjunction with both poltergeists and the appearance of Ultra-Terrestrials, or your more common variety of "alien."

The girls were understandably terrified by this new development. They could by no means be familiar with the later outbreak of such "super canines," which had not really begun to show up in any large numbers at the date of their experience – or at least had not been substantially reported on in the UFOlogical community, which is often slow to progress to the next state of consciousness. Even now, they are still attempting to hang on to their single-minded theory that all unknown aerial craft must be from other planets, which is a near impossibility, given the laws of physics and Einstein's theory of relativity as it concerns the speed of light.

Cowering in fear, Mickie happened to glance into the rearview mirror. What she saw only added fuel to a fire of panic that was so near to bursting out of control within them. "I saw what appeared to be a kid with his arms bunched together on the back seat." The girls got out of the car in an attempt to escape this potential menace. Luckily, the dog-like creature they had seen was nowhere in sight

However, directly behind them were two bright lights which were joined by several other duller looking lights. After several minutes they all blended into one light. "As the light went past us, it was no longer just a light, but a ship. We heard this rumbling sound and our hair stood on end. Our skin was covered with goose-bumps."

ENTERING ANOTHER DIMENSION OF THE STRANGE AND SUPERNATURAL

Inspirational Art by Carol Ann Rodriguez

At this point, it seemed as if Mickie and Kathy had been transported to another dimension, another sphere of reality, for all at once things started looking peculiar, totally out of whack "Then the sun started to come up, but it was really an orange ball and it was coming toward us. And then it was not orange anymore, but its color turned suddenly to gray, and it was about 100 feet across, just enormous. And people started to appear out of nowhere, walking across the freeway carrying tubes or pipes. We didn't actually see them come out of any ship because the sun – or whatever it was – had landed in a valley out of our immediate viewing range."

The beings – or whatever they were – were standing in the middle island that separates the north and southbound traffic. "There was this bunch of blue lights and we knew something was going to happen. We were terrified. We felt like we were going to be taken to another planet and would never be heard from again."

Without warning the car started up. "I got mad at Kathy because I thought she had slammed on the brakes and I hit my head on the dashboard. We saw this ship coming down the Interstate and we also saw an 18-wheeler pickup truck towing one of the sports cars we had seen earlier in the evening. Something pushed us from behind but we couldn't get the car to run of its own accord."

From out of nowhere a man appeared and asked the girls where they were headed. "He said he was heading toward Chicago and we said that's where we were going, too. I'd have gone to Timbuktu just to get out of the spot we were in." From what I was able to gather, the man did not know anything was happening. He seemed totally unaware of the frightful state of the girls' minds caused by a terror that was real enough to them even if nobody else was able to perceive what was transpiring around them.

"I was so scared that I crawled all over the driver. He stopped at a truck stop to get coffee and we got out and walked to a nearby motel. We didn't have very much money. But we had about $35 and so we got a room. We unlocked the door and turned on the light and the TV went on by itself. Also, this little teeny light flittered around the room and we knew we hadn't escaped."

Realizing that they were being observed, the girls tried to intimidate the light that was buzzing around their room.

"'Kathy, did you mail that letter telling about the flight pattern of the UFOs to my lawyer?' I asked with a purposeful slowness. She said she had, playing along with the game.

"We called the police and finally, at 5 o'clock the next afternoon, they came and took us back to the spot where we had abandoned the vehicle. As it turned out, the car wasn't where we had left it. And when we went back to the valley where the ship had been, the area wasn't the same. There was no little road on the side of the road. The freeway railing wasn't even the same. There was a sign "MOUNTAIN ROAD 189." There is no Mountain Road 189 in all of Wyoming. We had a full tank of gas and we were about 250 miles into the state and there wasn't a gas station anywhere."

It was like they were driving without consuming fuel.

Knife-Wielding Demons and Murderous Ghosts

Of further interest were the corpses of a cow and a sheep off in a nearby field. "The cow was all bones and the sheep had all of its skin peeled off, which made it look like a blanket lying there."

Mickie says that the police made them fill out a complete report. "After they had finished hearing our entire story they shrugged and told us we'd seen swamp gas!"

Moving the tape recorder closer to Mickie, she reported that both her life and that of her friend have been drastically altered because of the events of that night "Kathy is only 31 years old, but she's been in the hospital at least 20 times since this happened. It's hard to explain, but somehow I feel we are the same people, but, then again, we aren't. Kathy had always been a slob and I have always been neat and clean. Now my house looks like the wreck of the Hesperus, and Kathy's is really neat, tidy, and very well cared for.

"Before, I had always been the type to make my kids breakfast, lunch and dinner, while Kathy believed her children should prepare their own meals. It's just the other way around now. It's almost as though we've somehow exchanged personality traits. In other words, I'm still me, but it's as though I'm having my personality altered – taken over. I have always been a reader, for instance, and now I'm reading much more. I'm reading as much as I can on UFOs; that's the one subject that fascinates me the most."

Under hypnosis, Mickie was made to draw what she had seen. When it came to sketching the trucks that had appeared on the highway, she rendered a skeleton-type being instead of a moving vehicle. "Is it possible that they altered your whole thinking process that night?" I asked the witness. Mickie admitted that this is what might have happened and that what really transpired could be entirely different from what she perceived. For some unexplainable reason, Mickie and her friend, Kathy, have grown farther apart in their friendship. "Before the experience, we had been the best of friends for 17 years. Now we speak to each other only once a week, tops."

Mickie is anxious to undergo further hypnosis. She wishes to find out what really took place on July 22, 1978. She is not satisfied with just forgetting about the incident. The whole episode is a true puzzle. Taken as an isolated encounter, most UFOlogists would probably do their utmost to doubt the word of those individuals who were personally involved. The rule of thumb seems to be, "If you can't explain it, or it doesn't support existing evidence, brush the whole affair under the carpet." If we were to do this, we wouldn't be any better than the government agencies who have tried so hard to hide the very existence of UFOs from the public.

JOHN DE HERRERA ADDS HIS THOUGHTS AND OPINIONS

"My interrogation of the two witnesses, on four separate occasions, amounted to approximately twelve hours. It takes almost two hours for each one to tell her story! This account is incredibly detailed and the testimony from each lady is the same. Months later the repeat story matches the original account. I cannot imagine anyone investing this much effort to fabricate and memorize so much detailed information.

"If we stop and compare the information in this case to the multitude of similar cases, we find many parallels. The 'ball of light' phenomenon is frequently observed and has baffled men for thousands of years. These lights through the years have acquired many names: Ball of Fire, Orange Fire, Ghost Lights, Foo Fighters, etc. Strange glowing balls of light are seen, and have been photographed, as religious apparitions.

"Phantom helicopters are a persistent phenomenon in the Midwest. Many people have reported other phantom aircraft in the skies also. They glide silently by without making any noise. Has our government developed some extraordinary aircraft or is someone playing tricks on us? There have been many apparitions of things – from aircraft to creatures. Yes, even that dog with its glowing eyes."

Yes! John did say "dogs with glowing eyes." And we have not heard the last of them, as the world Beyond Amityville becomes increasingly strange and more tangled.

THE NIGHT ET RETURNED HOME
A First Person Experience

Sometimes a single event seems to trigger a set of weird and bizarre circumstances, as in the case recorded here of a New Jersey family whom I can vouch for as they are part of my extended family. Their sincerity is not to be disputed, whether you like it or not. This incident has the earmarks of both a confrontation with your standard-type poltergeist and some rather unwelcome interlopers from another dimension.

This particular series of bizarre happenings began when a UFO hovered across the street. Soon shadows were seen in the house, objects began to disappear, electrical devices malfunctioned and an eerie presence could be felt, as if something "new" had joined the family.

The Boyers (a pseudonym) are a large, loving family who occupy a modest home in a rural area of New Jersey. Ellen and her husband have six children, ranging in age from two years to twenty-seven. Ellen's daughter, Rita, is married, having children who, along with her husband, occupy the family basement apartment. Because they are not looking for any publicity this story might bring them, we have agreed to keep the identity of the family involved in this ongoing incident a secret. However, their total sincerity can be attested to by the author of this book, who has known them personally just about all of his life.

The bizarre happenings began in the late summer of 1982 when a mysterious object was observed hovering over some trees across the street at approximately five in the morning by Mr. Boyer, who was returning home from an emergency call. Though nothing unusual happened for quite some time after the sighting, it later became apparent that the UFO directly tied in with the many manifestations which threatened to alter the course of the family's lives and was probably the catalyst which triggered the start of this unearthly series of events, events which finally ended when their unseen visitor – their poltergeist-like manifestation – returned home, wherever that might be. Perhaps either Hell or Heaven, or somewhere in between?

Though there have been numerous incidents in which households have literally been besieged by invisible entities, the assumption is normally made that the disturbance is caused by the spirits of the dead and not alien beings. In recent years, however, there has been an increasing awareness of the fact that quite often UFOlogical events can closely parallel those of a psychic or parapsychological nature and that not all extraterrestrials need necessarily be flesh and blood creatures. Research has established the fact that unseen beings who exist in different dimensions or vibratory levels are around us all the time but can only be "felt" or "sensed" occasionally. Apparently, this is one such case, which proves that there is more in heaven and on Earth than most of us have imagined – or had nightmares about.

"I have reason to believe that an ET resided in our home for over a year, and that we felt his presence, though we might not have realized the identity of our uninvited visitor.

"We first noticed something strange going on when the weather started to turn warm last summer and the dogs in our yard began to act peculiar. They would bark all night long, keeping the family awake. One night my dog, Max, began to shake like a leaf. His tongue was hanging out and he was dripping saliva, though there was absolutely no reason for him to be acting this way.

"My daughter, who first brought my attention to the dog, suggested I bring him indoors. I told her I wanted to, but I was afraid that he might get sick in the house. No matter what I did, I couldn't shut him up. I couldn't stop him from shaking. I tried giving him water, but he wouldn't drink. He didn't want anything. He just kept running around and barking all night long.

"One of my five sons also said there was something wrong with his dog. He said all the animals seemed to be nervous. His dog almost hung himself trying to jump over the fence.

"The next day the three littlest children in the house, Danny, three, J.R., four, and Glen, four, went outside to play. They took a jar of jelly beans and some toys with them and had a picnic. I was doing the laundry indoors when J.R. came inside and told me and my daughter (his mother) that he was through. He said, 'The man told us, no more picnic.' We didn't think anything of it until the following afternoon when another of the kids told us that he had seen a man standing in the woods in back of the house and that they were told to go inside and not to play there.

"Naturally, I was worried about any strangers who might be wandering about where young children are concerned, and so I tried to get more information about the man, but all J.R. would say was, 'No more picnic, all finished, all gone.'

"Later we gathered all three children together and asked them to show us where the man had been. They all pointed to the same spot over by the garden where the fence is that the dog almost caught himself on.

"Interestingly enough, in the summer there is no way that anyone can get back there because the bushes are so thick and nobody trims them. Quite a few times the dogs have barked and the kids have come in and said they saw the man. We would run outside and wouldn't see anyone. The kids described him as wearing a suit jacket and a pair of pants. Sometimes they said there were two men.

"Shortly thereafter, it would feel like someone would come into the bedroom at night and would push against the bottom of my mattress. Sometimes I would be overcome by the feeling that I wasn't alone, although nobody was physically in the room with me. One time, I was lying on my left side facing the wall and I felt a poke like someone's finger jabbing into my shoulder.

"The business with the mattress happened almost every night. In addition, a photograph of my youngest son, aged two, kept falling from the wall This happened so frequently that finally I decided to leave it down where it couldn't break.

"One night, I got bumped on the mattress and I thought that someone was trying to speak to me. I sat up in bed and said, 'What did you say?' I was able to hear the sound of someone talking but was unable to distinguish any words.

"Later, when my daughter arrived home, I told her about the voices and she said she'd heard them a few times as well. Actually, she seemed truly petrified. It seems that they had been bothering her for a while, but she was afraid to mention it to anyone for fear we would all think she was crazy. She said the voices would call her by name, but even though I was in her company when this happened, I could never hear anything.

"Things really got out of hand the day before Labor Day. Everybody had gone out to see the fireworks display put on by our neighborhood carnival and I was sitting around the kitchen getting the food ready for the next day when I heard a sound coming from the basement. It was the sound of someone walking across a board that had been placed at the bottom of the stairs to cover an open sewer pipe. When you step on it, it makes a little plunking sound, and someone was going back and forth across it repeatedly and it was driving me crazy.

"Not wanting to get hysterical and trying to brush the matter aside, I kind of laughed and thought, 'Oh, I've got company.' It was like a feeling of not being alone. Now and then, I got a little upset because it plunked a little too loud. I would stand out on the porch for a little while just to clear my head and then go back into the house.

"When the family got back from the fireworks display, I told them what had happened and that I had this strange feeling that I wasn't alone. When I explained what had happened to the boards, my daughter replied they had been hearing that all day long but didn't want to say anything about it. Her husband and my oldest son also heard it. My daughter's husband even got up a couple of times to see if it was the kids fooling around and there was nobody there. He said, 'It would sound just like someone was walking around down there and then when you went to look, you couldn't find anything.'

"Our 'friend' seems to like my air conditioner. One night the dogs were barking out back and there was nothing outside. I shut off the air conditioner in order to go and check on the dogs. When we were below my bedroom window, my husband said, 'The air conditioner isn't on.'

"I said, 'No, I shut it off so I could hear the dogs better.'

"So, we were out back of the house trying to figure out what was wrong with Max. He had plenty of water and food. It wasn't that. He wasn't nervous, like he was that other time. He wasn't shaking. The dog was upset about something in the air.

"All of a sudden, my husband turned and said, 'What was that?'

"I asked him, 'What's what?'

"He said, 'The air conditioner just went on. Then it went off again. But just as we went by the window, it went on again.' There is no way to shut it off and turn it on without pushing the buttons. When I had shut it off, it was on 'Off.' When we went back indoors it was 'On.'

"I said, 'Well, thank you, whoever you are. It is hot in there.'

"My husband said, 'I know that thing was off. I know that thing went on and off a couple of times.'

"I said, 'I know, it's George.'

"He said, 'Well, tell your friend to leave. I don't want him hanging around here.'

"I said, 'You tell him to leave.' We went to bed and there wasn't any more trouble that night.

ENTER A SHADOWY FIGURE

"The next incident was about a month later. I was in bed and I had to go to the bathroom. So, I walked out to the living room, where the children were sleeping. There were no lights on. I stopped in the middle of the living room and looked into the kitchen. There was someone standing there. I couldn't see any clothes on him, so I thought it was my daughter's husband. He often walks around in only his shorts. It was very dark so it was difficult to see really well.

"I was just getting ready to say, 'What the hell are you doing here?' when I thought, 'No, wait a minute, that's not my daughter's husband. How come it's so dark and I can still see him? There's something wrong.' I didn't want to take any chances in case it was someone who broke in.

"As I backed up to hit the light switch, he started leaving, moving behind the refrigerator. As the light came on, he disappeared right through the wall.

"Then I grabbed my flashlight, went into the bedroom, and turned it on my husband. He asked me what the matter was. I said, 'There was a man out in the kitchen.'

"He said, 'Yeah? Let me go get him.'

"I said, 'Forget it, he just went through the wall.'

"He said, 'What are you talking about?'

"I had not been scared. I would have been more frightened if it was a human. When I thought about it, I realized it couldn't have been human, because it was like a shadow. I wasn't scared of him, because if he wanted to do anything, the two kids were in there. He could have done something to them. He doesn't seem to bother anyone, outside of scaring my poor daughter to death. I don't particularly like it when he comes into the room at night. He has grabbed my foot at times, which I don't like.

"Objects in the house have disappeared from time to time. For example, one morning I woke up and I didn't notice anything until I was talking on the phone. I went to rub my rings, which is a habit that I have, and they were gone from my fingers. I found the one which wasn't worth anything on the bed. I could see that one coming off because it's big.

"On the other hand, I could never get my wedding ring off. I looked all over the house for it. I couldn't get any work done. I paced back and forth and said, 'Look, I thought you were a nice guy. Taking the ring off my hand is not very nice. That's stealing.'

"I had just about given up when I went into the living room to straighten up. There I found the ring, on the floor, by the door. This was strange because I had looked all over the house. It could easily have been seen there. Also, it's just not possible to get the ring off my finger. This really bothered me...that 'he' could come into the room and had taken the ring, which is impossible to remove, without my knowing about it.

"There was another incident where one of my sons was lying on the living room floor and someone booted him smack in the behind.

A Shadowy Figure In An Otherwise Quiet Household.

"He gave out a loud yelp and before I knew it he was knocking on my door wanting to know if he could crash in my room, since he was afraid to stay by himself.

"Another time, two of the kids said they had seen two men, a short one and a tall one, standing on the roof of the house and that they had coveralls on and that when they unzipped them they had some sort of strange suit on underneath their outerwear. I was in the living room later and I felt someone standing near me and heard the sound of a zipper being pulled up and down.

"Still, at other times, I saw weird white-blue lights in my bedroom at night that were not reflections from the street. The whole house was being turned upside down. Things were missing that would show up in unpredictable places, there would be eerie sounds and a creepy feeling as if we were never alone.

"The second Sunday in October, at about 5:00 AM, I was lying in bed and I heard what sounded like a motor running. I woke my husband up and he mumbled something about someone trying to steal his truck. He jumped up and flew outside while I looked for my slippers. I was still looking for them when he came running back, slamming the door and bolting the latch behind him.

"'What did you see?' I asked him.

"'Never mind. It's nothing. Let's forget it and go back to bed.'

"Even the next day, my husband wouldn't talk about it. All that I could get out of him was, 'The last time I told you I saw something, you said I was nuts. So I'm nuts.' He was referring to an incident that happened the previous year when he saw a UFO above the trees across the street. It was about the same time, early in the morning, and I had poked a bit of fun at him for seeing things. After this incident, things quieted down in the house and eventually returned to normal. I've talked about this experience to Tim Beckley and he says there have been other cases where invisible entities have come into a person's house and made themselves right at home."

Yes! I believe I have said just about as much. Some call these bewildering entities poltergeists, while others might best refer to them as Ultra-terrestrials. You can make up your own mind, but they are certainly way beyond the vision of Amityville we started out with in our research.

THE CRAWLING LIGHTS

In the mid-1960s, when I first investigated the case of the "crawling lights," I didn't believe we had much to compare it to. But now, other cases involving roaming beams of light have become a bit more frequent.

The case that most immediately comes to mind is the famous "Bentwaters Affair," involving a spacecraft that landed near a NATO base in England and included the sightings of humanoids and possible contact with U. S. military forces. At Bentwaters, rays were seen to shoot out of the forest and actually pass through the solid trunks of trees as well as parked military vehicles. So, in a sense, this incident we relate here was sort of a forerunner of what was to come.

Normally, Toledo, Oregon, is an extremely quiet community. Situated far from the bustling city of Portland, it is located in what can only rightfully be termed logging country. Yet the residents of Toledo and nearby Siletz are considered city folk to those husky backwoodsmen who make up the large percentage of homeowners on Pioneer Mountain.

Knife-Wielding Demons and Murderous Ghosts

Typical of these residents was the Douglas Reeves family. Or we should say "former" residents, because they have since relocated from their modest mountain dwelling. In back of their decision to leave is one of the most harrowing and baffling UFO incidents to date. Their account may well go down in UFOlogical history as the first attempt by UFO occupants to observe the daily actions of a rather typical, hard-working Earth family.

A total of some 35 to 40 persons claim to have witnessed some type of strange phenomena near the Reeves property. These strange phenomena ranged from spaceship-like crafts to pulsating, doughnut-shaped lights that crawled along the walls of the house to strange stump-like creatures.

The beginning of these weird events on Pioneer Mountain was in early March of 1966. During a walk through the woods, the Reeves' 16-year-old daughter, Kathy, and a girlfriend suddenly glimpsed an apparent fire burning in an open section of ground some distance away that had been cleared of trees. Approaching closer, the teenagers noticed that instead of a fire there was some type of object hovering a few feet above the ground. The object, as the girls later described it, appeared to be giving off a "ruddy glow" which could be seen for some distance.

The object appeared to be dome-shaped with sparks and smoke flying in all directions, as if the craft were burning. Finally managing to get up some nerve, the two frightened girls headed for their nearby homes to get some older witnesses to back up their observations.

Hurrying now through the woods, they suddenly found themselves confronted with what appeared to be a large searchlight beacon. Thinking that someone was either trying to frighten them or play a joke on them, they both picked up some rocks and threw them at the light's source.

Suddenly, and without warning, they found themselves surrounded by identical lights which seemed to be moving in on them from all sides. Now near panic, the two raced at top speed to tell their parents.

On arriving home minutes later, the two teenagers managed to blurt out to Kathy's mother, Evelyn Reeves, what had happened. At first, Mrs. Reeves didn't take the girls seriously. She felt that they must be trying to pull her leg, having never taken UFO reports seriously before. However, she noted that they were extremely frightened and would not retract their story no matter how hard she tried to get them to.

Knife-Wielding Demons and Murderous Ghosts

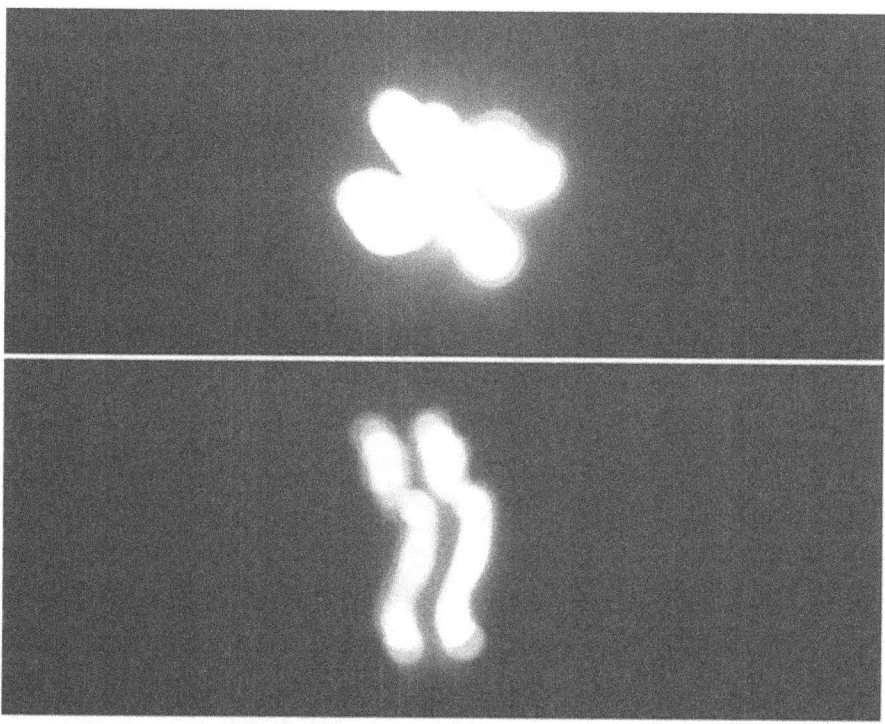

Mysterious hovering and crawling lights have become a frequent factor in many poltergeist- and alien-related breakouts, such as the one that occurred on Pioneer Mountain.

Normally the town of Toledo, Oregon, is a peaceful, very scenic community with covered bridges and less than 3500 residents. Yet at one point there was an outbreak of poltergeist and UFO activity in and around the Reeves property on Pioneer Mountain.

Knife-Wielding Demons and Murderous Ghosts

After talking with her husband and the parents of the other girl, Mrs. Reeves decided the best thing to do was to keep quiet about what had supposedly happened. After all, even if these weird things had occurred, who would believe them? They figured that the entire family would be held open to ridicule.

However, had the family known about what was to happen that very same night...

At about midnight, after everyone had retired for the evening, Mrs. Reeves was awakened from a sound sleep to find the air filled with a strange high-pitched hum like nothing she had ever heard before. Getting up to investigate, her eyes were at once attracted to the partly opened window of her bedroom. In between the curtains she could make out a light that appeared to be pulsating. As she drew the curtains apart, the entire bedroom was suddenly filled with a harsh glow emanating from what appeared to be a large object sitting in her yard. Suddenly all the rooms in the house were filled with the same glow. Likewise, appearing from nowhere were strange doughnut-shaped lights which seemed to be creeping up the walls of their dwelling.

By this time the rest of the family was also awakened. The high-pitched hum was louder and more menacing than ever and the weird crawling lights were rapidly increasing in number.

Grabbing a gun from its rack in the living room, Mr. Reeves ran to the window and pointed it toward someone or "something" he thought he had seen moving outside. Suddenly the house sparkled anew with bright lights. Many more "crawling lights" also appeared on the walls and for a time it seemed as if the family would be overcome by hundreds of these strange doughnut-shaped lights.

Then the original reddish glow gradually dimmed and disappeared; the humming sound faded away and the night was black and still once again.

Although the Reeves were very frightened, they still felt it to their advantage to keep their "invaders" secret. And with the dawn of a new day, all seemed back to normal again. It was as if the previous night's happenings had been part of another world, totally separated from normal reality.

By and by the family forgot about the strange sounds, the bright red lights in their yard, and most of all the lights that had seemingly crept up their very walls. They soon dismissed the entire affair, feeling it would be best to leave well enough alone. They felt as if the worst had passed and they could again live a normal existence.

But their hopes were soon to be shattered, for the weird sights and sound quickly returned to haunt their home on Pioneer Mountain, just as in the worst of other poltergeist attacks.

In the weeks to come the Reeves family was continually shaken out of a sound sleep about two or three o'clock in the morning to find the entire room filled with a rosy glow, which they described as being so intense that "you could read a newspaper by it." In fact, these occurrences became so frequent and annoying that they finally boarded up their windows in an attempt to keep the lights out. Even this failed, and the crawling doughnut-shaped lights continued to creep up the walls.

On one particular occasion, Mrs. Reeves happened to look toward the door leading into their darkened living room and saw a cloud about the size and shape of a watermelon, but transparent, just hanging in midair. It seemed to hover there for minutes before it dissipated into nothing.

It was at this point that the family agreed it would be best to call in outsiders to have a look at their UFO phenomena.

One of these "outsiders" was Delbert Mapes, who told investigators how he had himself seen various lights and objects flying in a helter-skelter fashion through some trees in the Reeves' apple orchard. He described the phenomena as consisting of small round disc-shaped objects, giving off a bright light and traveling at high speeds. He also indicated that they produced a high-pitched hum that was almost inaudible.

Another of the witnesses was Max W. Taylor, a personal friend of the family. Taylor is a chemist employed by the Georgia Pacific Corporation. At the request of Mr. Reeves, he and a group of neighbors camped out on their property in an attempt to find a rational explanation for the phenomena. Although Taylor was highly skeptical when first contacted, he soon joined the ranks of believers. For he was not on the site more than a half hour when he saw a number of strange pulsating spots of bluish light. According to Taylor and the other witnesses, one spot turned up on the outside wall of the living room while the other spot appeared at the opposite end of the home, on the outside wall of the kitchen. Surprisingly enough, there was no apparent source for the light and no beam could be seen in-between.

Making a call to the local police, Taylor brought in a deputy sheriff, Thomas W. Price, from Lincoln County. At about 1:30 AM, Price arrived at the

Reeves home, and as he was disembarking from his squad car he glanced upward and saw a fast-moving object that was flying from northeast to southeast. It was accompanied by a high-pitched whine.

Writing in the police log, Price said that the UFO itself was orange color and appeared to be spinning on end. As it headed in a southeasterly direction the object suddenly came to a complete stop and then made a sweeping motion toward the southwest and disappeared over the horizon.

Deputy Price stated further that before this incident, "I had never believed in UFOs – but I can only report what I myself was a witness to. It actually made the hair on the back of my neck stand on end."

Other residents, likewise skeptical, also reported odd occurrences. Five or six persons, who the police termed "apparently sober," insisted that they had seen "stump-like" creatures moving across an open field near the Reeves residence on two occasions.

A 17-year-old high school senior, Douglas Whitlow, found himself being followed by an object down the Siletz-Toledo Highway. The object remained visible for nearly an hour over the area and witnesses told how it crisscrossed the open highway, following the auto's bright lights, at low altitude. The description of the UFO tallied with the objects seen on the Reeves property.

But perhaps the best look at the UFOs came from a group of six teenagers who told reporters they had viewed the objects through binoculars near the Reeves home. They described the craft as "oval-shaped with a string of red, blue and green lights on their upper sections." Peering at the objects even closer, they felt that there were searchlights inside that appeared to be scanning the nearby earth, perhaps taking photographs. This light also seemed to change color from red to blue and then to a bright shade of green.

Nor was the Pioneer Mountain area free of what appeared to be physical evidence of these strange visitors. As early as May, 1966, Ed Keenon, a logger, came upon a large chunk of metal, which, under analysis, turned out to be pure sodium. This find was made by Keenon as he walked along a path which passes by a small creek bed on the outskirts of Kernville. To this date no one has been able to locate the source of the sodium or discover what its use might have been.

Also discovered near the Reeves Pioneer Mountain home was a large quantity of aluminum-looking shavings which an analysis showed was composed of magnesium. Taylor suggested that the pilots of the strange craft might be dropping the shavings in an attempt to jam nearby radar tracking stations.

Now the Reeves are gone and so are the lights, the spaceships, and the stump-like creatures. The new owner of the Reeves' former home denies seeing anything unusual now, although he had witnessed various phenomena before the Reeves' sudden departure.

Here indeed is a classic case where apparently the operators of the UFOs seen in the Taylor, Oregon, area were keeping watch on a single Earth family, perhaps with the intention of recording their daily activities, much the same as we would do upon the discovery of new life forms, whether it be microscopic or something higher on the evolutionary scale.

Did the strange phenomena follow the Reeves family to wherever they had fled, as has happened in many, seemingly-related poltergeist cases? We may never know, because so many years have passed and the family informed nobody of their destination. Perhaps someone from the Reeves family might read our version of their stranger-than-science fiction experience and update us or make any corrections that might be necessary in the telling of their story.

SUGGESTED READING – BOOKS BY TIMOTHY G. BECKLEY

UFOS – WICKED THIS WAY COMES

ROUND TRIP TO HELL IN A FLYING SAUCER

EVIL EMPIRE OF THE ETS AND ULTRA-TERRESTRIALS

THE BELL WITCH PROJECT

THE AUTHENTIC BOOK OF ULTRA-TERRESTRIALS

CRYPTID CREATURES FROM DARK DOMAINS

SCREWED BY THE ALIENS

ALIEN STRONGHOLDS ON EARTH

DAVID BOWIE, UFOS, WITCHCRAFT, COCAINE AND PARANOIA

Mr. UFO's Secret Files – Subscribe to our YouTube Channel

Knife-Wielding Demons and Murderous Ghosts

SERVANTS OF THE DARK SIDE: CULTS THAT KILL
By Scott Corrales

EDITOR'S NOTE: While ghosts, spirits, demons and poltergeists can be associated with devilish deeds that go so far as murder and mutilation, there have been various groups, and cults, which seem to open themselves up to the most primitive of terrors lifted right out of the likes of the *"Hell Raiser"* movie franchise, thus giving the public the wrong impression of legitimate UFO and paranormal groups operating within the boundaries of decency and good taste.

Scott Corrales has long been a valuable contributor to both our past newsstand magazine publications like *"UFO Universe"* and *"UFO Files,"* as well as providing valuable chapters in books such as **"Screwed by the Aliens,"** **"UFO Hostilities,"** and – most impressively – **"Alien Blood Lust,"** for which he was the main researcher.

Scott became interested in the UFO phenomenon as a result of heavy UFO activity while he was living in both Mexico and Puerto Rico. Early on he became an advocate for the paranormal, interdimensional interpretation of the enigma. In 1996, Scott documented the terrifying manifestation of the entity popularly known as the Chupacabras which resulted in three works, including **"The Chupacabras Diaries."** Since 1998, Scott has edited the online publication *"Inexplicata: The Journal of Hispanic UFOlogy."*

http://inexplicata.blogspot.com

* * * * * * * * *

Knife-Wielding Demons and Murderous Ghosts

In a world still reeling from the nearly one thousand dead at the People's Temple in Guyana and the more recent UFO-related suicides of the Heaven's Gate cult in California and Switzerland's Solar Temple, the news that thirteen children had been murdered by a South American cult did not raise eyebrows anywhere. Brazilian authorities had rounded up Dr. Anisio Ferreira de Souza, a respected physician, for the heinous crime of having "created an organization dedicated to murdering minors and removing their vital organs" that was active in several Brazilian states, notably Pará, Goias and Espiritu Santo. The specific charge was for having for his role in the deaths of thirteen children in Pará, who were first raped and later suffered genital mutilation "for purposes of a satanic ritual."

The police had also identified him as being a member of an obscure cult known as *LUS* – a play on the Spanish word for "light" – or Lineamiento Universal Superior (Superior Universal Guideline), an organization founded by a woman named Valentina de Andrade, who began preaching the "good news" of the benevolent Space Brothers in 1981 after having received allegedly extraterrestrial messages through her former husband, Argentinean national Roberto Olivera, her accomplice in the sect until 1987.

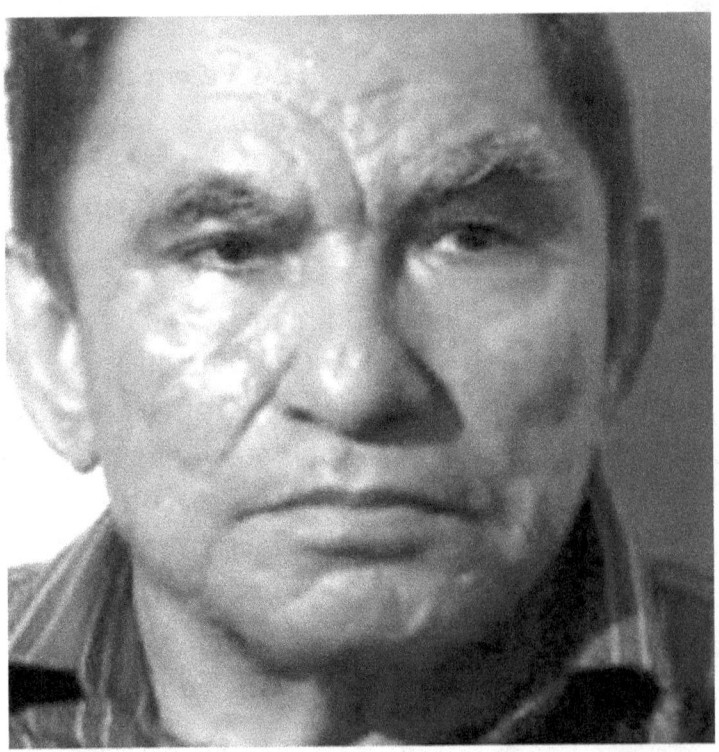

A Brazilian doctor and serial killer who ran a "satanic" ring, was convicted of murder having been linked to the deaths of 19 children.

Schisms occurred in the group – a common occurrence – as other members accused Ms. de Andrade of "betraying the mission and using her extraterrestrial-imparted knowledge for her benefit [rather than] for the common good, for which reason the teachings [received] must be purified from her distortions and rescued from the ridicule she created by her ravings."

The contactee appears to have disappointed her space brother contacts even further by trading them for darker masters: In 1992, de Andrade and the LUS group had experienced a brush with the law due to the fact that a child had vanished under mysterious circumstances from the isle of Guaratuba in southern Paraná, allegedly a victim of ritual crimes performed by the cult. Prosecution was avoided due to legal technicalities ("inconsistent evidence") and the LUS cult quit Brazil, relocating to Argentina instead, where the contactee cult leader lived large. However, hundreds of LUS members deserted her, apparently after having become "aware of the psychological manipulation and economic exploitation to which they had been subjected under the Brazilian's leadership."

Fearful of meeting the same fate as Dr. Ferreira de Souza, the former cult members left in Brazil testified before Judge Luis Ernane Ferreira Malto of the Third Court of Altamira that Valentina de Andrade had not engaged in any ritual crimes or child abductions, while accusing her of having persuaded a husband and wife who joined the LUS cult to leave their new-born daughter in the care of grandparents, so that the couple would be able to "leave the planet" aboard the spacecraft whose imminent arrival was a mainstay of de Andrade's teachings, which posited the belief that children were "negative energies" to be left behind.

Judge Ferreira Malto nevertheless mandated preventive custody for other members of the LUS cult suspected of involvement in the thirteen deaths. Among these were another doctor, a former military police corporal, and Valentina de Andrade. "As of today, they shall be hunted throughout the country and even abroad," stated the judge.

WHEN RITUALS GO BAD

On August 16, 2000, Mexico's "*El Norte*" newspaper ran an account of four people – two of them *curanderas*, or faith healers – who died while conducting the cleansing ritual known as a *limpia* in the village of San Buenaventura. The healers involved were two sisters – Blanca Esthela and Adriana Gutierrez – who apparently did not realize that the room in which they were cleansing the negative energies of an unnamed couple was quickly filling up with another lethal force: carbon monoxide. The four bodies were found the next day by Joel Villanueva, the husband of the woman who had gone seeking spiritual help.

The husband told authorities that his wife had gone to see the Gutierrez sisters because the pair had informed her that she had been "bewitched" and required their assistance. Mrs. Villanueva had been accompanied by her brother-in-law, who was interested in how the healers conducted their rituals.

Villanueva added that when the family reached the Gutierrez sister's apartment, the ritual started with the use of aromatic herbs, prayers and the ingestion of liquid essences. "We were led into a room that had a lit brazier, images of saints, holy water and some eggs." So far, the typical accoutrements of a Mexican faith healer. However, Villanueva added a further detail. "Miss Esthela told us that they worked with a spirit known as *Hermanito* – 'Little Brother' – and that through his aid they would try to expel the demon that was tormenting my wife.

"After that," he continued, "[they] told me to leave the room and place a gold crucifix around my neck, since things could get rough when they confronted the spirit. I went out and heard them shouting: 'Leave her! You're not from this world! Go away!'"

The article does not say at what point Villanueva left the healing session, but when he returned, the sad scene he had to face made him believe that the faith healers had lost the battle.

In May 2000, teenager Erika Guillén riddled her parents' bodies with bullets and dispatched her 10 year-old brother by stabbing him over forty times. The crime shocked Mexico and was compared to the murders committed by the Menéndez Brothers in California in the late '80s. Authorities established that the material culprit of the triple murder was Erika's boyfriend, Jorge Hernández, 22, a practitioner of black magic who convinced his young girlfriend that she must "purify her parents' souls."

Desecration of religious imagery and the proliferation of cults has become a critical factor in the state of Michoacan's so-called Tierra Caliente region. According to the November 20, 2000, edition of "*El Norte,*" the Municipality of Turicato, located some one hundred miles distant from Morelia, the state capital, boasts the "New Jerusalem" – a 25-year-old cult whose numbers exceed four thousand faithful. The cult holds the belief that the End Times are at hand, and praying the Rosary 30 times is therefore commanded. Residents of this community affect the lifestyle found in Palestine during Christ's lifetime: the women are covered head-to-toe in pastel colored gowns, cannot wear makeup or pants. Miniskirts and plunging necklines represent a mortal sin. Nor can they wear their hair short, become pregnant – abstinence is preferable in the face of the "inevitable end" -- or listen to music other than their prayers. The community is spearheaded by "Papa Nabor," the spry 81-year-old who founded the cult in 1974.

A supposedly Millennialist sect made its appearance in the town of Zacapu in 1999, as its members feverishly made preparations for an end of the world which never came. Mexican law enforcement paid careful attention to this group – which dubbed itself *Oracion Espiritual* (Spiritual Prayer) – fearful of the possibility of a mass suicide. The group's spiritual leader, Francisco de la Cruz, 70, is allegedly manipulated by a U.S. cult which still remains unknown within the state. Cruz successfully convinced his followers to rid themselves of all their worldly possessions by convincing them that it was necessary to do so in order to "enter into the Kingdom of Heaven." According to the testimony of neighbors and relatives of some of the cult members, there was talk that "a long journey" would be necessary to reach salvation (echoes of the initial version of the "Heaven's Gate" cult in the U.S.). Police work may have thwarted any mass suicide that may have been in the works, but their raid resulted in the religious group's disappearance to parts unknown.

Limpia rituals in Latin communities are often credited with the spiritual and physical healing of those attending.
www.joygallerysf.com

BLACK ROBES AT NIGHT

It came as a surprise to readers of Chile's *"La Tercera"* newspaper that the nation's Chamber of Deputies (similar to the U.S. House of Representatives) had held hearings in relation to the existence of eighty active satanic groups in their country – 40 of them classified as "dangerous clandestine groups." The cults are allegedly involved in such ghastly acts as consuming human flesh, necrophilia and self-mutilation.

According to sociologist and cult researcher Humberto Lagos, satanic groups were proliferating throughout Chile since the year 2000. The groups are never large – size not being a consideration, rather, the amount of damage they can cause being the major factor – and are formed by young males (30 and younger) who cut off one of their fingers as a sign of belonging to the cult. Lagos, the government's main consultant on the matter, added that lonely, elevated areas such as La Piramide are frequented by these cultists for their weekly rituals. A cross-section of the cult members would reveal disaffected youth who blame society for their ills and – in a Catholic country – rebel against one of the most visible societal symbols.

Police officers report that these places are often marked by a hexagon with the number "666" and fenced with inverted crosses. The cultists drink alcohol and take drugs prior to engaging in sexual rituals. However, the Vitacura sheriff's department, which is in charge of the La Piramide sector, has not recorded any reports from local residents regarding strange rituals or situations in the area.

It is believed that three hundred such groups exist throughout Chile, acting in small cells, much like terrorist outfits. Many of them are not satanic, but rather practitioners of Santería or other Afro-Caribbean religions, which have gained considerable followings in South America.

The Chamber of Deputies' committee on cults was empaneled as a result of charges of white slavery leveled against the "Center for Tibetan Studies" in the city of Viña del Mar. The new anti-cult legislation would follow the European model, which makes "manipulation of conscience" and any form of mental manipulation or obfuscation a crime

None of this, according to the information in *"La Tercera,"* compares with the most violent case recorded: the 1994 incident involving a Satanic/neo-Nazi cult engaging in child abductions in order to torture them and subject them to all manner of sexual outrages. The cult celebrated its rituals at night in the vicinity of the sports club of the town of Sausalito.

Knife-Wielding Demons and Murderous Ghosts

The Chilean newspaper does not go on to state if there was any link between the cultists and the members of the upper class athletic club. While such a connection may at first seem startling, it has been seen elsewhere, as in the case involving a group of Mexican Satanists who carried out their rituals in Chapultepec Park, not far from the elite Restaurante del Lago eatery. Another case involving upper middle class practitioners of ritual magic appeared in Spain's *"El Pais"* newspaper on March 23, 1999, when it was reported that members of the *Fraternidad Blanca Universal* (Universal White Fraternity) had performed a ritual designed "to enhance both pleasure and longevity" in the coastal resort town of L'Alfás del Pi which resulted in the death of Natalie Castleford, 38, a Belgian national. According to the press, the cultists placed a blanket over Castleford's body and several people proceeded to sit on her in order to interrupt her breathing process – a method which, according to the cult's beliefs, causes intense pleasure, extends natural life span and purifies the body.

At this point it must be added that police officials in these countries, while at first baffled by the nature of the crime, tend to react swiftly and usually "get their man" after diligent detective work, often resorting to infiltrating the cults. In October 2002, Spain's *"El Mundo"* newspaper carried a story on how Italian law enforcement had successfully broken up the Angels of Sodom, a satanic cult in the city of Pescara in eastern Italy, led by a 32-year-old reverend known as Jan Ash. This cult leader had allegedly belonged to a number of U.S. cults, but decided to establish his own seven years ago because of his interest in "vampiric practices," according to the newspaper.

The police apprehended "Reverend Ash" and three associates during the Pescara raid, and confirmed fourteen cases of abuse to minors, adding that "the total list may number in the hundreds, since the cult had been operating clandestinely for seven years and reputedly had a considerable number of customers."

"YOU WILL FEEL HOW THE GROUND SHAKES"

The most frightening cult, however, is the one that lacks the trappings of satanic worship. This is certainly the case in a truly bizarre event which befell bus driver Efraín Zet and his three sons in January 2002, when they drove a religious youth movement known as "los Exploradores del Rey" – the King's Pioneers – to the recreational facility known as Lican Ray, a nature site enjoyed by families from all over the Santiago de Chile region, for what appeared to be a Christian youth gathering.

After depositing his passengers at the site where the religious gathering was to be held, Efraín Zet and his eldest son, Felipe, began to cook a meal while the two younger boys, Horacio and Matías, hung out near the platform where the meeting was being held and broadcast over loudspeakers.

"Suddenly, the master of ceremonies announced the appearance of a 15-year-old girl who had supposedly traveled all over the world, healing many different types of people," Zet told reporters from the *"Diario Austral de Temuco."* The young woman spoke in oddly-modulated tones. "Her voice rose and dropped. Listening to her made one feel very sleepy, like some sort of hypnosis."

The father and eldest son continued their preparations for the evening meal as the girl continued to address the gathering. "When the girl finished speaking, everyone was sort of 'bemused' and I will never forget how the girl raised her hands and said: 'You will feel how the ground shakes, how you will burn for not having respected Jesus, your brother!'" Zet reported.

Dozens of teenagers began weeping in what appeared to be a trance-like state. Efraín Zet and Felipe scoffed at what they took to be theatrics aimed at recruiting new adepts into the group, until the young woman began toppling the weeping teens. "We felt nervous when we saw her knocking guys over without even touching them, and seeing the guys fall to the ground like sacks of potatoes."

But panic gripped Felipe Zet when he realized his two younger brothers were among the screaming and sobbing mass. The father plunged into the crowd to retrieve his boys, finding Horacio "totally gone" and Matías lying on the floor. What truly unnerved the bus driver was that, while rescuing his children, the girl used her uncanny powers to direct some kind of "force" against him which hurled him to the ground.

Managing to flee, the bus driver and his eldest son took the two children out the area. "I would say [to the boys]: 'Hey, what's the matter with you?' but they wouldn't answer me. For some reason, they weren't my brothers. They would answer, but as though someone else was talking through them," Felipe told the media.

A vacationing physician offered assistance to the bus driver's young sons. According to Zet, little Matías appeared to be in shock, and the physician counted up to three and caused the boy to snap out of the state he was in.

In a state of sheer terror, Efraín and Felipe Zet headed for the Lican Ray state police station. They asked the law enforcement personnel to please go back and retrieve their belongings, since they refused to go back to the scene where the unnatural events had transpired. Officials told the newspaper that no formal complaint was made because there was no way of classifying the crime. In the main assistance center of the lake community, the minors were cared for by Dr. Alejandra Bahamondes Soto, who signed the certificates dated February 5th. The documents show that both minors were diagnosed with post-traumatic shock of unknown origin.

"This parent's dramatic account leads to several questions regarding the event," says the article in *"Diario Austral."* "Is it possible that some religious rituals may produce negative effects in persons foreign to the church that engages in them? Can anyone have the power to produce hypnotic effects in nearly 100 people?"

CONCLUSION

The reader should not infer from these cases that cult activity is safely restricted to the world's Spanish-speaking populations: the U.S. has been the proverbial heavyweight – and at the forefront of such developments – decades before the first *sectas*, as cults are known in Spanish, appeared in these countries. It is important to note that despite lurid newspaper accounts going back to the Manson Family and even earlier, a more skeptical approach has developed toward events in this field.

Of a number of examples that could be presented, perhaps the best of these is author Jeffrey S. Victor's **"Satanic Panic"** (Chicago: Open Court, 1993), which points to such factors as economic hardship, family breakdown and unstable relationships as "stressors" that lead to the belief that groups living in the margins of society are the focus of the problem. While the 1950s pointed the finger at "juvenile delinquents," and the 1960s did the same to "biker gangs," the '70s and subsequent decades found ready-made culprits in satanic cults, the Moonies and assorted groups.

Victor's book studies the hysteria that occurred in Jamestown, New York, in the late 1980s, when rumors that a satanic cult was active in the area and that a "blond virgin" was going to be sacrificed led police on wild-goose chases and women to reach for the hair dye. A number of societal pressures, he suggests, had led residents to find convenient scapegoats in some unusually-garbed students (either goths or punks) at the local high school. Fundamentalist groups also took advantage of the instability for proselytizing, handing out cartoon gospel leaflets about devil worship. One of these, *"The Poor Little Witch,"* was found at one of the Jamestown locations supposedly employed by the Satanists in their assemblies.

This contrarian viewpoint has its merits, particularly when it comes to keeping levels of hysteria from becoming unmanageable. But it is nevertheless hard to dismiss the accumulated evidence that something truly extraordinary is going on, at least in light of the cult activity in Chile and Spain (where police departments have availed themselves of the help offered by researchers of the occult in solving crimes).

Social psychologist Richard Ofhse defines a cult as an authoritarian movement, presented under the guise of a religious, cultural or miscellaneous grouping or association that requires absolute devotion by its members toward an individual or ideas, employing manipulation, persuasion and control techniques aimed at achieving the leader's own ends.

These concepts may apply to "traditional" cult activity in which children or young adults are drawn into the spiral of mind-controlling and behavior-altering situations that have traditionally been associated with cult activity in the media. But there are other examples of cult activity, as we have seen, which may simply be said to border on madness.

Scott Corrales

Knife-Wielding Demons and Murderous Ghosts

"Satanic panics" in the 1980s and 90s were fostered by rumors of satanic ritual abuse alleged to be occurring in places such as daycare centers and funeral homes.

Knife-Wielding Demons and Murderous Ghosts

No one really understands the origins of a poltergeist. Is it the spirit of a deceased person? The unleashed energies of a troubled mind? Or something completely beyond our understanding?

WHEN THE POLTERGEIST FINDS ITS VOICE
By Tim R. Swartz
Co-Host of "Exploring the Bizarre," KCORradio.com

It can be terrifying enough when a poltergeist makes its appearance in a household. Rocks thrown about, strange bangs on the walls, moving furniture, items disappearing and then reappearing – this is enough to set anyone on edge. However, when a poltergeist finds its voice and starts to talk, you know that events have decidedly taken a turn for the worse.

Poltergeist activity has been recorded throughout history and is probably the most prolific of all supernatural events. One of the earliest accounts is from around 500 C.E. when St. Germain, Bishop of Auxerre, was bothered by a spirit that battered the walls of a shelter the Bishop was spending the night in with showers of rocks. Another early case was the Bingen poltergeist, which comes from the "***Annales Fuldenses***" or "***Annals of Fulda.***" This incident happened near Bingen, in present-day Bavaria, around 856-858 C.E. A farmer was plagued by a stone-throwing ghost who shook the walls of his house "as though the men of the place were striking it with hammers," set crops on fire and also shouted obscenities and accusations at the farmer suggesting that he had slept with the daughter of his foreman. The poltergeist would follow the man around, and fearful neighbors would refuse to allow him near their homes.

The Bishop of Mainz sent priests with holy relics who attested to hearing the poltergeist denouncing the farmer for adultery. When the priests sang hymns and sprinkled holy water, the poltergeist threw stones and cursed at them.

The Bingen poltergeist had many typical features of a poltergeist that are still repeated in modern times. The fact that this poltergeist could talk is something that has been seen in other cases, but, nevertheless, it really doesn't happen that often.

IS A POLTERGEIST A GHOST?

The poltergeist phenomenon is often placed in the same niche as ghosts and hauntings. The implication is that a poltergeist is a ghost, i.e. a human that has died and returned in spirit form. There is no doubt that there are similarities between ghosts and poltergeist activity. However, a ghostly haunting often tends to have the visual element; for example, a glowing figure dressed in old fashioned clothes is seen walking down a hallway. A haunting also repeats in the same way on a regular basis, much like a recording that is played back over and over. In long-term ghostly hauntings, a ghost will usually ignore entreaties from the living and show no sign of awareness of its surroundings.

Poltergeist activity, instead, operates in a completely different fashion. A poltergeist almost never makes an "appearance" and becomes visible, but, as with ghostly hauntings, there are always exceptions. A poltergeist can do things such as move heavy furniture, instantaneously teleport objects, produce explosive sounds and disgusting odors, create rain inside a building, cause spontaneous fires and other things that seem to be outside of our current understanding of physics.

A poltergeist is extremely aware of its surroundings and will often quickly respond to suggestions by observers and other external stimuli. This shows that there is some kind of "intelligence" behind its pranks and not just some random psychokinesis (PK). This intelligence, along with an ability to communicate, will manifest in a myriad of ways. Pieces of paper with strange messages appear; writing on the walls; children's toys will be arranged to make words; and, perhaps the most shocking, they will sometimes start to speak out loud.

When a poltergeist achieves speech, it generally starts out as animal-like growls and whispers that slowly evolve into discernible words. Most poltergeists never reach this stage of their development, but, once they do, a clear "personality" emerges from what were previously just random events.

L'ANTIDEMON DE MASCON

One early case of a talking poltergeist happened in Mâcon, France, in 1612, when a Calvinist pastor named Francois Perreaud, (or Perrault) became the target of a very unsettling poltergeist. Perreaud's poltergeist made its first appearance on September 19, 1612, when invisible hands started shaking bed curtains and tossing bed clothes onto the floor. This continued for several nights and then escalated when Perreaud and his family heard "a frightful din in the kitchen consisting of unearthly rumblings and knockings, accompanied by the sounds of plates, pots, and pans being hurled against the walls." Perreaud rushed to the kitchen, expecting to find his kitchen destroyed, but was shocked to find that everything was normal and the kitchenware was in its place.

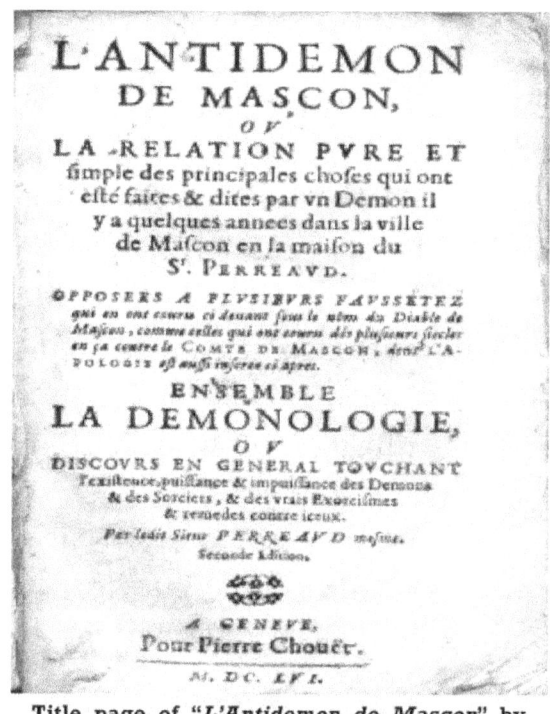

Title page of "L'Antidemon de Mascon" by pastor Francois Perreaud, detailing his experiences with a talking poltergeist.

Eventually a voice that was "very distinct and understandable, although somewhat husky" was heard in the house. It sang, "Twenty-two pennies, twenty-two pennies," then repeated the word "Minister" several times. Perreaud said to the voice, "Get thee behind me, Satan, the Lord commands you."

The voice kept saying "Minister, minister" until the exasperated Perreaud snapped, "Yes, I am indeed a minister and a servant of the living God before whose majesty you tremble."

"I am not saying otherwise," the voice replied.

Once the poltergeist began speaking, it proved to be difficult to shut it up. It recited the Ten Commandments, followed by the Our Father, the Apostles' Creed, and other prayers. It also sang Psalms and recited accurate personal details about Perreaud's family. The voice claimed that it was from the Pays de Vaud, which was at that time infamous for its witch hunts.

The voice told wild stories, made inappropriate jokes and often acted like a child and teased the maid. It was also able to expertly mimic the voices of various Mâcon residents. It also took on several different identities. At one time the voice claimed to be the valet of the original entity, who had left the house and was now in Chambery.

On November 25, the voice announced that it would no longer speak, but its antics in the form of throwing stones, tying knots in the mane and tail of Perreaud's horse, and other typical poltergeist stunts continued through until December, when it finally disappeared forever.

Knife-Wielding Demons and Murderous Ghosts

DIFFERENT PERSONALITIES, DIFFERENT VOICES

The Bell Witch poltergeist in 1817 was very similar to the Mâcon poltergeist due to the fact that "the witch" was extremely talkative and could imitate the voices of people from the area. The poltergeist was said to speak at a nerve-racking pitch when displeased, while at other times it sang and talked in low musical tones. In one instance, it was alleged to have repeated, verbatim, sermons administered by two preachers, occurring at separate locations, that took place simultaneously. The sermons recited by the witch were verified by people attending the churches as being identical in voice, tone, inflection, and content. The poltergeist was even known to attend church and sing along with the congregation, using the most beautiful voice anyone had ever heard.

As well, the poltergeist had the ability to change personalities in the middle of conversations with the Bells or their visitors. The witch had five distinct personalities, each with different voices and traits, which made it easy for the family to separate the perpetrator of the moment. These voices were named "Black Dog," "Mathematics," "Cypocryphy" and "Jerusalem."

This ability to produce "different personalities" also shows up in other poltergeist cases, creating a belief that there are a number of different entities haunting a house.

The Bell Witch was very fond of talking about religion and philosophy for hours on end, especially with John Bell, Jr. The witch had developed a respect John Bell, Jr., due to his tendency to stand up to its abusive behavior. In 1828, the poltergeist reappeared to John Bell, Jr., telling him, "John, I am in hopes you will not be as angry at me on this visit as you were on my last. I shall do nothing to cause you offense; I have been in the West Indies for seven years."

Despite his misgivings, the poltergeist had long talks with him about the past, the present and the future. Years later, he told his son, Dr. Joel Thomas Bell, the details of the poltergeist's discussions. A book was published in 1934, "The Bell Witch – A Mysterious Spirit," which supposedly was met by outrage by other members of the Bell family who felt that details of "the family problem" should not have been made public.

For a more complete history of the Bell Witch poltergeist, see "**The Bell Witch Project**" by Timothy Green Beckley, published by Inner Light-Global Communications.

Above: The home of John Bell and his family. The focal point for the Bell Witch haunting.

Right: The Dagg home as it looks now. The Shawville poltergeist, also known as the Dagg poltergeist, is a historical and well-documented case in Canada.

THE SHAWVILLE POLTERGEIST

When a poltergeist does find its voice, it seems to take great delight in spinning wild tales of its identity and origin. It may at one time say it is the ghost of someone who died years before, only to change its tune later and profess to be the devil or a demon. Like the Bell Witch, the Shawville poltergeist (also known as the Dagg poltergeist) enjoyed entertaining visitors by telling obscene stories and, conversely, singing hymns in an "angelic voice."

The Shawville Poltergeist events took place in the Ottawa Valley, Quebec, in 1889, and centered on the farm and family of George Dagg. The incidents started with what appeared to be animal feces streaked along the farmhouse floor. At first, a young farmhand named Dean was blamed since he was known to come into the house with dirty shoes. Nevertheless, after the boy had been fired, the strange incidents continued, with crockery moving, fires starting spontaneously and windows being smashed.

The Dagg family's eleven-year-old adopted daughter, Dina-Burden McLean, was also physically attacked by the entity when it pulled her hair so hard that her braid was almost torn off. Later, when Dina's grandmother was making up one of the bedrooms, the girl shouted, "Oh grandmother, see the big, black thing pulling off the bed clothes!" The woman could see the sheets being pulled up but couldn't see what was doing it. She handed Dina a whip, telling the girl to strike out at the invisible being. Dinah struck the air a few times and both the girl and her grandmother heard a sound like a pig squealing.

Knife-Wielding Demons and Murderous Ghosts

POTATO HEAVING GHOST?
Charlie Harris of R R. 2 Shawville was hit on the head by a hat with a potato in it when he peeked into the room where the voice of the ghost seemed to be coming from way back in 1889. A neighbor of the Daggs, he recalls the "hullabaloo" the ghost caused—and the bump on his head the potato caused.

Charlie Harris was a witness to the Dagg Poltergeist when he was a boy in 1889. He claimed to have been hit on the head by a hat with a potato in it that had been flung from an empty room.

A few days later a piece of paper bearing the message "You gave me fifteen cuts" was found nailed to the wall.

After this incident, Dina claimed that she was hearing a strange, gruff voice that followed her around while saying bad words to her. Soon, the entire family and others could hear the gruff, man's voice who identified itself as "the Devil." Not everyone was convinced the voice was a supernatural being and blamed Dina for everything. At one point, her mouth was filled with water, yet the voice could still be clearly heard by everyone in the room.

Much like the Bell witch, the Shawville poltergeist enjoyed the attention and would talk for hours. It would often give conflicting stories on what it was. Previously it had said it was the devil, but later it claimed to be the spirit of an old man who had died 20 years earlier. When George asked it why it was bothering his family, it replied, "Just for fun."

It also admitted setting small fires in the house, but again only for its amusement. "I set the fires in the daytime, when you could see them. I like fires, but I didn't want to burn the house down."

After several months of activity, the voice announced that it was going away. When word got out, crowds began gathering at the house to witness the event. The voice was happy to answer questions from the crowd, but now it claimed, "I am an angel from Heaven, sent by God to drive away that fellow."

"You don't believe that I am an angel because my voice is coarse," it said to the crowd. "I will show you I don't lie, but always tell the truth." Instantly its voice took on an "incredible sweetness" and it started singing a hymn:

"I am waiting, I am waiting, to call you, dear sinner, Come to the savior, come to him now, won't you receive Him right now, right now, Oh! List, now he is calling today, He is calling you to Jesus, Move! Come to Him now, Come to Him, dear brothers and sisters, Come to Him now."

Witness testimony agreed that the poltergeist sang with such a beautiful voice that many of the women were reduced to tears. After several hours of singing, the poltergeist said goodbye, saying it would return the next morning and show itself to Dinah and the other children.

The next morning the children breathlessly told their parents that "a beautiful man, he took little Johnny and me in his arms... he went to Heaven and was all red."

Under questioning, the children described a man dressed in white with a lovely face with long white hair. He also had ribbons and "pretty things" all over his clothes and a gold object with stars on his head. The man reached down and picked them up, saying that they were fine children.

Dinah said he had spoken to her as well, telling her that everyone thought he was not an angel, but he would show he was. Then he had "gone up to Heaven." Questioned further, she said he seemed to rise up in the air and disappear in a kind of fire that blazed from his feet.

The Shawville poltergeist was almost forgotten until 1957 when 64-year-old Thomas Dagg, who was born after the events, confirmed that his parents and older siblings were convinced that everything that had happened to them was true and not a hoax. Thomas told reporters that he was sure that the uncanny episode "was the work of the Devil."

Compared to other poltergeist events, talking poltergeists seem to be in a category all by themselves. They may start out the same, manifesting with annoying pranks, strange noises, showers of rocks and other debris, but then they seem to turn a corner and gain energy to a point where a consciousness and personality emerges. The personality is much like a child or mentally challenged adult, but it is a personality nevertheless.

Both the Bell Witch and the Shawville poltergeist exhibit almost identical personality traits. Both were fond of using obscene language and taking on the roles of different characters. Both entities were never shy about talking for hours in front of multiple witnesses. In fact, they seemed to thrive on the attention. They also claimed the ability to travel instantaneously to far-off locations, bringing back information that could be verified later.

Knife-Wielding Demons and Murderous Ghosts

GEF THE TALKING MONGOOSE

So much has been written about the "Dalby Spook" over the years that there really is nothing new that can be added for this chapter. However, considering the similarities between "Gef" and other talking poltergeists, this amazing case does need to be included.

The case of "Gef the Talking Mongoose" started in 1931 on the Isle of Man, located in the Irish Sea between England and Ireland.

The farm, located on an isolated hilltop, was home to 60-year-old Jim Irving, his wife Margaret, and their 12-year old daughter, Voirrey.

Jim had been a travelling salesman before taking up farming in his retirement. The farm was not a success and the family struggled to make ends meet. Doarlish Cashen (Manx for "Cashen's Gap") was extremely isolated, with no electricity, no phone and no radio. By all descriptions, life on the Irving farm was dreary and offered few pleasures.

This all changed when Gef made his appearance. The family started hearing strange "blowing, spitting and growling" sounds coming from behind the wooden paneling lining the farmhouse walls. Eventually these sounds turned into recognizable words spoken with a very high-pitched voice. The voice introduced itself as Gef and claimed to be "an extra-clever mongoose" born in Delhi, India in 1852.

Gef was soon holding regular conversations with the Irving family. He would travel in the space between the interior wooden paneling and the exterior walls of the house. He reportedly would throw objects like pins or rocks from the cracks and holes in the paneling. Although Jim and Margaret both caught brief glimpses of Gef, only Voirrey was allowed to look at him directly. She described him as being the size of a small rat, with yellowish fur, a flat snout like a hedgehog, and a long bushy tail.

Even though Gef acted like a poltergeist, he once told Jim that he was a living creature and was, in fact, terrified of ghosts. Like other talking poltergeist's, Gef's voice had an inhuman quality about it. Those that heard him said his voice was high-pitched, at least an octave above a human voice. Unlike other talking poltergeist's, Gef did not like to talk to others outside of the Irving family. Paranormal investigators Harry Price and Nandor Fodor went to great lengths to travel to Doarlish Cashen, but Gef refused to speak to them. However, there were

Knife-Wielding Demons and Murderous Ghosts

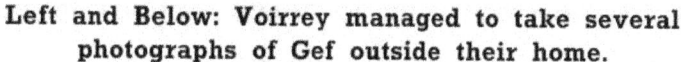

Above: Jim Irving and his daughter Voirrey in front of their home on the Isle of Man.

Left and Below: Voirrey managed to take several photographs of Gef outside their home.

plenty of witnesses to Gef's ability to speak, enough to convince both men that there was some sort of unusual activity at the Irving house.

In their book about Gef, ***"The Haunting of Cashen's Gap: A Modern Miracle Investigated,"*** Harry Price and R. S. Lambert noted some parallels to poltergeist cases. They wrote:

"Many of the events related by Irving can be classified by those experienced in psychical research as belonging to the class of 'poltergeist' phenomena. Amongst these are Gef's habit of throwing sand and small stones, also metal, wooden, and bone objects, at persons in or near Doarlish Cashen; the thumping, scratching, rapping, and banging noises which he makes behind the paneling and in the rafters of the house; and the movement of furniture."

Nandor Fodor thought differently, though. He discounted that Gef was a poltergeist and instead thought Gef was what he claimed to be, an extra-clever mongoose that had somehow developed the ability to speak. Later, Fodor would change his opinion, speculating that Gef was an animal who had somehow become psychically possessed by "a split-off part" of Jim Irving's personality.

In 1970, Voirrey agreed to be interviewed by Walter McGraw for *"FATE"* magazine. Voirrey denied any involvement and seemed rather bitter about the whole experience, stating, "It was not a hoax. Gef was very detrimental to my life. We were snubbed. The other children used to call me 'the spook.' I had to leave the Isle of Man, and I hope that no one where I work now ever knows the story. Gef has even kept me from getting married. How could I ever tell a man's family about what happened?"

She continued by saying that Gef "made me meet people I didn't want to meet. Then they said I was 'mental' or a ventriloquist. Believe me, if I was that good, I would jolly well be making money from it now!"

Gef remains a true enigma in the hallowed halls of paranormal research. One side thinks that Gef was a poltergeist, while the other side thinks he was something else. If you were to compare Gef to other talking poltergeists, the similarities are obvious. Like the Bell Witch and the Shawville poltergeist, Gef enjoyed singing hymns. On January 19, 1935, Gef was in "high spirits" and sang the hymns, "Jesus, my Savior, on Calvary's Tree" and six verses of "The King of Love my Shepherd is."

As well, like other talking poltergeist's, Gef's voice was said to be strange and not like human speech. Jim Irving also said that Gef's laughter ranged from what sounded like a precocious child to the chuckling laugh of an aged person to a distinct type of maniacal laughter that caused the Irving's to think that they were living with some kind of psychotic demon.

Because Gef was seen several times, and even interacted with the household physically, it was widely believed that Gef couldn't be a poltergeist. However, a talking poltergeist is often able to make itself visible, but, much like the way it can talk in different voices, it can also appear in different forms.

In the same time period that Gef was active, another talking poltergeist appeared in Zaragoza, Spain. The Palazon family was living in an apartment complex on Gascón Gotor Street when, in September 1934, they started to hear maniacal laughter and voices coming from inside their home. At first, the voice sounded like a woman, but later it would change and appear to be a man speaking. The family was perplexed by the strange sounds, but kept it to themselves for fear of ridicule.

Above: Maid Pascuala Alcocer in front of the stove from which the mysterious voice emanated.

Left: The police in Zaragoza were never able to determine the source of the strange, taunting voice.

Knife-Wielding Demons and Murderous Ghosts

When the din coming from the apartment became too much, neighbors called the police. The voice then started shouting: *"Cowards, cowards. You called the police. Cowards!"*

When they arrived, the household's young maid, named Pascuala Alcocer, told police that when she was trying to light the wood stove, she heard a loud voice coming from the stove saying, *"You're hurting me!"*

The police checked the apartment but couldn't find any source for the mysterious voice. Word quickly spread and hundreds of people gathered outside of Building #2 in hopes of hearing the "duende" (goblin) for themselves.

Local police and judges personally investigated the home, forcing the family to move out. The authorities shut off the electricity and phone service and tore the place apart. This enraged the voice, and it shouted to everyone that it would kill them and all the residents in the building.

Authorities also brought in psychiatrists to question Pascuala, whom they suspected of hoaxing everything. The doctors suggested that Pascuala was mentally ill and that she was producing the voice through subconscious ventriloquism. At one point they sent the maid on a vacation along with the family, yet the voice continued to speak. Even moving every resident out of Building #2 failed to stop it.

Whatever the source, the voice was able to see what was going on around the building. It would guess the number of people that were in a room at a time and it would interact with police officers directly when they asked it what it wanted.

"Do you want money?"

"**No!**"

"Do you want a job?"

"**No!**"

"Every man wants something."

"**I'm not a man!**"

One of the original builders was brought in to take measurements of the kitchen, but the voice interrupted saying: "Don't worry, it measures 75 centimeters." The mason was so scared he left the building never to come back, leaving his tools behind in a closet.

Eventually the voice vanished just as mysteriously as it arrived. Pascuala Alcocer went into seclusion, and like Voirrey Irving, Pascuala lamented up until her death years later that "the voice from the wall ruined her life."

THE POLTERGEIST AS AN ELEMENTAL

There are many more cases of talking poltergeists that have been carefully researched and chronicled, and probably hundreds more that were never reported for fear of ridicule. The poltergeist by itself is an oddity in the world of paranormal research, and the talking poltergeist goes even further as a head-scratcher due to its outright off-the-wall high strangeness.

All kinds of theories on the true nature of the poltergeist have been suggested. Black magic and curses as the cause of poltergeists are popular in countries such as Brazil, where spiritism is still practiced. Folklore concerning elemental spirits such as fairies, hobs and goblins show that they were also fond of mischievous tricks such as throwing rocks, starting fires and stealing household objects.

Middle Eastern folklore and Muslim theology concerning the djinn and their amazing powers also have similarities to the poltergeist. The djinn are beings with free will that once lived on Earth but were sent away by God to a world parallel to mankind. The word "djinn" comes from an Arabic root meaning "hidden from sight," so they are physically invisible to man, as their description suggests.

The djinn will take possession of buildings or locations and torment any person who goes to live there. They throw rocks at people. They can levitate and cause objects to disappear. A djinn can quickly travel great distances. One of the powers of the djinn is that they are able to take on any physical form they like. Thus, they can appear as humans, animals and anything else. They can mimic the voices of deceased humans, claiming to be spirits or Satan. They enjoy playing tricks and frightening people. In fact, they can feel strong emotions such as fear or grief and gain energy from these powerful feelings.

Like humans, the djinn have distinct personalities. There are those who are of low intelligence, quick to anger and fond of playing tricks. Others have a superior intellect and act more along the lines of guardian angels rather than tricksters.

It is interesting to consider that the poltergeist could be an elemental spirit rather than a human one. This could explain why poltergeists (especially the more energetic talking poltergeist) are resistant and very hostile to attempts to get rid of them by using religious methods. If a poltergeist is not a human spirit or a demon in a Christian, Jewish or Muslim tradition, attempts to use exorcism are pretty much useless.

COULD THE POLTERGEIST BE AN ARTIFICIAL INTELLIGENCE?

Considering that the poltergeist could be something other than a human spirit, the website *"The State of Reality"* (www.thestateofreality.com) declares itself to be "the combined effort of four professional remote viewers that have set out to share their project findings regarding socially significant, anomalous target sets." On this site there is an interesting article concerning their remote viewing of the Bell Witch incident.

Jeff Coley writes that the team's remote viewing attempt produced the concept of "Something contained, or restrained, inside an enclosure. Often this container was sketched and described as being like a bottle, while at other times as a box of some kind which acted as an enclosure or a tomb. One viewer's session described this object as an ossuary, similar to what a collector of antique relics might possess within their private collection. Other sessions described what looked suspiciously similar to the idea of a Genie bottle."

According to Coley, something had been contained inside a bottle or box. The viewers described it as a phantom, an intelligence and a thought form. The remote viewing work described the purpose of this thing as having to do with amusement, recreation, performance and the idea of sending a message. The viewers also described that the phenomenon was associated with something destructive in nature. One viewer notes that it is like a parasite or a time bomb that somehow escaped or was accidently released.

The opinion by the remote viewers was that whatever the Bell Witch was, it had been deliberately contained as a punishment eons ago. Three of the viewers described guards who seem to be keeping this thing bottled up. One viewer described these guards as ethereal, floating, muscular "brutes," almost like otherworldly prison guards, while another viewer described something like a sentry, guarding and patrolling.

It almost sounds like the Bell Witch (and it even admitted to John Bell, Jr., that it was millions of years old) was an artificial intelligence that had been created by a highly advanced and now-vanished civilization that could have been terrestrial or even extraterrestrial. Its purpose might have been to entertain and teach but somehow became uncontrollable and had to be contained.

This is just speculation, of course. But considering how unusual and powerful talking poltergeists can be, is it really so far-fetched to say that these invisible entities might be a form of artificial intelligence? Not an intelligence contained within a machine, but an artificial intelligence without a physical form; in other words, an artificial "spirit."

Perhaps millions of years ago, these AI's were locked away for some reason. As time wore on, some have managed to escape their confinement and then proceeded to wreak havoc in the area where they were kept. Perhaps they have limited energy that can no longer be "recharged." This could explain why they disappear so abruptly and completely, never to be heard from again.

When you look at past cases of talking poltergeists, they display personalities that, if they were human subjects, doctors would describe as psychotic, or schizophrenic. If my theory is correct, this madness could be the result of millions of years of lonely confinement, with little hope of rescue. The human mind would self-destruct in a matter of months. Consider what this amount of time could have done to an artificial mind.

Rather than fear and loathe these tortured entities, a better solution would be to offer them kindness and understanding. For any creature with a soul, even if it's artificial, deserves happiness and even love. This is a difficult concept considering the torture these things have brought upon their victims, but even a savage dog will eventually respond to a kind heart.

Could the poltergeist respond as well?

SUGGESTED READING

THE LOST JOURNALS OF NIKOLA TESLA

TIME TRAVEL: FACT NOT FICTION

ADMIRAL BYRD'S SECRET JOURNEY BEYOND THE POLES

UFO REPEATERS: THE CAMERA DOESN'T LIE

MEN OF MYSTERY

GEF THE TALKING MONGOOSE: THE "EIGHTH WONDER OF THE WORLD"

Knife-Wielding Demons and Murderous Ghosts

There are ultra-dimensional beings that seek to invade and possess the bodies and psyches of vulnerable men and women.

THE PASSING OF BRAD STEIGER – NOW A PART OF "THE OTHER"
A Retrospect By Timothy Green Beckley

Year of Birth: **1936** - Passing: **May 5, 2018**

Place of birth: **Iowa, U.S.A.**
Occupation: **Author and Teacher**.
Spouse: **Sherry Hansen Steiger**.
Education: **University of Iowa**.

If I had my way I would canonize him the Patron Saint of the Paranormal.

For there is no other individual that I can think of who for over half a century did more to popularize the existence of the paranormal, UFOs, cyyptozoology, reincarnation, bigfoot, psychic pets and above all else life after death. He probably did more to turn on the "young and uninitiated" to the esoteric and the plain old strange and unexplained than anyone else who ever came into and impacted our lives. Indeed, if we had a tinge of interest in such topics within our soul it is likely that he bought us out of the sensory closet at a very early age.

With a grand total of over 170 books to his credit, and worldwide sales up around the astounding twenty million mark, Brad Steiger reigned supreme in a rather offbeat world to a multitude of literary fans who scooped up his paperbacks when they were fashionable and could be found at almost every checkout counter, to his more recent volumes larger and thicker and certainly more pricey in this day of runaway inflation than even the spirits could have predicted during a turn of the century séance.

Knife-Wielding Demons and Murderous Ghosts

I first met Brad at a UFO conference held in New York City back in 1967. He had recently come out with a pulp pot boiler **"Ghosts, Ghouls and Other Peculiar People"** followed up quickly by **"Strangers From the Sky,"** his first of many books on aliens and unidentified flying saucers (by far what was to become his favorite topic of continued exploration).

One thing I quickly found out, when it came to his research and writing, Brad was not pragmatic. He let the chips fall where they may. He let the witnesses and experiencers tell their own stories in the own way without editorial colorization. This is one of the reasons why he was genuinely loved and appreciated far and wide – as well as I knew him I don't believe I ever heard Steiger say anything negative about anyone.

And well I knew him. We became so close over the years that he would call me "Brother Tim," and I would refer to him as "Brother Brad," as if we were really part of one big extended family. And I suppose in a sense we certainly were – as we often exchanged a wealth of arcane information on everything from conspiracies to the mysteries of the pyramids. Brad became a regular contributor to my books as, in exchange I willing shared my own experiences with his followers. For years, Brad made his home in Phoenix, Arizona where he lived with his wife Sherry Hansen Steiger who often shared by lines with him. To get away from pressures that only living in Manhattan (or London) can bring I traveled once or twice a year to his home in the Southwest. We did autograph signings together and a couple of times he stunned me with a surprise birthday party. He spoke at the conferences I organized both on the paranormal as well as at writing seminars which those interested in becoming published authors flocked to. Brad managed to inspire many, several attendees going on to have their life's ambitions fulfilled because of his ability to see their talents. A former teacher of literature and creative writing on both the secondary school and college levels, the prolific author saws no reason not to share his knowledge of the written word and how best to express oneself in such a manner.

What made Brad's writing on the paranormal so unique – especially in the earlier days when most failed to see the interconnection between the majority of the topics he wrote about – was that he eventually realized there was an overall structure – not yet understood or fully explained – that linked together UFOs, life after death, astral travel, spiritualism, bigfoot to a sort of parallel universe which might be entered through portals around the planet.

Overall he saw the big picture and realized that many of the things he wrote about were of a symbolic nature that were meant to teach us some aspect of living together on this planet. He once told me: "I tend to believe that things we call UFOs are other dimensional intelligent beings who share our turf – and that they have been with us since before the beginning of recorded history. I truly believe that there is a symbiotic relationship between man and UFOs and the afterlife, and I suggest that UFOs are not only vehicles we see, but a perspective and dimension of our own psyche."

Clumping them together Brad called the entities that inhabit this vast unseen universe – *"THE OTHER,"* a term that has stuck to this very day.

Using documented sightings and testimony of people who have been contacted by a variety of entities, Steiger concludes that these episodes are part of mankind's common experience. "There are certain archetypes which have been seen through the ages and which are apparently a part of our thought fields accessible through dreams, meditation, and other altered states of consciousness. These archetypes seem to exist in a grander, paraphysical scale from where they appear to influence and guide the affairs of this world. It's been the same source, the same intelligence, and the same message throughout, but it takes on different forms according to our level of understand."

There is much more that I could say about "our friend" – as Brad belonged to the entire world and will surely be missed (crack open one of his books and keep his legacy alive). As cryptozoologist Loran Coleman so amply put it:

"There is a rip in the fabric of the veil as the portal to the other side opens for Brad Steiger."

Perhaps we shall be hearing more from him!

Author's Note: You can listen to Brad's final interview on my podcast *"Exploring The Bizarre,"* located on my YouTube channel, "Mr UFOs Secret Files."– www.youtube.com/watch?v=RpcOad3Cs4s&t=182s

A Mere Sample of Brad's Nonfiction Works Include:

"Conspiracies and Secret Societies: The Complete Dossier" – *"Cat Miracles: Inspirational True Stories of Remarkable Felines"* – *"Real Encounters, Different Dimensions and Otherworldy Beings"* – *"The Werewolf Book: The Encyclopedia of Shape-Shifting Beings"* – *"Real Ghosts, Restless Spirits, and Haunted Places"* – *"Four-Legged*

Miracles: Heartwarming Tales of Lost Dogs' Journeys Home" – *"Real Monsters, Gruesome Critters, and Beasts from the Darkside"* – *"Real Aliens, Space Beings, and Creatures from Other Worlds"* – *"Santa Miracles: 50 True Stories that Celebrate the Most Magical Time of the Year"* – *"Project Blue Book"* – *"Horse Miracles: Inspirational True Stories of Remarkable Horses"* – *"Totems: The Transformative Power of Your Personal Animal Totem"* – *"Worlds Before Our Own"* – *"Real Vampires, Night Stalkers and Creatures from the Darkside"* – *"Kahuna Magic"* – *"The Source: Journey Through the Unexplained"* – *"Mysteries of Time and Space"* – *"The Star People"* – *"Real Zombies, the Living Dead, and Creatures of the Apocalypse."*

KNOCK, KNOCK – THERE ARE DEMONS IN THE HOUSE
By Brad Steiger

One can spend hours upon end thinking of the implications of the "Other," a collective term I have derived for what may be the consciousness behind the Ultra-terrestrials who have been encamped on our cosmic shoreline from when we started recording extraordinary events in human history.

And while some among the rank and file of UFOlogy and the "star-seedlings" of the New Age variety may see this planetary "intrusion" in a warm and welcoming light, there are many among us who have every reason to accept the Ultra-Terrestrials as demonic, akin to the poltergeists that plague our darkest nightmares and create havoc all around those they decide to target.

Since my early investigation into the UFO enigma in the late 1960s, it has seemed apparent to me that if humankind is indeed interacting with an extraterrestrial species, then those UFOnauts, the "Grays" as they are currently nicknamed, may be representatives of technologically superior reptilian or amphibian humanoids. Furthermore, it also seems evident that these Serpent People have been interacting with Earth for millions of years – either appearing in cycles of programmed visitations or steadily monitoring our species' technological and societal development from underground or undersea bases.

It also seems evident to me that at some point in their many centuries long interaction, some Ultra-terrestrial entities began to exploit humankind in foul, lascivious and wicked ways. Whether they be extraterrestrial or multidimensional in origin, they have become known to those unfortunate humans with whom they have interacted as evil, cruel and demonic beings.

Susan Koebler, a young attorney from the Ft. Worth, Texas, area, stated in her report to me that it is her habit to take a hot bath after concluding the day's work schedule. She lights a number of aromatic candles and places them around the tub to add to the therapeutic fragrance emitted by the powders and oils that she sprinkles into the steaming water.

"I stretch out in the tub, adjusting the water until it is as hot as I can comfortably stand it, then I sip a glass of white wine and listen to some New Age type music," Susan said. "This ritual not only completely relaxes me, but I sometimes slip into a meditative state and really clear my consciousness of all the uglies and nasties that might have beset me at the office that day."

On this particular evening in late October of 1997, Susan found herself entering a very strange "mental place." As she was driving home to her apartment, she thought that she had sighted a strange light in the evening sky and she wondered if she had experienced a UFO sighting. She had never had an interest in stories of extraterrestrials or outer space exploration, but she was open to the subject.

As she slipped into the tub of warm water, she began to feel herself drifting into an altered state of consciousness in which she saw herself with a group of other young women in a forest. "I was linking arms with other girls and dancing under a full moon," she recalled. "It was so real, so detailed."

After at least half an hour relaxing in this visionary experience, Susan emerged reluctantly from the tub, dried herself, and draped a robe loosely about her body. "I was still feeling extremely relaxed," she said, "so I walked into the bedroom and lay down on my stomach across the bed, my feet sticking out over the sides. I had lain there, nearly asleep, when I felt someone grab my ankles and start to turn me over on my back!"

Susan screamed her surprise, shock, and rage, feeling certain that someone had forced his way into her apartment and was now attempting to force himself upon her. But the scream became a stunned kind of gasp of horror when she saw that there was no one there.

"Yet someone, something, invisible, but of tremendous strength, was trying to spread my legs apart," Susan stated. "I fought against the thing with all my will. The struggle must have continued for several minutes. Every muscle in my thighs and lower back was burning with the pain of the constant tension – yet I would not yield and permit my genitals to be exposed in such a vulnerable manner."

At last the pressure ceased, and Susan lay gasping on the bed. "Then, suddenly, he was there – solid, visible, repulsive," Susan said. "His eyes were cat or snakelike with the pupils thin slits against yellow-gold retinas. His skin appeared smooth, kind of grayish-green in color. And his teeth! They were rotted, brownish stumps that almost appeared to be set in double-rows in purplish jaws. And this thing was very large and very muscular."

Susan stated that she could never be certain if the grotesque creature actually spoke aloud or if she perceived his thoughts telepathically. However the communication was accomplished, the effect was the same. "You will want me. You will desire me," the monster told her.

Susan lay on the bed before the creature, sprawled out as if she were some kind of sacrificial offering to the dragon-like beast.

"The ugly thing smiled and reached out a hand with long fingernails to caress my hair, still soaked from the tub," Susan said. "The monstrous gargoyle was changing its tactics. It was moving away from attempted rape to seduction. But those putrid brown teeth jutting from its jaws in its pathetic attempt at a smile made a travesty of gentleness and compassion. It was only after one thing from me – and by now it was very apparent that the creature was very definitely male."

And then, Susan wrote, there was something about the monster's eyes that had suddenly become very compelling, very hypnotic.

"There was something in those reptilian eyes that wanted to make me stop resisting its sexual advances," Susan said. "I found myself staring into their depths, and it suddenly seemed as though I had been mistaken. My uninvited guest was really not so bad. In fact, he was really quite handsome and virile."

Susan will forever be thankful that she realized what the creature was doing to her, that it was seducing her with an almost irresistible hypnotic power.

"I cried out for my guardian angel to help me," she said. "I started to cry out for all things holy and of the Light to drive away this creature of darkness."

Susan concluded her report by stating that she is thankful to her guardian angel and all benevolent entities who rallied around her that terrible evening to drive away whatever the grotesque monster was that materialized in her apartment and tried to force itself upon her.

Quite likely the entity that appeared to Susan Koebler was a type of ultra-terrestrial entity that has sought to sexually molest human beings ever since our species became "fair" and appeared capable of providing a warm, fleshly body for a spirit being to possess for minutes, weeks, months – or permanently. In my over 50 years of researching the strange, the unusual and the unexplained, I have come to understand that as much as our materialistic and scientific age might wish it could relegate such supernatural sexual molesters to a much less sophisticated past – somewhere around the Dark or Middle Ages – these ultra-terrestrial demons have not relinquished their grip on the human psyche. According to a good many men and women, such sexual offenders from other dimensions are as much a nasty nuisance in the shadow world of our supermarket and space-age culture as they were in the superstition-saturated and sexually tortured Middle Ages.

While those ultra-dimensional beings that seek to possess and enjoy sexually the physical bodies of mortals are terrible and demeaning enough, even worse are those fiends who invade the psyches of men and women and command them to maim, mutilate or murder their victims. Perhaps the most monstrous of all the frightening creatures that issue forth out of the dark claim those tortured individuals who heed fiendish commands to kill. The media proclaim in each day's newspaper headlines and news broadcasts that these disciples of murder and mayhem are very real. And so are the demons who scream at them relentlessly to do their awful bidding and kill without mercy.

Here is what Dr. Morton Kelsey, an Episcopal priest and a noted Notre Dame Professor of Theology, had to say: "Most people in the modern world consider themselves too sophisticated and too intelligent to be concerned with demons. But in thirty years of study, I have seen the effect of demons upon humans."

The Rev. James LeBar, an exorcist for the Archdiocese of New York, commented in September 2000 that there had been a "large explosion" of exorcisms in recent years. In New York alone, he said, the number had accelerated from none in 1990 to a total of 300 in the last ten years. Rev. LeBar said that men and women have diminished self-respect for themselves and decreased reverence for spirituality, for other human beings and for life in general.

All right, you protest, Rev. LeBar is a priest, an exorcist. His theological training has conditioned him to believe in demons. Then take into serious consideration the comments of Dr. Ralph Allison, senior psychiatrist at the California state prison in San Luis Obispo: "My conclusion after thirty years of observing over one thousand disturbed patients is that some of them act in a bizarre fashion due to possession by spirits. The spirit may be that of a human being who died. Or it may be a spirit entity that has never been a human being and sometimes identifies itself as a demon, an agent of evil." A good definition of an ultra-terrestrial entity with evil intent toward humans.

In a recent report released by the American Psychological Evaluation Corporation, Dr. Andrew Blankley, a sociologist, issued alarming statements about the rise in contemporary sacrificial cults, warning that society at large might expect a "serious menace" to come. According to Dr. Blankley, human sacrifice constitutes an alarming trend in new religious cults: "Desperate people are seeking dramatic revelation and simplistic answers to complex social problems. They are attracted to fringe groups who provide the ritualistic irrationality that they crave. In the last ten years, fringe rituals often include the sacrifice of a human being."

Dr. Al Carlisle of the Utah State Prison System has estimated that between 40,000 and 60,000 humans are killed through ritual homicides in the United States every year. In the Las Vegas area alone, Dr. Carlisle asserts, as many as 600 people may die in demon-inspired ceremonies each year.

Mutilated bodies of hitchhikers and transients are being found in forested regions, beside lonely desert roads and alongside river banks – their hearts and lungs removed, strips of flesh slashed from their bodies.

Devil-worshipping rites are being held in our state and national parks. Human blood is mixed with beer and drunk by all participants. Human bone fragments, teeth, and pieces of flesh are discovered in the ashes of campfires.

The terrible power which drives and compels those obsessed with sacrificial murders is something so much more insidiously evil and complex than can be created by the distortion of creeds, ecclesiasticisms or belief structures. The monstrous voices that command men and women to kill others are not those of mortals. Those who have fallen under the deadly spell of the possessing ultra-terrestrial-multidimensional entities claim to have been controlled by something outside of themselves – usually personified as Satan or one of his demons.

However one wishes to identify these Parasites of the Spirit, they have the ability to sense and to seize the moments of vulnerability in the strongest of men and women. They possess the uncanny power of knowing the precise moments when even the most righteous can be tempted, when even the most devout can be led astray, when the most disciplined moralist may be seduced.

Knife-Wielding Demons and Murderous Ghosts

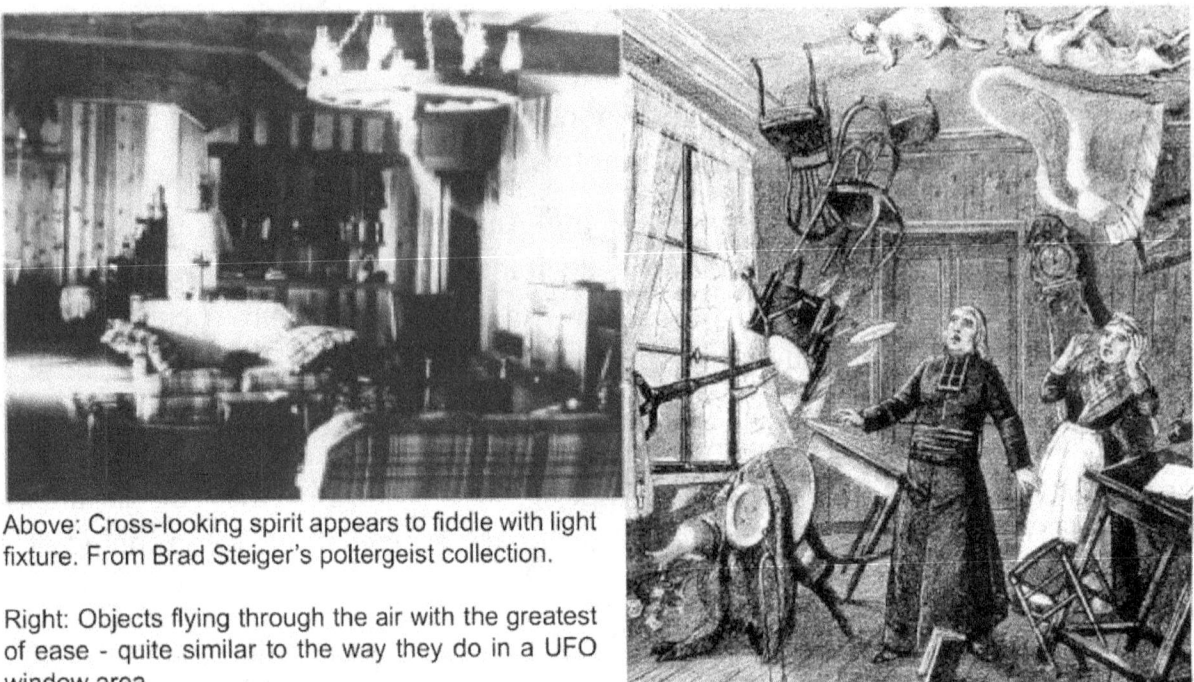

Above: Cross-looking spirit appears to fiddle with light fixture. From Brad Steiger's poltergeist collection.

Right: Objects flying through the air with the greatest of ease - quite similar to the way they do in a UFO window area.

Left: An authentic picture or a hoax? Said to be a spiteful alien seen cavorting around tombstones.

Headline story in UK where many believe poltergeists and aliens go hand-in-hand.

Knife-Wielding Demons and Murderous Ghosts

Here is only a sampler of men and women who were apparently possessed by multidimensional demons and commanded to kill:

* On January 5, 1990, authorities searching an Ohio farm commune found the slain bodies of a family of five – all victims of human sacrifice. Jeffrey Lunden, a self-declared prophet of a new religion, had decreed the sacrifices necessary to persuade the "forces" to present the cult with a magical golden sword.

* Daniel Rakowitz couldn't quite understand whether or not the voices said that he was actually Jesus reborn, but he knew that they were insistent that he was a messiah. The voices also told him to form a new satanic religion to be named the Church of 966, thereby discarding the old and familiar 666 label. To insure his messiah-ship, in September of 1989, he sacrificed his girlfriend.

* The voices told Herbert Mullin that California was about to be destroyed by a cataclysmic earthquake and a giant tidal wave unless he immediately began sacrificing human life to Satan. The voices nullified Mullin's squeamishness by declaring that the sacrificial victims would actually be grateful for being given the opportunity to serve the greater good of California. Before he was stopped on February 13, 1972, Mullins had sacrificed thirteen victims and, in his mind, become the Savior of California.

* While other households in the Queens District of New York watched the Thanksgiving Day parade on November 22, 1990, Joseph Bergamini honored the satanic promise that he was immortal by stabbing and killing his mother and wounding his father.

* As a teenager, Mark David Chapman had experienced a vision of Jesus which led him to become an advocate for the common man. When the visions later revealed the popular idol John Lennon was no longer a working-class hero, but a prosperous businessman, the voices decreed that the former Beatle must die on the night of December 8, 1980.

* Inspired by the vampire movie "Lost Boys," Tim Erickson and other Minnesota teenagers decided to form a vampire cult in March 1987. They murdered a drifter and drank his blood.

* July 1991, Jaime Rodriguez was convicted and sentenced to life for beheading a teenage runaway as a sacrifice to Satan. He also severed one of her fingers to wear as a charm around his neck. Augustin Pena, a fellow Satanist, kept the girl's head in his refrigerator.

Knife-Wielding Demons and Murderous Ghosts

* December 2000, prosecutors charged a man in Great Falls, Montana, with killing a 10-year-old boy, butchering him, eating his flesh in specially prepared dishes, then feeding the remains to his unsuspecting neighbors. A psychiatric evaluation indicated demonic fantasies about cannibalism and the taste of human flesh. Encrypted writings found in the suspect's home revealed a list of recipes involving the bodies of small children.

The list of assaults by demonic ultra-terrestrial/multidimensional beings on the U.S. Presidency is a frightening one:

* When John Wilkes Booth, the assassin of Abraham Lincoln, was but an infant in his crib, his mother, Asia Booth, had a horrid vision of her son being one day transformed into a monster with a grotesque hand that would commit a terrible deed.

* On the morning of July 2, 1881, Charles Guiteau could no longer resist the demon voices that commanded him to kill President James Garfield. The President clung to life through the agony of a long summer before yielding to the assassin's bullet in his back. Guiteau was relieved that he had fulfilled his mission. He went to the gallows confident that the demon he hailed as "Lordy" would take care of him in the afterlife.

* Lee Harvey Oswald was obsessed with his fears that "devil-men" would usurp all earthly governments. The death of JFK would serve as a kind of sacrifice to keep them at bay.

* Sirhan Sirhan's legal defense in his trial for the murder of Robert Kennedy strongly considered arguing that he had been possessed by the fanatical spirit of a dead Arab nationalist.

* Squeaky Fromme, one of Charles Manson's family, received mental instructions from her imprisoned master to murder President Gerald Ford on August 5, 1975.

* John Hinckley was literally possessed with the belief that the assassination of Ronald Reagan would somehow impress the actress, Jody Foster.

* On January 11, 1990, the Secret Service arrested John S. Daughetee, a medical school dropout, who was acting under the orders of his "voices" when he robbed eight banks to finance his assassination attempts on Presidents Reagan and Bush.

Knife-Wielding Demons and Murderous Ghosts

On September 19, 2000, the *"Chicago Sun-Times"* reported that the Archdiocese of Chicago had appointed a fulltime exorcist for the first time in its 160-year history.

In the November 28, 2000, issue of the *"New York Times,"* an article by John W. Fountain (*"Exorcists and Exorcisms Proliferate Across U.S."*) quoted Rev. Bob Larson, an evangelical preacher and author who heads an exorcism ministry in Denver, as saying that he had 40 "exorcism teams" across the nation. "Our goal is that no one should ever be more than a day's drive from a city where you can find an exorcist," said Rev. Larson.

If, as some theologians and scholars predict, there is soon to take place a major conflict between the Forces of Light and the Forces of Darkness, one would be well-advised to be wary of those seductive creatures of the shadows, the multidimensional/ultra-terrestrials who have for centuries sought to confuse us humans into believing that their counterfeit illumination is truly a Guiding Light.

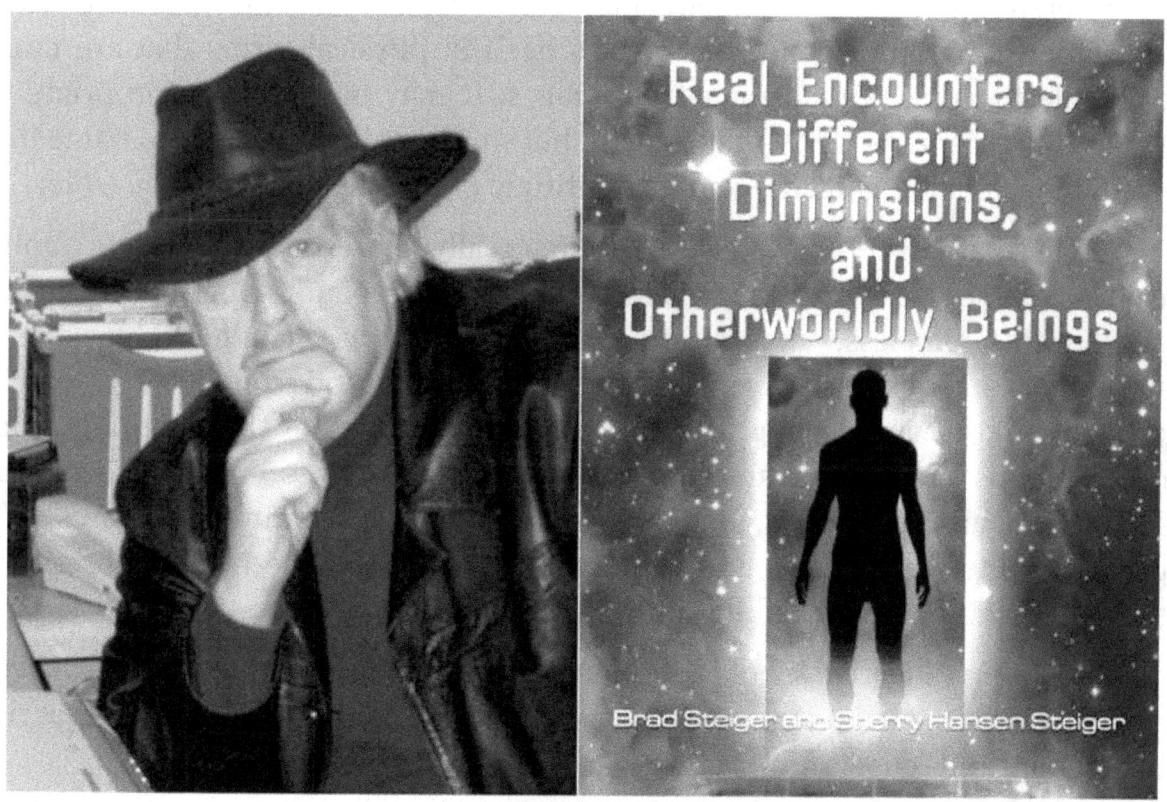

Above left: Brad Steiger looks like he is about to do battle with the poltergeist at large.

Above right: A recent book by Steiger, one of almost 200 he has penned since the mid-1960s.

Knife-Wielding Demons and Murderous Ghosts

Brad and Sherry Steiger's views on the *"Other"* are applauded in this review by Robert A. Goerman, which also touches on the link between the UFO phenomenon and ghosts.

****

"Real Visitors, Voices from Beyond, and Parallel Dimensions," by the amazing Steiger duo is a lighthouse guiding us through the murky realm of the *Other*. Decades of diligent research and professional writing have rewarded this couple with a smorgasbord of fascinating colleagues and access to literally thousands of personal narratives from readers and fans everywhere. Brad and Sherry Steiger maximized these assets and created another volume that will dominate paranormal libraries for many years to come. What is the *Other*?

The authors explain: "We are now comfortable with the thesis that the aliens, angels, spirit guides, demons, fairies, elves, and gods and goddesses encountered by receptive percipients may actually be the product of a multidimensional intelligence that masks itself in physical forms that are more acceptable to humans than their true images. It may be equally appropriate to refer to this enigma as UFO Intelligences, but we chose to define and to name this multidimensional intelligence and its multitude of manifestations as the *Other*.

"These are ageless mysteries. Do they really share a mutual origin? John Keel thought so. He coined the terms "Ultra-terrestrial" and "super-spectrum" to describe this timeless, shapeshifting intelligence. Dr. J. Allen Hynek, the astronomer and professor best remembered for his enduring UFO research, suggested that we are dealing with "meta-terrestrial" entities that originate from unseen realms beyond our three-dimensional world. Jacques Vallee believes that religious apparitions, UFOs, and appearances by supernatural creatures rely upon the same mechanisms and share similar effects on the human observers, interpreted within the prevailing cultural environment.

As an investigative scholar of the unknown and unexplained, this reviewer has also researched the apparent overlap between nonhuman creatures, aerial phenomena, and "ghosts."

Certain locations have been haunted by a medley of otherworldly visitors. These phenomena can materialize, affect our reality, and disappear again. Time and space become "terra incognita."

Knife-Wielding Demons and Murderous Ghosts

Stranger still, unsuspecting folks have even briefly stepped over into so-called parallel worlds.

Brad and Sherry Steiger write that "readers may find that they will learn of more possibilities and probabilities than final answers to some age-old dilemmas and puzzles, but that is because there can be no dogma in a serious study of the paranormal and the UFO Mystery."

The greatest strength of this book is its thought-provoking variety. Facets of encounters with every manner of entity are described by every manner of experiencer, scientist, engineer, and scholar. Many have contributed their own unpublished accounts, theses, papers, and research data. I have followed Brad Steiger since "***Strangers from the Skies***" in 1966. His early writings and my personal encounters with the *Other* triggered my own lifelong role as an author and researcher. "***Real Visitors, Voices from Beyond, and Parallel Dimensions***" is an enjoyable read that entertains and enlightens. This book easily deserves my highest recommendation.

SUGGESTED READING

REAL GHOSTS, RESTLESS SPIRITS AND HAUNTED PLACES

REAL CREATURES, DIFFERENT DIMENSIONS AND OTHER WORLDLY BEINGS

REAL VISITORS, VOICES FROM BEYOND AND PARALLEL DIMENSIONS

MYSTERIES OF TIME AND SPACE

THE RAINBOW CONSPIRACY

- Nearly 200 books in print!

Knife-Wielding Demons and Murderous Ghosts

Often centered around an individual, a poltergeist can produce strange physical phenomena that have been known to be dangerous and cause serious harm.

THE AMHERST POLTERGEIST – A KNIFE-WIELDING SPIRIT

In the past, there were poltergeists that have been not only annoying, but also devilish and destructive. One can't easily forget the havoc created by Tennessee's Bell Witch. This crazed head-turner even drove a future U.S. President into the dampness of an early American dawn, so anxious was he to get out of town and forget about the spirit that had kept him up all night and made him fear for his political life.

Up in Northeastern Canada, in Nova Scotia to be more specific, a poltergeist had gotten totally out of control and was heaving knives and throwing heavy paper weights at the occupants of what had been a normal, family-occupied dwelling.

Circa 1879, the "Amherst Mystery," as it is best known, centered on Esther Cox, who lived in a small house with her married sister Olive Teed, Olive's husband Daniel, and their two young children. A brother and sister of Esther and Olive also lived in the house, as did Daniel's brother John Teed.

According to Walter Hubbell's account, events began at the end of August 1878, after Esther Cox, then aged 18, was subjected to an attempted sexual assault by a male friend. This left her in great distress, and shortly after this the physical phenomena began. There were knockings, banging's and rustlings in the night, and Esther herself began to suffer seizures in which her body visibly swelled and she was feverish and chilled by turns. Then objects in the house took flight.

The frightened family called in a doctor. During his visit, bedclothes moved, scratching noises were heard, and the words "Esther Cox, you are mine to kill" appeared on the wall by the head of Esther's bed. The following day the doctor administered **sedatives** to Esther to calm her and help her sleep, whereupon more noises and flying objects manifested themselves. Attempts to communicate with the "spirit" resulted in tapped responses to questions.

Many parapsychologists became armchair investigators over the many decades since this poltergeist conjured itself up and threatened the lives of an entire family. One of those who wrote extensively on the case was veteran

Knife-Wielding Demons and Murderous Ghosts

investigator Susy Smith, who authored 40 or so books during her career before converting to Christianity and never writing about the occult again. Maybe this case set her off and frightened her beyond repair.

Said Smith in a 1960 article in *Tomorrow Magazine*: "Lighted matches floated slowly from ceiling to floor; a kettle of boiling water and a frying pan with a medium-rare steak in it moved from the stove to the back door stop; a dinner fork escaped from its drawer and hit the Clerk of the County Court on the back of his head."

The poltergeist was known for being a bit pesky and perhaps a bit of an exhibitionist. "One day Esther told her married sister that the ghost was wearing black-and-white striped stockings.

'Take off my stockings this very instant, you naughty ghost,' she said. And immediately the black-and-white stockings dropped from the air in the middle of the room to the floor – with no one anywhere near them."

As one would expect, there were the usual knockings and poundings and talk of a haunted box. The author of this book of occult wonderment, which was published about a century and a half ago, said that one evening he was "in the house only a few minutes when my umbrella was thrown across the room by no visible agent. A few minutes later, as Esther walked out of the pantry with a large dish in both hands, a big carving knife came whizzing through the air, passing closely over her head.

"Those present thought the knife had come from the pantry, but no one was there to throw it! Knives and forks were thrown with such force that it is said they 'would stick into doors; foods disappeared from the table; and worse than all, strange, unnatural voices could be heard in the air, calling us by our names...'"

Decades upon decades have gone by and the Amherst Poltergeist continues to be spoken about as if it were still alive.

BUT IT SURE AS HELL ISN'T – RIGHT?

We hereby present the original manuscript written by Walter Hubbell and first published in 1879.

THE HAUNTED HOUSE: A True Ghost Story

Being an account of the Mysterious Manifestations that have taken place in the presence of ESTHER COX, the young girl who is possessed of Devils and has become known throughout the entire Dominion as:

THE GREAT AMHERST MYSTERY.

By Walter Hubbell
The author lived in the house and witnessed the manifestations.

INTRODUCTION

The manifestations described in this story commenced in 1878. No person has yet been able to ascertain their cause. Scientific men from all parts of Canada and the United States have investigated them in vain. Some people think that electricity is the principal agent; others, mesmerism; whilst others, again, are sure they are produced by the devil. Of the three supposed causes, the latter is certainly the most plausible theory, for some of the manifestations are remarkably devilish in their appearance and effect. For instance, the mysterious setting of fires, the powerful shaking of the house, the loud and incessant noises and distinct knocking, as if made by invisible sledgehammers, on the walls; also, the strange actions of the household furniture, which moves about in the broad daylight without the slightest visible cause.

As these strange things only occur while Miss Esther Cox is present, she has become known as the "Amherst Mystery" throughout the entire country.

The author of this work lived for six weeks in the haunted house, and considers it his duty to place the entire matter before the public in its true light, having been requested to do so by the family of Miss Cox.

Knife-Wielding Demons and Murderous Ghosts

Part I

THE HOME OF ESTHER COX

Amherst, Nova Scotia, a beautiful little village on the famous Bay of Fundy, has a population of about three thousand souls, and contains four churches, an academy, a music hall, a large iron foundry, a large shoe factory, and more stores of various kinds than any village of its size in the Province.

The private residences of the more wealthy inhabitants are very picturesque in their appearance, being surrounded by beautifully laid out lawns, containing ornamental trees of various kinds and numerous beds of flowers of choice and sometimes very rare varieties.

The residences of Parson Townsend, Mr. Robb, Doctor Nathan Tupper, and Mr. G.G. Bird, proprietor of the Amherst book store; also that of Mr. Amos Purdy, the village Post Master, and others too numerous to mention, are sure to attract the visitor's attention and command his admiration.

On Princess Street, near Church, there stands a neat two story cottage, painted yellow. It has in front a small yard, which extends back to the stable. The tidy appearance of the cottage and its pleasant situation are sure to attract a stranger's attention. Upon entering the house, everything is found to be so tastefully arranged, so scrupulously clean, and so comfortable, that the visitor feels at home in a moment, being confident that everything is looked after by a thrifty housewife.

The first floor consists of four rooms: a parlor, containing a large bay window, filled with beautiful geraniums of every imaginable color and variety, is the first to attract attention; then the dining room, with its old fashioned clock, its numerous homemade rugs, easy chairs, and commodious table, makes one feel like dining, especially if the hour is near twelve; for about that time of day savory odors are sure to issue from the adjoining kitchen.

The kitchen is all that a room of the kind in a village cottage should be, is not very large, and contains an ordinary wood stove, a large pine table, and a small washstand, has a door opening into the side yard near the stable, and another into the wash shed, besides the one connecting it with the dining room, making three doors in all, and one window. The fourth room is very small and is used as a sewing room; it adjoins the dining room, and the parlor, and has a door opening into each. Besides the four rooms on the first floor, there is a large pantry, having a small window about four feet from the floor. The door of this pantry opens into the dining room. Such is the arrangement of the first floor.

Upon ascending a short flight of stairs, and turning to the left, you find yourself in the second story of the cottage, which consists of an entry and four small bedrooms, all opening into the entry. Each one of the rooms has one window and only one door. Two of these little bedrooms face towards the street, and the other two towards the back of the cottage. They, like the rest of the house, are conspicuous for their neat, cozy aspect, being papered and painted and furnished with ordinary cottage furniture. In fact, everything about the little cottage will impress a casual observer with the fact that its inmates are happy and evidently at peace with God and man.

This humble cottage is the home of Daniel Teed, shoemaker. Everybody knows and respects honest, hardworking Dan, who never owes a dollar if he can help it, and never allows his family to want for any comfort that can be procured, with his hard-earned salary as foreman of the Amherst Shoe Factory.

Dan's family consists of his wife Olive, as good a soul as ever lived, always hard at work. From early morning until dusky eve she is on her feet. It has always been a matter of gossip and astonishment, among the neighbors, as to how little Mrs. Teed, for she is by no means what you would call a large woman, could work so incessantly without becoming weary and resting for an hour or so after dinner. But she works on all the same, never rests, and they still look on her with astonishment. Dan and Olive have two little boys. Willie, the eldest, is five years old; he is a strong, healthy-looking lad, with a ruddy complexion, blue eyes, and brown curly hair; his principal amusements are throwing stones, chasing the chickens, and hurting his little brother. George, the youngest of Dan's boys, is the finest boy of his age in the village and is only a little over a year old; his merry little laugh, winning ways, and cunning actions to attract attention have made him a favorite with all who visit at the cottage.

Besides his wife and two little boys, Dan has under his honest roof and protection his wife's two sisters, Jane and Esther Cox, who board with him. Jane is a ladylike, self-possessed young woman of about twenty-two, and is quite a beauty; her hair is very light brown and reaches below her waist when she allows it to fall in graceful tresses. At other times she wears it in the Grecian style; her eyes are of a greyish hue; a clear complexion and handsome teeth add to her fine appearance. In fact, Jane Cox is one of the village belles, and has hosts of admirers, not of the male sex alone, for she is also popular among the ladies; she

Knife-Wielding Demons and Murderous Ghosts

is a member and regular attendant of Parson Townsend's Church, which, by the way, the good Parson has had under his care for about forty-five years.

Esther Cox, Dan's other sister in-law, is such a remarkable girl in every respect that I must give as complete a description of her as possible. She was born in Upper Stewiacke, Nova Scotia, on March 28th, 1860, and is consequently in her eighteenth year. Esther has always been a queer girl. When born she was so small that her good, kind grandmother, who raised her (her mother having died when she was three weeks old), had to wash and dress her on a pillow, and in fact keep her on it all the time until she was nine months old, at which age her weight was only five pounds.

When she was quite a little girl, her father, Archibald T. Cox, married again and moved to East Machias, Maine, where he has since resided. Having followed his second wife to the grave, he married a third with whom he is now living. Esther's early years having been spent with her grandmother, she very naturally became grave and old-fashioned without knowing how or why. Like all little girls, she was remarkably susceptible to surrounding influences, and the sedate manner and actions of the old lady made an early impression on Esther that will cling to her through life.

In person Esther is of low stature and rather inclined to be stout; her hair is curly, of a dark brown color, and is now short, reaching only to her shoulders; her eyes are large and grey, with a bluish tinge, and an earnest expression which seems to say, "Why do you stare at me so? I cannot help it if I am not like other people." Her eyebrows and eye-lashes are dark and well-marked; that is to say, the lashes are long and the eyebrows very distinct. Her face is what can be called round, with well-shaped features; she has remarkably handsome teeth and a pale complexion. Her hands and feet are small and well-shaped, and, although inclined to be stout, she is fond of work and is a great help to her sister Olive, although she sometimes requires a little urging.

Although Esther is not possessed of the beauty that Jane is famous for, still there is something earnest, honest and attractive about this simple-hearted village maiden that wins for her lots of friends of about her own age; in fact, she is quite in demand among the little children of the neighborhood also, who are ever ready to have a romp and a game with Ester, as they all call her. The truth is, a great many of the grownup inhabitants of the village call her Ester also, dropping the "h" entirely, a habit common in Nova Scotia.

Esther Cox of Amherst, Nova Scotia, was the center of bizarre poltergeist activity that tormented, injured, and traumatized her and her family beginning in 1878.

Knife-Wielding Demons and Murderous Ghosts

Esther's disposition is naturally mild and gentle. She can at times, however, be very self-willed and is bound to have her own way when her mind is made up. If asked to do anything she does not feel like doing, she becomes very sulky and has to be humored at times to keep peace in the family. However, all things considered, she is a good little girl and has always borne a good reputation, in every sense of the word.

There are two more boarders in the little cottage who require a passing notice. They are William Cox and John Teed. William is the brother of Olive, Jane, and Esther, and is a shoemaker by trade and one of Dan's workmen in the factory.

The other boarder, John Teed, is Dan's brother. John, like his brother, is an honest, hardworking young man, has been raised a farmer, an occupation he still follows when not boarding with Dan in Amherst.

As the reader may, perhaps, be anxious to know how Dan, good, honest, hardworking Dan, and his thrifty little wife, Olive, look, I will endeavor to give a short description of each. So here goes. Dan is about thirty-five years old and stands five feet eight in his stockings. He has light brown hair, rather thinning on top, a well-shaped head, blue eyes, well defined features, a high nose, and wears a heavy moustache and bushy side whiskers; his complexion is florid; rheumatism of several years standing has given him a slight halt in the left leg. He does his work, spends his salary as he should, and leads a Christian life, has a pew in the Wesleyan Church of which Rev. R.A. Temple is pastor, belongs to a temperance society, and, I dare say, when he dies will be well rewarded in the next world.

Olive, as I have already said, is not a very large woman. She is good and honest, like her husband, and goes to church with him as a wife should. Her hair is dark brown, eyes grey, complexion pale and slightly freckled. Although not as beautiful as Jane, nor at any time as sulky as Esther can be, she has those motherly traits of character which command respect. Being older than her sisters, she is looked up to by them for advice when they think they need it and consolation when they are in sorrow. Olive's wise little head is sure to give the right advice at the right time, and in the family of the cottage her word is law. I do not mean to say that she rules her husband. No! Dan is far from being a henpecked man, but, as two heads are always better than one, Dan often takes her advice and profits by it.

Such is the cottage and household of honest Dan Teed.

Knife-Wielding Demons and Murderous Ghosts

Today is cool and pleasant. The hour is nearly twelve noon, the hour for dinner in the cottage. Esther is seated on the parlor floor playing with George to keep him from running out in the hot sun. Willie is out in the yard near the stable tormenting a poor hen, who has had a log of wood tied to one of her legs by Olive to prevent her from setting in the cow's stall; but master Willie seems to think she has been tied so that he may have a good time banging her over the head with a small club, which he is doing in a way that means business.

Suddenly his mother comes out of the kitchen, and, after soundly boxing his ears, sends him howling into the house, much to the relief of the poor hen who has just fallen over with exhaustion and fright, but upon finding her tormentor gone is soon herself again. Presently Olive hears Dan at the gate, and comes to the front door to meet him and tell him that dinner is almost ready, remarking that he cannot guess what she has for dessert. Honest Dan replies that no matter what it is he is hungry and will eat it, for he has been working hard. So in he goes to wash his hands and face at the washstand in the kitchen.

Jane is coming down the street. Esther, who is seated on a chair with George on her lap, sees her sister from the bay window in the parlor. Jane has a position in Mr. Jas. P. Dunlap's establishment and goes to her work every morning at seven o'clock. As soon as Esther sees Jane she takes George up in her arms and runs in to tell Olive that Jane is coming, and suggests that dinner be served at once, for she feels hungry. So Olive, with Esther's assistance, puts the dinner on the table, and they all sit down to enjoy the meal.

And a good substantial meal it is: plenty of beefsteak and onions, plenty of hot mashed potatoes, plenty of boiled cabbage, and an abundance of homemade bread and fresh butter made that very morning from the rich cream of Dan's red cow. Little George, who is seated in his high chair at his mother's right hand, commences to kick the bottom of the table in such a vigorous manner that not one word can be heard, for he makes a terrible noise, the toes of his shoes being faced with copper to prevent the youngster from wearing them out too soon.

Olive asks Esther to please get the old pink scarf and tie his feet so that he will be unable to make such a racket. Esther does not move, but upon being requested a second time gets up rather reluctantly, goes to the hat rack in the hall, gets the scarf and ties the little fellow's feet, as requested. Upon reseating herself at the table, it is noticeable that she has a sulky expression, for she does not like to be disturbed while enjoying dinner, nor in fact any meal, for the simple reason that her appetite is voracious, being particularly fond of pickles, and she has been known to drink a cupful of vinegar in a day.

All ate in silence for some minutes, when Jane inquires if the cow was milked again last night? "Yes," says Dan, and "I only wish I could find out who does it; it would not be well for him, I can tell you. This is the tenth time this fortnight that she has been milked. Oh! If it was not for this rheumatism in my hip, I would stay up some night and catch the thief in the act, have him arrested, and ——"

"And then," remarks Esther, with an eye to the financial part of the milk question, "we should have just two quarts more to sell every day; that would be — let me see how much it would come to."

"Never mind," remarks John Teed, "how much it would come to, just hand me that dish of potatoes, please. They are so well-mashed that I must eat some more. I can't bear potatoes with lumps all through them, can you Jane?"

"No, John, I cannot," replies Jane.

"Neither can I," joins in William Cox. "If I ever marry, I hope my wife will be as good a cook as Olive; if she prove so I shall be satisfied."

"Gimme 'nother piece of meat, do you hear?" is the exclamation which comes from Master Willie.

"Ask as a good boy should," remarks Dan, "and you shall have it."

"Gimme 'nother piece of meat, do you hear?" says the young rascal a second time, louder than before.

A good sound box on the ear from his father prevents further remarks coming front the unruly boy during the rest of the meal. However, after a slight pause, Dan gives him a piece of beefsteak, while his mother in the meantime says:

"I wonder how that boy learned to be so rude."

"Why," replies John Teed, "by playing with those bad boys down near the carriage factory. I saw him there about nine o'clock this morning, and what's more, I can tell you that unless he keeps away from them he will be ruined."

"I'm going to take him in hand as soon as he gets a little older and make him toe the mark," says Dan. "Well, Mudge," — Dan nearly always calls his wife Mudge, for a pet name — "give me another cup of tea, woman, and then I'll go back to the factory, that is as soon as I have taken a pull or two at my pipe."

Knife-Wielding Demons and Murderous Ghosts

"What! Are you going without eating some of the bread pudding I went to the trouble of making because I thought you would like it?" asks Olive.

"Oh, you've got pudding have you? All right, I'll have some if it's cold," replies Dan.

"Oh, yes, it's cold enough by this time. Come, Esther, help me to clear away these dishes, and you, Jane, please bring in the pudding. It is out on the doorstep near the rainwater barrel."

The dishes having been cleared away, and the pudding brought, all ate a due share, and after some further conversation about the midnight milker of the cow, Esther remarks that she believes the thief to be one of the Micmac Indians from the camp up the road. Everybody laughs at such a wild idea, and they all leave the table.

Esther takes George from his chair, after first untying his feet, and then helps Olive to remove the dishes to the kitchen, where she washes them and then goes to the sofa in the parlor to take a nap. Dan in the meantime has enjoyed his smoke and gone back to the factory, as has also William Cox. John Teed has gone up the Main Street to see his sister Maggie, and Jane has returned to Mr. Dunlap's. Willie is out in the street again with the bad boys, and Olive has just commenced to make a new plaid dress for George, who has gone to sleep in his little crib in the small sewing room.

Esther, after sleeping for about an hour, comes into the dining room where Olive is sewing and says, "Olive, I am going out to take a walk, and if Bob should come while I am out, don't forget to tell him that I will be in this evening and shall expect him."

"All right, Esther," says her sister, "but you had better be careful about Bob and how you keep company with him. You know what we heard about him only the day before yesterday."

"Oh, I don't believe a word of it," replied Esther. She looked at her sister for a moment and then said in an injured tone, "I guess I am old enough to take care of myself. What! Half-past two already? I must be off;" and off she went.

Supper being over, Esther put on her brown dress and took her accustomed seat on the front doorstep to talk to Dan as he smoked his evening pipe. Jane, dressed in her favorite white dress, trimmed with black velvet, her beautiful hair fastened in a true Grecian coil, and perfectly smooth at the temples, is in the parlor attending to her choice plants. Presently her beau comes to spend the evening with her.

So the evening passes away. Olive has sung little George to sleep, carried him up to bed and retired herself. Dan has smoked his pipe and retired also. It was now ten o'clock. Esther still sat on the front step humming the tune of a well-known Wesleyan hymn to herself as she gazed up at the stars; for it must be remembered that although she was not by any means pious, still, like a dutiful girl, she went to church with Dan and Olive. As the girl was just passing into womanhood, and felt that she must love something, it was perfectly natural for her to sit there and wait for Bob to make his appearance. About half-past ten, Jane's beau took his departure, and Jane, not having anything further to keep her up, decided to retire, and advised Esther to follow her example.

The poltergeist made itself right at home in the Teed family home in Nova Scotia.

It's a wonder more individuals haven't been "taken down" when a poltergeist erupts and throws things such as sharp knives...which might end up in the wall, or IN your head!

Esther took a last look up and down the street and then went into the house with much reluctance. After locking the front door, the girls went into the dining room and Jane lighted the lamp. Esther had taken off her shoes and thrown them on the floor, as was her custom, when it suddenly occurred to her that there was buttermilk in the cellar, and the same instant she made up her mind to have some. Taking the lamp from Jane, she runs into the cellar in her stocking feet, drinks about a pint of buttermilk, and runs up again, telling her sister, who has been meanwhile in the dark dining room, that a large rat passed between her feet while in the cellar.

"Come right up to bed, you silly girl," said Jane, "and don't be talking about rats at this time of night." So Jane took the lamp and Esther picked up her shoes and they went to their bedroom.

After closing the door of their room, "Esther," said Jane, "you are foolish to think anything at all about Bob."

"Oh, mind your own business, Jane," Esther replied. "Let's say our prayers and retire." And so they did.

Part II

THE FATAL RIDE

Esther and Jane arose on the morning of August 28th, 1878, as was their usual custom, at half-past six, and ate breakfast with the rest of the family.

After breakfast Jane went to Mrs. Dunlap's, Dan to his shoe factory with his brother-in-law, William Cox. John Teed also went to his work, and none of the family remained in the house but Olive and Esther, who commenced to wash up the breakfast dishes and put the dining room in order so that part of their work at least should be finished before the two little boys came downstairs to have their childish wants attended to. What with making the beds and sweeping the rooms, and washing out some clothing for the boys, both Esther and Olive found plenty to occupy their time until the hour for preparing dinner arrived.

When Olive commenced that rather monotonous operation, assisted by Esther, who, as she sat on the doorstep between the dining room and kitchen paring potatoes, and placing them in a can of cold water beside her, attracted her sister's attention by her continued silence and the troubled expression of her countenance.

"What in the name of the sun ails you today, Esther?" inquired Olive, really worried by her little sister's sad appearance.

"Oh, nothing, Olive! Only I was thinking that if — that if — that if –"

"Well! Well, go on, go on, it is not necessary to say 'that if' five or six times in succession, is it? Before telling me what's the matter with you, you nonsensical, giddy, hardheaded girl. I believe you have fallen in love so deeply with Bob McNeal that you are worrying yourself to death because you know he is too poor to marry you and you are afraid some rich girl will fall in love with him, and that he will marry her and give you the cold shoulder. There, that's just what I think is the matter with you, and I can tell you one thing, my young lady, and that is that the sooner you get over your infatuation for that young man, the better for you, and the better for us all. There now, I'm done. No I'm not either. Listen to me, girl, and don't make me angry by turning up your nose while I am giving you good advice."

"I'm not turning up my nose at you, Olive. I only felt like sneezing and wanted to stop it before it had fully commenced. And how could I try to stop it except by working my nose in that way, when I have a big wet potato in one hand and this ugly old knife in the other, and all wet, too?"

"Oh, nonsense, girl, don't keep on talking about ugly old knives and wet potatoes, but listen to me. I feel it in my bones that trouble is in store for us, and all through Bob McNeal. Now do be a good girl, and take my advice and never invite him to call again; because I tell you, Esther, that trouble is coming to you through that young man, for I feel it in my bones."

"Well, Olive, I will tell you the truth; the fact is that — why here's Jane! Why, Jane, what has brought you home at this time of day? It is only eleven and dinner won't be ready for an hour."

Jane, who had just taken off her hat and hung it up in the hall, replied that as there was nothing more to be done at Dunlap's until the afternoon, she thought she might as well be at home attending to her plants as at the shop.

After looking at Esther and Olive a moment, she said, "What were you two putting your heads together about when I came in? Esther stopped talking as soon as she saw me, and Olive, I noticed that you went to the stove and poured so much water into the teakettle from the bucket that it ran over, just because you were looking at me instead of at the kettle. You are both up to something, I know you are. Now come, tell me all about it; is it a great secret? I won't tell anybody; tell me, do."

Esther, who has just finished paring the potatoes and is now putting them on the stove to boil, takes a seat in the dining room on the settee and has one of her sulky moods, during which she always declines to speak when spoken to.

Jane looks at her a second and then says in a playful manner, "Oh, it's all right, Esther, I can guess what it was; what nonsense. I'll go and attend to my plants. Why, I declare it's a quarter past eleven already, and I have got to comb my hair before dinner, too. Oh, my, how time flies!"

So off Jane goes to her plants in the parlor, leaving Esther in the dining room and Olive in the kitchen getting dinner ready as fast as she can.

Olive had just gone behind the kitchen door that leads into the yard to get another stick of wood for the fire when she was startled by a scream; she feels instinctively that one of her children is in danger, and she is right, for little George has just been saved from a horrible death by Maud Weldon, their next door neighbor. The little scamp had managed to crawl through the fence and get as far as the middle of the street, when Maud saw him, and was just in time to prevent him from being run over by a heavy wagon drawn by a pair of horses that were being driven at a breakneck pace past the house.

Of course the fair Maud screamed, young women generally do at such times; but she saved George all the same. Her piercing shriek brought the stately Miss Sibley and her mother to the door of their house, which is almost directly opposite Dan's, and also caused Mrs. Mitchell and Mrs. Bell to become so nervous that they kept their children in the house for the rest of the day when they heard of the dangerous adventure George had had, for they both arrived too late to witness the rescue. The watchfulness and care they both bestowed on their little ones for the next week was so much time thrown away, however, for it so happened that no more fast teams came through that particular street for about a month.

Well, after the brave blonde, Maud Weldon, had become the heroine of the hour, she went into Dan's cottage with Esther and Jane, who both ran out when they heard the scream. Olive had already taken her boy in, washed his little hands and face, put on his clean overdress, and was now holding him in her lap in the large rocking-chair. Maud Weldon was in the parlor with Jane and Esther looking at the flowers and telling them about her new beau, how handsome he was, and

Knife-Wielding Demons and Murderous Ghosts

that she intended to marry him if he asked her, winding up her conversation on the subject of beaux with the remark that she was bound not to die an old maid but was going to get married, for she wanted to have a house of her own to keep. And so the conversation ran on between the three girls in the parlor until dinner was nearly ready, when Mrs. Hicks, Maud's aunt, called her and she went home.

After dinner, Esther and Olive were washing the dishes in the kitchen and talking over George's narrow escape when Esther suddenly made up her mind to tell her sister what she was about to do when Jane's rather unexpected return from the shop put an end to their conversation. So, after having put all the dishes away in the pantry, she told Olive that, if she would promise not to tell anybody, not even Dan, then she would tell her something that must be kept a secret because if it became known it might make people nervous and could do no good.

"Very well," replied Olive, "wait until I get my sewing, then we will go into the parlor, you can tell me all about it, and I promise that I won't tell."

So they went into the parlor. Esther sat in the rocking-chair and Olive on the sofa.

"Well, Olive," said Esther. "Now, don't laugh, for it is about a dream."

"A dream!" exclaimed Olive. "A dream! Go on, let me hear it."

"Well," began Esther, "last night I sat for two hours on the front step looking at the stars. After I came in I went down into the cellar in my stocking feet and drank about a pint of buttermilk and a large rat ran between my feet; then Jane and I went to our room, shut the door, said our prayers and went to bed. In a short time we both fell asleep, and I dreamt that when I got up in the morning everything and everybody was changed except myself. This cottage, instead of being yellow, was green; you, Dan, Jane, brother William, John Teed, Willie and George, all had heads like bears, and you all growled at me, but yet could talk, and, what was very strange, you all had eyes as large as horses eyes, only they were as red as blood.

"While I was talking to you I heard a noise in the street and, upon going to the door, I saw hundreds of black bulls with blue eyes, very bright blue eyes, coming towards the house. Blood was dripping from their mouths and their feet made fire come out of the ground. On they came, roaring very loudly all the time, right straight for the house. They broke down the fence. I shut the front door, locked it and then ran to the back door and fastened it. Then they all commenced to butt the house so violently that I had fallen over. It shook so that I woke up and found that I had fallen out of bed without waking Jane. So I got in again and soon fell asleep; but the dream is still in my mind. I can see it still, and wonder what it means until I get the headache.

"What do you think about it, Olive? Do you think there is any truth in dreams? Did you ever know of one to come true, or do you think it was all caused by the pint of buttermilk and my going into the cellar in my stocking feet, and the rat?"

"Well," said Olive, "I never could make up my mind fully on that subject; but of this I am certain: whatever Dan dreams comes true; there is no doubt about that. But don't tell him anything about this dream, Esther, or he will be floundering around all night trying to find out what it means; or Jane either, because, perhaps, it will scare her so that she will be unable to sleep."

"Don't believe it, Olive. I have told Jane, and she says it was all caused by the buttermilk I drank. She says it made me see a rat in the cellar just after I had drank it, and that it was no wonder I saw bears and bulls, too, after I went to sleep. Oh, my sakes alive, if I only had a dream book, like the one Mrs. Emery used to have. I'd soon find out what it means. Do you know, Olive, I have a great mind to go out to the Indian camp this very afternoon and try if that fortune-telling squaw who told Maggie Teed's fortune, and Mary Miller's, too, can't tell me all about it. I want to know if it means that something terrible is about to happen or not."

"Well," said Olive, "Esther, don't talk any more about it but read your Bible, go to church, say your prayers, and ask God to take care of you; then you need never fear dreams or anything else, for you must always remember that God has more power than the devil, and always will have."

"Oh!" replied Esther, with a smile, "it is all very well for you to talk in that way, but I shouldn't wonder if the devil saw more of me than he ever has yet before I die."

"Oh, Esther, how can you talk so; you ought to be ashamed of yourself, and to think that you were brought up by grandmother, too."

And so the afternoon passed slowly away, the beautiful blue sky which had been so clear all day began to assume a darkish aspect and threatening clouds spread themselves between the earth and heaven. By the time Dan and the rest had come home to supper, it looked very much like rain. Dan said it was going to rain sometime during the night; he knew it, because his rheumatism was bad.

Knife-Wielding Demons and Murderous Ghosts

Supper being ready, they all sat down and enjoyed it. After supper Dan took a smoke, Jane went to her accustomed seat in the parlor near her plants, William Cox and John Teed went out to see their girls, Olive put the boys to bed, and Esther sat down on the front doorstep all by herself and sang "The Sweet Bye-and-Bye" in a low voice.

The hands of the old fashioned clock in the dining room indicated ten minutes to eight, when a carriage drove up to the gate, and a well-built young man jumped out, opened the gate and came in. As he entered the house he shook hands with Esther, saying as he did so: "Go and put on your hat and sack and take a ride with me, Esther, and I will tell you why I did not call last evening as I promised." This young man was Bob McNeal, by trade a shoemaker, and a fine-looking young fellow he was, too. His hair and eyes were black, features rather handsome, and he wore a small black moustache.

As soon as Esther had received his invitation she ran upstairs, got her hat and sack, ran down again, jumped into the carriage, which was a buggy with room for two only, and off they drove. Jane came out to the front door and called after them, just as they were driving away: "You had better put the top up Bob, for it will certainly rain before long."

Dan, who had been sitting in the dining room in one of the easy chairs, remarked to Jane as he was going upstairs: "What a pity Bob McNeal is such a wild fellow. I'm afraid he will never amount to much. He is a remarkably fine workman, too; he has improved in his work since I took him into the factory with me. Oh well, I suppose it's all right; good night Jane."

"Good night Dan," said Jane. "I hope your rheumatism will be better in the morning."

"So do I," replied Dan. And up he went to bed. Jane returned to the parlor to wait for her beau.

Bob and Esther drove through Amherst and turned down the road leading to the marsh. They were going to take a ride into the country. Bob said that was the best road to take, and Esther did not care much which way they went, so she got a ride.

While driving through a small wood, Bob seemed to be suddenly seized with an attack of what lawyers are pleased to term "emotional insanity," for he dropped the reins and leaped from the buggy. Upon reaching the ground, he drew from the side pocket of his coat a large revolver, and, pointing it at Esther, told her, in a loud voice, to get out of the buggy or he would kill her where she sat. She, of course, refused to do as he requested or rather commanded, and, as it was raining and becoming quite dark, she told him to get into the buggy and drive her home and not act like a crazy man.

The remark about acting like a crazy man seemed to enrage him past endurance, for he uttered several terrible oaths, and, aiming the revolver at her heart, was about to fire, when the sound of wheels were heard rumbling in the distance. He immediately jumped into the buggy, seized the reins and drove at a breakneck pace through the pouring rain to Dan's cottage. Esther was wet through by the time they had arrived at the gate. She jumped out, opened the gate, entered the cottage and ran upstairs without noticing Jane, whom she passed in the hall. Bob, as soon as she got out, drove rapidly down the street.

As the hour was now ten o'clock, Esther immediately retired and, after crying herself to sleep, slept until morning. Jane entered the room about half an hour after her sister, engaged in prayer and then retired without disturbing her.

For the next four days Esther seemed to be suffering from some secret sorrow. She could not remain in the house, but was continually on the street, or at some of the neighbors' houses, and every night she cried herself to sleep.

Of course her woebegone appearance was noticed by the family, but they refrained from questioning her, for the simple reason that they supposed she and Bob had quarreled; and, as they did not approve of the attachment between him and Esther, they were rather glad that his visits had ceased, and gave no further attention to the matter, supposing that she would be herself again in a week or two. Bob's continued absence from the cottage — for he used to be there every other day — strengthened them in the belief that they were right in their supposition, and so they let the matter rest.

Part III

THE HAUNTED HOUSE

Supper is just over. Dan and Olive are in the parlor. Jane is upstairs in her room, talking to Esther, who has retired early. It being only seven o'clock, she asks Esther how long she is going to continue to worry herself about Bob.

Not receiving a reply, she puts on her heavy sack and remarks: "I am going over to see Miss Porter, and will soon return; it is so damp and foggy tonight that,

Knife-Wielding Demons and Murderous Ghosts

I declare, it makes me feel sleepy, too. I think I will follow your example, and retire early. Good night. I suppose you will be asleep by the time I get back." And off she goes.

As the night is so very damp and disagreeable, all begin to feel sleepy long before half-past eight and go up to their rooms.

Before Dan goes upstairs, he takes the bucket and brings some fresh water from the pump which he, as usual, places on the kitchen table, taking a large tin dipper about half full up to his room for the children to drink during the night.

It is now about fifteen minutes to nine. Jane has just returned from her visit and has gone to her room, which is in the front of the house, near the stairway, and directly next to Dan and Olive's room. She finds Esther crying, as usual, for the girl has actually cried herself to sleep every night since the fatal ride. After getting into bed, she says: "Oh, my, I forgot to put the lamp out," rises immediately and extinguishes the light, remarks to Esther that "it is very dark," bumps her head against the bed post, and finally settles herself down for a good sleep.

Esther, who has just stopped crying, remarks to Jane that "This is a wretched night," and says, "Somehow I can't get to sleep."

"No wonder," says Jane, "you went to bed too early."

"Jane, this is September the fourth, aint it?" asks Esther.

"Yes," replies Jane. "Go to sleep and let me alone. I don't want to talk to you. I want to go to sleep. What if it is September the fourth?"

"Oh, nothing," replies Esther. "Only it is just a week tonight since I went riding with Bob! Oh, what will become of me?" And she instantly burst into another crying spell.

"Esther," said Jane, "do you know I think you are losing your mind, and that if you keep on this way you will get so crazy that we will have to put you in the Insane Asylum."

This had the desired effect, for she stopped instantly. For a few minutes everything was perfectly still. No sound was to be heard except the breathing of the two young girls as they lay side by side in bed.

They had remained perfectly quiet, for about ten or fifteen minutes, when Esther jumped out of bed with a scream, exclaiming that there was a mouse under the bed clothes.

Knife-Wielding Demons and Murderous Ghosts

Her scream startled her sister, who was almost asleep, and she also got out of bed and lit the lamp, for she is as much afraid of mice as Esther is. They both searched the bed, but could not find the supposed mouse, supposing it to be inside the mattress. Jane exclaimed "Oh pshaw, what fools we are to be sure to be scared at a little harmless mouse; if there really is one here it can do us no harm, for see, it is inside the mattress. Look how the straw is being moved about. The mouse has gotten inside and can't get out, because there is no hole in the ticking. Let us go back to bed, Esther. It can do us no harm now."

So they put out the light, and got into bed again. After listening for a few minutes without hearing the straw move in the mattress, they both fell asleep.

On the following night the girls heard something moving under their bed. Esther exclaimed: "There is that mouse again, Jane. Let us get up and kill it. I'm not going to be worried by mice every night."

So they both arose, and on hearing a rustling in a green pasteboard box, filled with patchwork, which was under the bed, they placed it out in the middle of the room and were much amazed to see the box jump up in the air about a foot and then fall over on its side. The girls could not believe their own eyes, so Jane placed the box in its old position in the middle of the room. Both watched it intently, when, to their amazement, the same thing occurred again. The girls were now really frightened, and screamed as loudly as they could for Dan, who put on some clothing and came into their room to ascertain what the matter was. They told him what had just taken place, but he only laughed, and after pushing the box under the bed, and remarking that they must be insane or perhaps had been dreaming, he went back to bed grumbling because his rest had been disturbed.

The next morning the girls both declared that the box had really moved; but, as nobody believed them, they saw it was of no use to talk of the matter. Jane went to the shop, Dan to his shoe factory, and William Cox and John Teed about their business as usual, leaving Olive and Esther to attend to their household duties. After dinner Olive took her sewing into the parlor, and Esther went out to walk. The afternoon was delightful, and there was quite a breeze blowing from the bay. Walking is very pleasant when there is no dust; but Amherst is such a dusty little village, especially when the wind blows from the bay, that it is impossible to walk on any of the streets with comfort on a windy day during the summer. Esther found this to be the case, so she retraced her steps homeward, stopping at the post office and at Bird's book store, where she bought a bottle of ink from Miss Blanche. On arriving at the cottage she hung up her hat and joined

Knife-Wielding Demons and Murderous Ghosts

Olive in the parlor, took little George on her lap, and, after singing him to sleep, lay down on the sofa and took a nap.

After supper Esther took her accustomed seat on the door-step, remaining there until the moon had risen. It was a beautiful moonlit night, almost as bright as day. While seated there gazing at the moon, she said to herself, "Well, there is one thing certain anyhow. I am going to have good luck all this month, for on Sunday night I saw the new moon over my shoulder."

At half-past eight o'clock, Esther complained of feeling feverish and was advised by Olive and Jane to go to bed, which she did.

About ten o'clock, Jane retired for the night. After she had been in bed some fifteen minutes, Esther jumped with a sudden bound into the center of the room, taking all the bed clothes with her.

"My God!" she exclaimed, "what can be the matter with me! Wake up, Jane, wake up! I'm dying, I'm dying!"

"Dying!" responded Jane. "Why, dying people don't speak in that loud tone. Wait until I light the lamp. Don't die in the dark, Esther."

Jane thought her sister had only had a nightmare, but, when she lit the lamp, she was considerably alarmed by her sister's appearance. There stood Esther in the center of the room, her short hair almost standing on end, her face as red as blood, and her eyes really looked as if they were about to start from their sockets, her hands were grasping the back of a chair so tightly that her nails sank into the soft wood. She was truly an object to look on with amazement, as she stood there in her white night gown trembling with fear.

Her sister called as loudly as she could for assistance; for Jane, too, was pretty well frightened by this time and did not know what to do. Olive was the first to enter the room, having first thrown a shawl around her shoulders, for the night was very chilly. Dan put on his coat and pants in a hurry, as did also William Cox and John Teed, and the three men entered the room about the same time.

"Why, what in the name of thunder ails you, Esther?" asked Dan. William and John exclaimed in the same breath, "She's mad!"

Olive was speechless with amazement while they stood looking at the girl, not knowing what to do to relieve her terrible agony. She became very pale and seemed to be growing weak; in fact, she became so weak in a short time that she had to be assisted to the bed. After sitting on the edge of the bed for a moment, and gazing about the room with a vacant stare, she started to her feet with a wild yell and said she felt like bursting into pieces.

"Great Heavens," exclaimed Olive, "What shall we do with her? Is she crazy?"

Jane, who always retains her presence of mind, took her sister's hand and said in a soothing tone: "Come, Esther, get into bed again." As they found that she could not do so without assistance, Olive and Jane helped her and placed the bed clothing over her again. As soon as she had been assisted to bed she said in a low choking voice, "I am swelling up and shall certainly burst, I know I shall."

Dan looked at her face and remarked in a startled tone. "Why, the girl is swelling, Olive, just look at her. Look at her hands, too. See how swollen they are, and she is as hot as fire."

She was literally burning up with fever and yet as pale as death, while only a few minutes before her face was as red as blood and her person as cold as ice. What a strange case, pale when hot, and blood red when cold, yet such was really the fact.

While the family stood looking at her, wondering what would relieve her, for her entire body had swollen to an enormous size and she was screaming with pain and grinding her teeth as if in a fit, a loud report like thunder was heard in the room. They all started to their feet instantly and seemed paralyzed with fear.

"My God!" exclaimed Olive, "the house has been struck by lightning and I know my poor boys are killed!"

After giving vent to this exclamation, she rushed from the room to her own where the children were and found them both sleeping soundly, so she returned to the room where they all stood looking at Esther, and wondering what had produced the terrible sound. On entering, Olive told them that the boys were both sound asleep.

"I wonder what that awful noise was?" she said. Going to the window and raising the curtain, she saw that the stars were shining brightly and was then satisfied that it had not been thunder they had heard. Just as she let the curtain drop, three terrific reports were heard, apparently from directly under the bed. They were so loud that the whole room shook, and Esther, who a moment before had been swollen to such an enormous size, immediately assumed her natural appearance and sank into a state of calm repose. As soon as they found that it was sleep and not death that had taken possession of her, they all left the room except Jane, who went back to bed beside her sister but could not sleep a wink for the balance of the night.

The next day Esther remained in bed until about nine o'clock, when she arose, seemingly all right again, and got her own breakfast. As her appetite was not as good as usual, all she could eat was a small piece of bread and butter and a large green pickle, washed down with a cup of strong tea. She helped Olive with her work as usual, and after dinner took a walk past the post office, around the block and back to the cottage again. At supper the usual conversation about the strange sounds took place, all wondering what had caused them. As no one could ascertain the cause they gave it up as something too strange to think about, and all agreed not to let the neighbors know anything about it, because, they argued, that as no one would be likely to believe that such strange sounds had been heard under the bed, the best thing to do was to keep the matter quiet.

About four nights after the loud reports had been heard, Esther had another similar attack. It came on about ten o'clock at night, just as she was getting in bed. This time, however, she managed to get into bed before the attack had swelled her up to any great extent. Jane, who had already retired, advised her to remain perfectly still, and perhaps the attack would pass off, but how sadly was she mistaken. Esther had only been in bed about five minutes when, to the amazement of the girls, all the bed clothing flew off and settled down in the far corner of the room. They could see them going because the lamp was burning dimly on the table.

They both screamed, and then Jane fainted dead away. The family rushed into the room as before and were so frightened that they did not know what to do. There lay the bedclothes in the corner, Esther all swollen up, Jane in a dead faint, and perhaps really dead for all they knew, for, by the glare of the lamp which Dan held in his hand, she looked more dead than alive. Olive was the first to come to her senses. Taking up the bedclothes, she placed them over her sisters. Just as she had done so, off they flew again to the same corner of the room. In less time than it takes to count to three, the pillow flew from under Esther's head and struck John Teed in the face. He immediately left the room, saying that he had had enough. He could not be induced to return and sit on the edge of the bed with the others, who in that way managed to keep the clothes in their place.

Jane had by this time recovered from her swoon. William Cox went down to the kitchen for a bucket of water to bathe Esther's head, which was aching terribly. Just as he got to the door of the room again with the bucket of water, a succession of reports were heard which seemed to come from the bed where Esther lay. They were so very loud that the whole room shook, and Esther, who had a moment before been swollen up, commenced to assume her natural appearance and in a few minutes fell into a pleasant sleep. As everything seemed now to be all right again, everybody went back to bed.

In the morning Esther and Jane were both very weak, particularly Esther. She, however, got up when her sister did and lay down on the sofa in the parlor. At breakfast they all agreed that a doctor had better be called in. So in the afternoon Dan left the factory early and went to see Dr. Caritte. The doctor laughed when Dan told him what had occurred. He said he would call in the evening and remain until one in the morning if necessary, but did not hesitate to say that what Dan had told him was all nonsense, remarking that he knew no such tomfoolery would occur while he was in the house.

As the hands of the clock pointed to ten, in walked the doctor. Bidding everybody a hearty good evening, he took a seat near Esther, who had been in bed since nine o'clock, but as yet had not been affected with one of her strange attacks. The doctor felt her pulse, looked at her tongue, and then told the family that she seemed to be suffering from nervous excitement and had evidently received a tremendous shock of some kind. Just as he had said these words, the pillow from under her head left the bed; with the exception of one corner, which remained under her head, it straightened itself out as if filled with air and then went back to its place again. The doctor's large blue eyes opened to their utmost capacity, as he asked in a low tone: "Did you all see that? It went back again."

"So it did," remarked John Teed, "but if it moves out again it will not go back, for I intend to hold on to it, even if it did bang me over the head last night."

John had no sooner spoken these words than out came the pillow from under Esther's head as before. He waited until it had just started back again and then grasped it with both hands and held on with all his strength. The pillow, however, was pulled from him by some invisible power stronger than himself. As he felt it being pulled away, his hair actually stood on end.

"How wonderful!" exclaimed Dr. Caritte.

Just as the doctor arose from his chair, the reports under the bed commenced, as on the previous night. The doctor looked beneath the bed, but failed to ascertain what caused the sounds. When he walked to the door the sounds followed him, being now produced on the floor of the room. In about a minute after this, off went the bed clothes again and before they had been put back on the bed, the sound as of some person writing on the wall with a sharp instrument was heard. All looked at the wall whence the sound of writing came, when to their great astonishment there was seen written, near the head of the bed, in large characters, these words: "Esther Cox, you are mine to kill." Everybody could see the writing plainly, and yet only a moment before nothing was to be seen but the blank wall.

The reader can imagine their utter amazement at what had just taken place. There they stood around the bed of this wonderful girl, each watching the other to see that there was no deception. They knew these marvelous things had taken place, for all heard them with their own ears and beheld them with their own eyes. Still, they could not believe their own senses, it was all so strange. But the writing on the wall — what did it mean, and how came it there? God only knew.

As Doctor Caritte stood in the doorway for a moment wondering to himself what it all meant, a large piece of plaster came flying from the wall of the room, having in its flight turned a corner and fallen at his feet. The good doctor picked it up mechanically and placed it on a chair. He was too astonished to speak. Just as he did so, the poundings commenced again with redoubled power, this time shaking the entire room.

It must be remembered that during all this time Esther lay upon the bed, almost frightened to death by what was occurring. After this state of things had continued for about two hours, everything became quiet and she went to sleep. The doctor said he would not give her any medicine until the next morning, when he would call at nine and give her something to quiet her nerves; for she was certainly suffering from some nervous trouble. As to the sounds and movements of objects, he could not account for them, but thought if she became strong again they would cease.

In the morning the doctor called, as he had promised, and was much surprised to see Esther up and dressed, helping Olive to wash the dishes. She told him that she felt all right again, only she was so nervous that any sudden noise made her jump. Having occasion to go down into the cellar with a pan of milk, she came running up, out of breath, exclaiming that there was someone down in the cellar, for a piece of plank had been thrown at her. The doctor went down to see for himself, Esther remaining in the dining room; for it must be borne in mind that the cellar door opens into the dining room. In a moment he came up again, remarking that there was nobody down there to throw a piece of plank, nor anything else.

"Esther, come down with me," said he. So down they both went, when, to their great surprise, several potatoes came flying at their heads. That was enough. They both beat a hasty retreat. The doctor left the house and called again in the evening, with several very powerful sedatives, morphine being one, which he administered to Esther about ten o'clock as she lay in bed. She still complained of her nervousness and said she felt as if electricity was passing all through her body.

He had given her the medicine and had just remarked that she would have a good night's rest when the loud sounds commenced, only they were much louder and in more rapid succession than on the previous nights. Presently the sounds left the room and were heard on the roof of the house. The doctor instantly left the house and went out into the street, hearing the sounds while in the open air. He returned to the house, more nonplussed than ever, and told the family that from the street it seemed as if some person was on the roof with a heavy sledgehammer pounding away to try and break through the shingles. Being a moonlit night, he could see distinctly that there was not any one out on the roof. He remained until twelve. Everything becoming quiet again, and he then departed, saying he would call the next day. When he had got as far as the gate, the sounds on the roof commenced again with great violence and continued until he had gone about two hundred yards from the cottage, at which distance he could still hear them distinctly.

The next week it became known throughout Amherst that strange things were going on at Dan Teed's cottage. The mysterious sounds had been heard by people in the street as they passed the house, and the poundings now commenced in the morning and were to be heard all day long. Esther always felt relieved when the sounds were produced by the unknown power.

Dr. Caritte called every night, and sometimes during the day, but could not afford her the slightest relief. One night, about three weeks after the doctor's first visit, as he and the family were standing around her bed listening to the loud knockings, Esther suddenly threw her arms up towards the head of the bed and seemed to be seized with a spasm, for she became cold and perfectly rigid.

While in this state she commenced to talk, and told all that had occurred between herself and Bob McNeal on the night of the fatal ride. This was the first

Knife-Wielding Demons and Murderous Ghosts

anybody knew of the affair, for she had never told of it, and Bob had never been seen in the locality after that night. When she came to her senses again, they told her what had been said by herself during the strange state from which she had just emerged. Upon hearing this she commenced to cry, and told them that it was all true; that he had threatened her with his revolver, but, becoming frightened by the sound of wheels in the distance, had driven her home without offering her any further show of violence.

"There!" exclaimed Olive. "Didn't I tell you that I felt it in my bones, that harm would come to you through that young man, and now you see he really is at the bottom of all this. Ah, it is Bob who makes all these strange sounds about the house; I know he is the cause." Instantly three distinct reports were heard, shaking the whole house with their violence.

"Do you know, doctor," said Jane, "that I believe that whatever agency makes these noises, it can hear and understand what we are talking about, and perhaps see us." The moment she had finished the sentence, three distinct reports were heard as loud as before.

"Ask if it can hear us, doctor," said Dan.

"Can you, whatever you are, hear what we say?" asked Dr. Caritte.

Again three reports were heard, which shook the entire house.

"Why, that is very singular," remarked the doctor. "I believe Jane was right, it can hear."

"Well, let us try again," said Dan. "If you can see and hear, tell us how many persons are in this room?" Esther did not know how many were present, for she was lying in the bed with her face buried in the pillow, trembling with fear. As Dan did not receive an answer, he asked again.

"How many persons are in the room? Give us a knock on the floor for each one."

Five distinct knocks were made by the strange force on the floor, and there were just five persons in the room, as follows: Dr. Caritte, Dan, Olive, Esther and Jane, William Cox and John Teed having left the room after Esther had buried her face in the pillow. "Well, it certainly is strange," remarked the doctor, "but I must go. It is getting late." So he departed after saying he would call the next evening.

Knife-Wielding Demons and Murderous Ghosts

The next evening the Doctor called and remained for about an hour, but as nothing occurred he departed feeling rather disappointed. For the next three weeks no one could tell when the manifestations would take place. Sometimes they would commence in the morning and continue all day, and at other times they would only take place after Esther had retired. It had now become a settled fact that Esther must be in the house or there would be no manifestations of any kind. They never occurred during her absence.

About one month after the commencement of the manifestations, Dr. Edwin Clay, the well-known Baptist clergyman, called at the home to behold the wonders with his own eyes. He had read come little account of them in the newspapers, but was desirous of seeing and hearing for himself, not taking much stock, as the saying is, in what other people told him about the affair. However, he was fortunate enough to have his desire fully gratified.

He heard the loudest kind of knocks in answer to his various questions, saw the mysterious writing on the wall, and left the house fully satisfied that Esther did not produce any of the manifestations herself and that the family did not assist her, as some people believed. He, however, was of the opinion that through the shock her system had received the night she went riding, she had become in some mysterious manner an electric battery. His theory being that invisible flashes of lightning left her person, and that the knocks, which everybody could hear distinctly, were simply minute claps of thunder. He lectured on his theory and drew large audiences, as he always does, no matter what the subject is. Perfectly satisfied that the manifestations are genuine, he has nobly defended Esther Cox from the platform and the pulpit.

Rev. R.A. Temple, the well-known Wesleyan minister and pastor of the Wesleyan Church in Amherst, has witnessed some of the manifestations. He saw, among other strange things, a bucket of cold water become agitated and, to all appearances, boil, while standing on the kitchen table.

As soon as people in the village found that such eminent men as Dr. Clay, Dr. Caritte and Rev. Dr. Temple took an interest in the case, it became quite fashionable for people in the village to call at Dan's little cottage to see Esther Cox and witness the wonderful manifestations. While the house was filled with visitors, large crowds often stood outside, unable to gain admittance. On several occasions the village police force had to be called out to keep order, so anxious were people to see and hear for themselves.

Knife-Wielding Demons and Murderous Ghosts

Many believed and still believe the whole affair a fraud, and others say that Esther mesmerizes people, and they think they hear and see things which never have an existence. Dr. Nathan Tupper is of this belief, although he has never witnessed a single manifestation.

Dr. Caritte, who continued to be one of the daily callers at the cottage, would have a theory one day that would seem to account for the manifestations he had witnessed, and the next day something wonderful would occur and upset his latest theory completely, so that he finally gave up in despair and became simply a passive spectator. Things went on in this way until December, when Esther was taken ill with diphtheria and confined to her bed for about two weeks, during which time the manifestations ceased entirely. After she had recovered from her illness, she went to Sackville, N.B., to visit her other married sister, Mrs. John Snowden, remaining at her house for about two weeks. While there she was entirely free from the manifestations.

On returning to Dan's cottage, the most startling part of the case was developed. One night while in bed with her sister Jane in another room, her room having been changed to see if that would put a stop to the affair, she told her sister that she could hear a voice saying to her that the house was to be set on fire that night by a ghost. The voice also said that it had once lived on the earth, but had been dead for some years.

The members of the household were called in at once and told what had been said. They only laughed and remarked that no such thing as that could take place, because there were no ghosts. Dr. Clay had said it was all electricity.

"And," added Dan, "electricity can't set the house on fire unless it comes from a cloud in the form of lightning."

As they were talking the matter over, to the amazement of all present, a lighted match fell from the ceiling to the bed and would have set it on fire had not Jane put it out instantly. During the next ten minutes, eight or ten lighted matches fell on the bed and about the room, but were all extinguished before any harm could be done.

In the course of the night, the loud knockings commenced. The family could now all converse with the invisible power in this way. It would knock once for a negative answer, and three times for an answer in the affirmative, giving two knocks when in doubt about a reply. Dan asked if the house would be set on fire, and the reply was three loud knocks on the floor, meaning yes; and a fire was started about five minutes afterwards.

The ghost took a dress belonging to Esther that was hanging on a nail in the wall near the door, rolled it up, and, before any of the persons in the room could remove it from under the bed, where the ghost had placed it before their very eyes, it was all in a blaze. It was extinguished, however, without being much injured by the fire. The next morning all was consternation in the cottage. Dan and Olive were afraid that the ghost would start a fire in some inaccessible place and burn the house down. They were both convinced that it really was a ghost, "For" said Olive, "nothing but the devil or a ghost with evil designs could do so terrible a thing as start a fire in a cottage at the dead of night."

Dr. Clay's theory might be true, but it was not clear to them how electricity could go about a house gifted with the cunning of a fiend. "It is true," said Dan, "that lightning often sets fire to houses and barns, but it has never yet been known to roam about a man's house, as this strange power does. And as Esther can hear it speak, and it does whatever it says it will, why I believe it to be a ghost, or else the devil."

While Olive was churning in the kitchen one morning about three days after the fire under the bed, she noticed smoke coming from the cellar. Esther was seated in the dining room when Olive first saw the smoke, and had been seated there for the last hour, previous to which she had been in the kitchen assisting her sister to wash the breakfast dishes, as was her custom. On seeing the smoke, both she and Esther were for the moment utterly paralyzed with fear. What they so dreaded had at last come to pass. The house was evidently on fire, and that fire set by a devilish ghost. What was to be done?

Olive was the first to recover from the shock. Seizing the bucket of drinking water, always kept standing on the kitchen table, she rushed down the cellar stairs and was horrified at the sight which burst upon her view. There in the far corner of the cellar was a barrel of shavings blazing almost to the floor above. In the meantime Esther had reached the cellar, and stood looking at the crackling flames in blank astonishment. The water Olive had poured into the barrel was not enough to quench the flames, for in the excitement of the moment she had spilled more than half of it on her way down. What was to be done? The house would catch and probably be burned to the ground, and they would be rendered homeless.

Knife-Wielding Demons and Murderous Ghosts

"Oh! If Dan were at home, he could put it out," Olive managed to articulate, for both she and Esther were nearly suffocated with the dense black smoke with which the cellar was filled, and now the barrel itself had caught. The cellar was very small, and everything in it would soon be blazing unless the fire could be extinguished at once.

"Oh! What shall we do?" cried Esther. "What shall we do?"

"Run out in the street and cry fire as loud as you can. Come, let's run at once or the whole house will burn down!" exclaimed Olive, by this time wild with fear.

So, both she and Esther ran upstairs and out into the street, crying "Fire! Fire!" Of course, their cries aroused the whole neighborhood. At that moment, a gentleman, a stranger in the village who happened to be passing, instantly threw off his coat, rushed into the cottage, picked up a mat from the dining room floor and was down in the cellar in a second. He put the fire entirely out, and then, without waiting to be thanked, walked out of the cottage and was soon lost to view in the distance. And, what is remarkably strange, nobody knows who he was or whence he came, for from that day he has not been seen.

The news of the fire which the ghost had set in Dan's cellar soon travelled all over the country and created a great deal of curiosity. People who had set the whole affair down as a fraud began to think that perhaps it was all true after all, for certainly no young girl could set fire to a barrel of shavings in the cellar and be at that instant in another part of the house, under the watchful eye of an older sister, who was continually at her side. The fact that both the little boys were out in the front yard at the time the fire was kindled, and consequently could not have had anything to do with setting it, was also calculated to throw an air of mystery around the whole affair.

The family believed that it had been started by the ghost. The fire marshals of the village seemed to be of the opinion that Esther set both fires herself; the villagers held various opinions. Dr. Nathan Tupper suggested that if a good rawhide whip were laid over her back by a strong arm, the manifestations would cease at once. Fortunately for Esther, no one had the right or power to beat her as if she were a slave, and so the mystery still remained unsolved.

For the next week, manifestations continued to take place daily and were as powerful as ever. The excitement in Amherst was intense. If the cottage in which Dan lived should catch fire when the wind was blowing from the bay, the fire would spread, and if the wind was favorable for such a terrible calamity, the whole village would soon be reduced to ashes.

As if to pile horror upon horror, one night, as Esther and the entire family were seated in the parlor, the ghost appeared. Esther started to her feet and seemed for the moment paralyzed with terror. In a second or two, however, she recovered her self-possession, and, pointing with a trembling hand to a distant corner of the room, exclaimed in a hoarse and broken voice:

"Look there! Look there! My God, it is the ghost! Don't you all see him? There he stands all in grey; see how his eyes are glaring at me and he laughs when he says I must leave the house tonight or he will start a fire in the loft under the roof and burn us all to death. Oh, what shall I do? Where shall I go? The ground is covered with snow. And yet I cannot remain here, for he will do what he threatens; he always does. Oh, I wish I were dead."

After this exclamation, she fell to the floor and burst into an agony of grief. "Well," said Dan, after lifting her up, "something will have to be done, and quickly, too. The wind is blowing hard tonight, and, if the ghost does as he threatens, the house will burn down sure, and perhaps the whole village. You must go, Esther. Remember, I don't turn you out; it is this devil of a ghost who drives you from your home."

They all knew none of the neighbors would shelter Esther, because they all feared the ghost. What was to be done? Heaven only knew. It suddenly occurred to Dan that John White would perhaps give her shelter, for he had always taken a deep interest in the manifestations, and had often expressed pity for the unhappy girl. So Dan, after putting on his heavy coat — for it was snowing fast, and the night was intensely cold — went to White's house. After knocking for some time, the door was opened by John White himself. He looked at Dan a moment in amazement, and then exclaimed in an inquiring tone:

"What's the matter, Teed? Has the house burned to the ground or has the girl burst all to pieces?"

Dan explained his mission in a few words. When he had finished, White thought a moment, and then said:

"Wait until I ask my wife; if she says yes, all right, you may bring her here tonight."

He asked his wife, and, fortunately for the miserable girl, she said "yes," and that very night Esther Cox changed her home.

Knife-Wielding Demons and Murderous Ghosts

Part IV

THE WALKING OF THE GHOST

When John White took Esther to his house to reside, he performed a charitable deed, which no man in the village but himself had the heart to do. Both he and his good wife showed, by the kindness with which they treated the poor unhappy girl, that Heaven had at least inspired two hearts with that greatest of all virtues: Charity.

It was now January, 1879, just four months since the manifestations first commenced. Esther had been at White's residence for two weeks and had not seen anything of the ghost. She had improved very much in that short time, her nervousness having almost subsided, and she was contented and happy. Mrs. White, who found her of great assistance in the house, had become much attached to the girl and treated her with the same kindness that she did her own children.

Towards the end of the third week her old enemy — the ghost — returned.

While Esther was scrubbing the hall at her new home, she was astonished to see her scrubbing brush disappear from her hand. When the ghost told her that he had taken it, she became much alarmed and screamed for Mrs. White, who, with her daughter Mary, searched the hall for it in vain. After they had abandoned their search, to the great astonishment of all, the brush fell from the ceiling, just grazing Esther's head in its fall.

Here was a new manifestation of the ghostly power. He was able to take a solid substance from this material world of ours and render it invisible by taking it into his mysterious state of existence; and, if he could take one object, why not another? If a brush, why not a broom? But why speculate on so great a mystery? The ghost did it, and as we must draw the line somewhere, it is better to draw it here than to allow our minds to become dazed by such fellows as ghosts.

Many other remarkable manifestations continued to take place almost daily for the next two weeks. The ghost could now tell how much money people had in their pockets, both by knocking and by telling Esther. He would answer any question asked in the abovementioned manner, and behaved himself very well indeed until the end of the sixth week, when his true devilish nature broke out again. He commenced setting fires about the house and walking so that he could be heard distinctly. Of course, John White would not run the risk of having his house burned down. So he persuaded Esther to remain during the day in his dining saloon, which stands opposite the well-known book store of G.G. Bird, on the principal street.

While standing behind the counter in the dining saloon, also while she worked in the adjoining kitchen, many new and wonderful things were witnessed by the inhabitants of Amherst and by strangers from a distance, and many plans were tried to prevent the manifestations. Among others, someone suggested that if she could stand on glass they would cease. So pieces of glass were put into her shoes, but as their presence caused her head to ache and her nose to bleed, without stopping the manifestations, the idea was abandoned.

One morning the door of the large stove in the kitchen adjoining the saloon was opened and shut by the ghost, much to the annoyance of Mr. White, who, with an old axe handle, so braced the door that it could not be moved by any known mundane power, unless the axe handle was first removed. A moment afterwards, however, the ghost, who seemed never to leave Esther's presence while she was in the saloon, lifted the door off its hinges, removed the axe handle from the position in which it had been placed, and, after throwing them some distance into the air, let both fall to the floor with a tremendous crash.

Mr. White was speechless with astonishment and immediately called in Mr. W.H. Rogers, Inspector of Fisheries for Nova Scotia. After bracing the door as before, the same wonderful manifestation was repeated in the presence of Mr. Rogers. On another occasion, a clasp-knife belonging to little Fred, Mr. White's son, was taken from his hand by the ghost, who instantly stabbed Esther in the back with it, leaving the knife sticking in the wound, which bled profusely. Fred, after drawing the knife from the wound, wiped it, closed it and put it in his pocket. The ghost took it from his pocket and in a second stuck it in the same wound. Fred again obtained possession of the knife, and this time hid it so that it could not be found, even by a ghost.

There is something still more remarkable, however, about the following manifestation: Some person tried the experiment of placing three or four large iron spikes on Esther's lap while she was seated in the dining saloon. To the astonishment of everybody, the spikes were not removed by the ghost, but instead became too hot to be handled with comfort and a second afterwards were thrown by the ghost to the far end of the saloon, a distance of twenty feet.

During her stay at the saloon the ghost commenced to move the furniture about in the broad daylight. On one occasion a large box, weighing fifty pounds, moved a distance of fifteen feet without the slightest visible cause. The very loud knocking commenced again and was heard by crowds of people, the saloon being continually filled with visitors. Among other well-known inhabitants of Amherst who saw the wonders at this period, I may mention William Hillson, Daniel Morrison, Robert Hutchinson, who is John White's son-in-law, and J. Albert Black, Esq., editor of the Amherst Gazette.

Towards the latter part of March, Esther went to Saint John, New Brunswick, and while there was the guest of Captain James Beck. She remained at his house for three weeks under the protection of his wife. Her case was investigated by a party of gentlemen, well known in Saint John as men whose minds have a scientific turn. Doctor Alward, Mr. Amos Fales, Mr. Alex Christie, Mr. Ritchie, and many others witnessed the manifestations and talked with the ghost by the aid of the knocks on the wall and furniture, and, strange to relate, other ghosts came and conversed also; among them one who said his name was Peter Cox, and another who gave the name of Maggie Fisher.

All claimed to have lived on the earth before they entered the land of ghosts, but none were apparently as strong and healthy as the old original fire fiend of the cottage, who now gave the name of Bob Nickle and said that when he lived on the earth he had been a shoemaker. The ghost who called himself Peter Cox claimed to be a relation of Esther's and said he had been in ghost land about forty years; he was a quiet old fellow, and did all he could to prevent Bob Nickle and Maggie Fisher from breaking the articles which they threw and from using profane language, a habit in which they were fond of indulging.

Dr. Alward and his scientific friends also conversed with the ghosts by calling over the alphabet, the ghosts knocking at the correct letters, and in that way long communications were spelled out to the satisfaction of those present.

After remaining in Saint John about three weeks. Esther returned to Amherst and accepted an invitation to visit Mr. and Mrs. Van Amburgh, who reside about three miles from the village. She remained eight weeks with them, during which period the ghosts allowed her to enjoy the calm repose of a life in the woods, the Van Amburgh farm being literally situated in the woods.

At the expiration of the eighth week she returned to Amherst and went back to Dan's cottage to reside, being employed during the day in White's Dining Saloon. The manifestations soon commenced again and were as powerful as when the author commenced his investigation of the case.

Knife-Wielding Demons and Murderous Ghosts

Part V

THE AUTHOR AND THE GHOSTS

I closed my engagement with the dramatic company, of which I was a member in Newfoundland, and went to Amherst to expose, if possible, Esther Cox, the great Amherst Mystery.

Where occasion requires allusion to myself, I shall simply say "the author."

At seven o'clock on the morning of June 21st, 1879, as the sun was shining brightly and the cool breeze was blowing from the bay, the author entered the haunted house. After placing his umbrella in a corner of the dining room, and his satchel on the table, he seated himself in one of the easy chairs to await results.

Esther and Olive were present. He had been in the room about five minutes when, to his great astonishment, his umbrella was thrown a distance of fifteen feet, going over his head in its flight. At the same instant a large carving knife came jumping over the girl's head and fell near him. Not at all pleased with this kind of a reception on the part of the ghosts, he left the room and went into the parlor, taking his satchel with him, and there sat down paralyzed with wonder and astonishment. He had been seated only a moment when his satchel was thrown a distance of ten feet. At the same instant a large chair came flying across the room, striking the one on which he was seated, nearly knocking it from under him. It suddenly occurred to him that he would take a walk, during which he could admire the beauties of the village.

On his return to the cottage, the ghosts commenced their deviltry again with redoubled violence. He had no sooner entered the house than all the chairs in the parlor — and there were seven by actual count — fell over. Concluding not to remain in that room, he went to the dining room, when the chairs in that, his favorite room in every house, went through the same performance. Feeling hungry, not yet having had his breakfast, he sat down to a good substantial meal, Esther sitting directly opposite. After pouring his coffee, she handed it to him with the remark, "Oh, you will soon get used to them; I don't think they like you."

"No," he replied, "I do not think they do either. In fact, I am satisfied they do not; but, having come here to investigate, I shall remain until they drive me from the house."

While eating breakfast, the ghosts commenced to hammer on the table. By the system in use by the family when conversing with them, he carried on a long conversation, they answering by knocks on the bottom of the table. Before

Knife-Wielding Demons and Murderous Ghosts

entering into the conversation, however, he sat so that Esther's hands and feet were in full view. The ghosts told the number of his watch, also the dates of coins in his pocket, and beat correct time when he whistled the tune of "Yankee Doodle." Chairs continued to fall over until dinner, during which there was a slight cessation of manifestations.

After dinner, the author lay down upon the parlor sofa to take a nap, as is his custom in the afternoon. Esther came into the room for a newspaper. He watched her very closely, keeping one eye open and the one next to her shut, so that she would think he was asleep. While watching her intently to see that she did not throw anything herself, a large glass paper weight, weighing fully a pound, came whizzing through the air from the far corner of the room, where it had been on a shelf, a distance of fully fifteen feet from the sofa.

Fortunately for the author, instead of striking his head, which was evidently the intention of the ghost who threw it, it struck the arm of the sofa with great force, rebounding to a chair, upon which it remained after it had spun around for a second or two. Being very anxious to witness the manifestations, he requested Esther to remain in the room, which she did. After seating herself in the rocking chair, little George came into the room, and she placed the little fellow on her lap and sang to him.

As the author lay there watching her, one of the child's copper-toed shoes was taken off by a ghost and thrown at him with great force, striking his head. The place struck was very sore for three or four days. The balance of the day passed quietly away. Evening came, and the author had a good night's rest in the haunted house of which he had heard so much. The next day being Sunday, everything was peaceful in the cottage, though why the ghosts should respect the Sabbath the author has never been able to ascertain; however, they always remain quiet on that day.

On Monday morning the ghosts commenced their mad pranks again and seemed ready for anything. At breakfast, the lid of the stone-china sugar bowl disappeared from the table, and, in about ten minutes, fell from the ceiling. After breakfast, over went the table; then the chairs all fell over, and several large mats were pitched about the room. The author immediately left the room and went into the parlor, when, to his astonishment, a flower pot containing a large plant in full bloom was taken from its place in the bay window and set down in the middle of the room, and a large tin can filled with water was brought from the kitchen and placed beside it.

Walter Hubbell (left) attracted a certain degree of literary attention with his book, "The Amherst Mystery."

Esther Cox (right) was at the center of all the ghostly attention. She was haunted by one of the worst poltergeists in history.

Knife-Wielding Demons and Murderous Ghosts

During the afternoon a large inkstand and two empty bottles were thrown at him. The ghosts also undressed little George, and, as if to make a final climax to the day's performance, Bob, the head ghost, started a small bonfire upstairs. Then he and the other ghosts piled all the chairs in the parlor one on top of the other, until they made a pile about six feet in height, when, as if in sport, they pulled out those underneath, letting all the others fall to the floor with a crash.

On Tuesday morning, when the author took his seat at the breakfast table, he placed the sugar bowl lid beside his plate so that he might have his eyes on it. In a second it disappeared and fell, in exactly eight minutes by the clock, from the ceiling, a distance of fully twenty feet from the table. The ghosts got under the table, as on the previous morning, and were so obliging as to produce any sounds called for, such as an exact imitation of the sawing of wood, of drumming and of washing on a washboard. During the morning several knives were thrown at him; a large crock of salt was taken from the kitchen dresser and placed on the dining room table; the teakettle was taken from the stove by one of the ghosts and placed out in the yard, as was also the beefsteak, pan and all, which was frying on the stove; and, after dinner, the table was upset.

During the afternoon, while in the parlor, the author made the acquaintance of all the ghosts: Bob Nickle, the chief ghost; Maggie Fisher, another ghost almost as bad as Bob; Peter Cox, a quiet old fellow of very little use as a ghost, because he never tries to break chairs, etc.; Mary Fisher (who says she is Maggie's sister), Jane Nickle and Eliza McNeal. The three last are "no good" as ghosts, as all they do is stalk about the house and occasionally upset something. As there are only six ghosts all told, and they were all present, the author asked them numerous questions, all of which were answered by loud knocks on the floor or on the wall, just as he requested — all seeming anxious to converse. The first question the author asked was:

"Have you all lived on the earth?"

"**Yes.**"

"Have you seen God?"

"**No.**"

"Are you in heaven?"

"**No.**"

"Are you in hell?"

"Yes."

"Have you seen the devil?"

Very loud: **"Yes."**

Many other questions were answered, but the answers are not worth repeating.

At the conclusion of the interview, one of the ghosts threw the author's bottle of ink from the table to the floor, spilling the contents on the carpet.

The next day, as the author and Esther were entering the parlor, both saw a chair fall over and instantly jump up again. Neither the author nor Esther were within five feet of the chair at the time.

During the whole of the next day, the ghosts stuck pins into Esther's person. These pins appeared to come out of the air, and the author pulled about thirty from various parts of her body during the day. In the afternoon the family cat was thrown a distance of five feet by one of the ghosts and almost had a fit from fright. She remained in the yard for the balance of the day, and, ever afterwards, while in the house, seemed to be on the lookout for ghosts; possibly she saw and heard them on several occasions afterwards, for her tail often became quite large, as cats' tails always do when they are frightened or angry, after which she would leave the house in a hurry. The author saw Esther coming downstairs late in the afternoon, and when she had reached the hall a chair from his room came down after her. The only other person in the cottage at the time was Olive, and she was at that instant in the kitchen.

On June 26th, two or three matches fell from the ceiling at the author's feet. Being a great smoker, he requested the ghosts to throw down a few more, which they did. He would simply say, "Bob, I would like a, few matches, if you please." Then down they would come from the ceiling. Forty-five were thrown during the day, and on another day during the afternoon forty-nine fell to the floor.

It must be remembered that all the manifestations witnessed by the author took place in the broad light of day and that the only other persons present were the various members of the family.

On June 28th, the sound of a trumpet was heard by the author and all the family. It continued to be blown about the house from early morning until late in the evening. The sound was very distinct and was at times close to their ears. Late

Knife-Wielding Demons and Murderous Ghosts

in the evening "Bob" let the trumpet fall in one of the rooms. It is composed of some metal very similar to German silver and is now in the possession of the author, who intends to place it in a museum on his return to the United States. Where the ghosts got it, no one knows. It had never been seen in Amherst, so far as has been ascertainable, until it fell upon the floor, and its true origin will doubtless always remain a mystery.

It is hardly necessary that the author should weary the reader with a minute account of the manifestations produced by these ghosts during his residence of six weeks in the haunted house. He could easily fill a book containing twice the number of pages that this one does with an account of what was done by the ghosts alone, without mentioning the name of a single living individual except Esther Cox; but I suppose the reader, by this time, is ready to cry "quantum sufficient." So by referring to a few more facts, he will end this chapter.

One afternoon, while Esther was out walking, she called on Rev. R.A. Temple. During the visit he prayed with her and also advised her to pray for herself. On her return to the cottage, one of the ghosts, either Bob or Maggie, cut her on the head with an old bone from the yard and a moment afterwards stabbed her in the face with a fork.

While the author lived in the house, scarcely a day passed that some article was not thrown by the ghosts. They would often steal small articles and keep them secreted — Heavens only knows where — for days at a time, and then unexpectedly let them fall in one of the rooms, to the amazement of everyone. In that way, shoes and stockings, knives, forks and other articles too numerous to mention would be missed, sometimes for weeks, and on one occasion some copper coins were taken from Dan's pocket and placed upon the author's knee.

It was a common thing for the ghosts to throw knives at the author, but fortunately they were all dull and he was never cut; he was, however, often struck by small articles, never sufficiently hard, however, to draw blood. During his stay in the house, Esther often went into a state very similar to the mesmeric sleep, during which she talked with people invisible to all present; among others, her dead mother. On coming out of this strange state she always said she had been to heaven among the angels.

On several occasions, Bob, the head ghost, tormented her so at night that it was with difficulty she could remain in bed. On one particular occasion the author was called up by Dan at midnight so that he might behold for himself what was going on. After dressing, he went into Esther's room, and was horrified by the sight which met his gaze. There, upon the bed, lay the poor, unhappy girl swollen to an enormous size, her body moving about the bed as if Beelzebub himself were in her, while between her gasps for breath she exclaimed in agonizing sobs: "Oh, my God, I wish I were dead! I wish I were dead!"

"Oh, don't say that, Esther," pleaded Olive. "Don't say that."

"Now, Mr. Hubbell," said Jane to the author, "you see how much she suffers."

"Yes, I see," said Hubbell, "but let us endeavor to hold her, so that this fiend cannot move her about the bed, and then, perhaps, she will not suffer so much." So Dan and he tried to hold her so that she could not be moved, but in vain.

"Well," said Hubbell, "one ghost is certainly stronger than two men. Are you sure nothing can be done to relieve her?"

"No," replied Olive. "Dr. Caritte has tried everything without affording her the slightest relief. Medicine has no more effect on her than water."

Jane, Olive, Dan and the author remained up with her for about three hours, during which time she continued to move about the bed, after which the ghost left her and she sank from sheer exhaustion into a state of lethargy. She had several attacks of this kind during the author's residence in the cottage, and on one occasion she was seen by Mr. G.G. Bird, Mr. James P. Dunlap, Mr. Amos Purdy and several ladies; on another occasion by Dr. E.D. McLean, Mr. Fowler and Mr. Sleep.

Towards the latter part of July the manifestations became so powerful that it was no longer safe to have Esther in the house. Fires were continually being started, the walls were being broken by chairs, the bedclothes pulled off in the day time, heavy sofas turned upside down, knives and forks thrown with such force that they would stick into doors, food disappeared from the table, finger marks became visible in the butter, and, worse than all, strange voices could be heard calling the inmates by name in the broad light of day.

This was too much; if the ghosts continued to gain in strength, they would take possession of the house and all in it, for there were six ghosts, and only five persons in the flesh all told, as follows: Dan, Olive, Jane, Esther and the author, not, of course, counting the two children — William Cox and John Teed having left the house before Esther went to St. John, literally driven away by ghosts.

THE

GREAT AMHERST MYSTERY

A TRUE NARRATIVE OF THE

SUPERNATURAL.

BY

WALTER HUBBELL.

BRENTANOS',

CHICAGO.   NEW YORK.   PARIS.
1888.

Front cover of Walter Hubbell's book "*The Great Amherst Mystery.*"

There was but one remedy, and that was that Esther Cox should leave the house, even though her sisters loved her dearly. Simple hearted village maiden! Fate decreed that she should be torn from their home, but not from their hearts, for the simple reason that her room was far more agreeable than her company.

So one morning, after packing up all her worldly possessions, she kissed the little boys, embraced her sisters, shook hands with the rest, bade them all farewell and departed, never to return.

Part VI

CONCLUSION

Esther is living with her friends, the Van Amburgh's, on their farm in the woods. The ghosts do not torment her now. With the Van Amburghs, she has a quiet, peaceful home. One thing is certain: if she returned to Dan's cottage, the manifestations would, in a short time, become as powerful as ever, and Heaven only knows where the matter would end.

The author went to see her at the farm on August 1st, 1879, and found her making a patchwork quilt, on which she stopped working every few minutes to play with the little children. She informed him that she read her Bible regularly every day and was contented and happy. Before departing, he advised her to pray earnestly that she might never again be possessed by devils. She promised to take his advice. So, hoping that her prayers would be answered, he bade her farewell forever.

In Dan's little cottage, all is now harmony and peace. Pretty Jane still tends her plants with loving care. Olive works as hard as ever, and so does honest Dan. And there may they reside for years to come, enjoying the blessings which the virtuous always receive from the hands of Providence.

Reader, a word. This account of the "Haunted House," in which Esther Cox suffered so much, and the author had such a remarkable experience, is no fanciful creation of the imagination, but really what it is claimed to be, "A True Ghost Story."

Write for our FREE catalog of mysterious books and other fascinating items.

Global Communications

P.O. Box 753

New Brunswick, NJ 08903

Email: mrufo8@hotmail.com

www.conspiracyjournal.com

BRAND NEW — SOMETHING UNIQUE AND DIFFERENT!

LEARN TO PRACTICE WHITE WITCHCRAFT UTILIZING TECHNIQUES USED BY CELEBRITIES DAVID BOWIE, UFOS, WICCA, DRUGS, AND A DOSE OF PARANOIA —THE SAGA OF WALLI ELMLARK, THE ROCK 'N' ROLL WITCH OF NY

Photo by Helen Hovey

This is the compelling story of the Wiccan lady Walli Elmlark who saved the life of David Bowie through witchcraft, and put a spell on pop stars and other high profile celebrities during the most dynamic period in rock music history– the 1970s.

This book also contains a "How To" section on Candle Burning Magick, plus spells for love and money that could work wonders for you. It explains how a knowledge of the true principles of positive witchcraft could empower your life, all adapted from the occult philosophy of the White Witch of New York. Walli was known for her dazzling beauty, her goth clothing, silver jewelry and a green streak in her hair, long before such attributes became fashionable. She befriended many confused and troubled celebrities, turning their lives around.

Through the pages of this book, the reader will go back in time to relive this celebrated period, mingling with those who were shaping the counter culture and causing a reconstruction of our social and political belief systems, both through the music and entertainment of this period, and the practice of witchcraft and the occult which was growing in popularity among the youth.

Much of the activities described took place backstage at the Academy of Music in Greenwich Village and as part of the inner circle of the N.Y. School of Occult Arts and Sciences hosted by the psychic world's "Grand Poobah" Tim Beckley. This enthralling work contains the "inside story" of David Bowie who had come under psychic attack, an evil spirit settling in his residence, and his belief that black magicians were trying to collect his semen so that they could create a demon baby. The Anti-Christ seemed to be looming in the pop star's future, untill Walli broke the curse... Many inspiring recollections of this revolutionary period as told by Tim Beckley, music promoter, radio host, publisher, widely known as "Mr UFO," (and editor of this publication).

☐ Order "David Bowie, Witchcraft, and the Occult," Black and white edition, $15.00.
Or ☐ Special all color, glossy, edition. $20.00.

TIMOTHY BECKLEY, BOX 753, NEW BRUNSWICK, NJ 08903
PayPal to mrufo8@hotmail.com

"BE YOUR OWN WITCH"

PRACTICE WICCAN MAGICK NOW!

This is a "starter kit" for those who want to get their feet wet in the ways of Witchcraft. We have kept the price low ao you can see if Wicca "is for you."

All Items In This Column For $50.00 +$6 S/H

 # 1— WICCA PENTAGRAM NECKLACE
Show you support of the craft, while at the same time the amulet brings miraculous good luck into your life. Measures approximately 1.25 inches in diameter. Color of stones may vary (blue is our favorite!).

 # 2 — "GOLDEN OPPORTUNITY" OILS

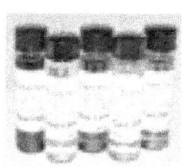

Five bottles of oil (2 drams each) for you to dress a candle, anoint ritual tools or talismans, and to diffuse in your sacred space. Can also be worn (one or two dabs) as a "spell perfume." Oils may differ. Use positively.

#3 — MIXED BAG OF MAGICAL HERBS
15 bags of herbs labeled with their common name listed along with their magical uses. We need to select depending upon availability, but will "do you good!"

Blessed Be

TIMOTHY BECKLEY, BOX 753
NEW BRUNSWICK, NJ 08903

PayPal mrufo8@hotmail (we will send you invoice). 646 331-6777 for credit cards

Our Dynamic Books Have Inspired Readers For Over Five Decades!

Maria D'Andrea
PSYCHIC AND SPIRITUAL COUNSELOR

631 559-1248 - mdanrea100@gmail.com

★★★★★★★★★★★★★

NOTE: Above information is for readings and counseling only. Books and kits this page to be ordered from the publisher (address below)

EXPERIENCE THE AMAZING POWERS OF ALADDIN'S LAMP

MARIA D' ANDREA TEACHES YOU TO CALL UPON THE UNSEEN KINGDOM OF MAGICKAL BEINGS

Maria D' Andrea

EXECUTE POSITIVE SPELLS AND UTILIZE MYSTIC POWERS

The following large format workbooks are based on the incredible occult knowledge and wisdom of Maria D' Andrea. Check off or list desired items.

- ☐ HEAVEN SENT MONEY SPELLS: DIVINELY INSPIRED FOR YOUR WEALTH
- ☐ OCCULT GRIMOIRE AND MAGICAL FORMULARY – A WORKBOOK FOR CREATING A POSITIVE LIFE
- ☐ POSITIVELY POSITIVE SPELL BOOK: VANQUISH ALL NEGATIVITY FROM YOUR LIFE
- ☐ SECRET MAGICAL ELIXIRS OF LIFE – LIVE LONGER, BE HAPPY, ATTRACT GOODNESS
- ☐ HOW TO ELIMINATE STRESS AND ANXIETY THROUGH THE OCCULT, CRYSTALS, GEMSTONES, MEDITATION, HERBS, OILS, MUSIC, INCENSE AND CANDLES
- ☐ SECRET OCCULT GALLERY AND SPELL CASTER. PLUS MARIA'S MOST POWERFUL SPELLS NEVER REVEALED PREVIOUSLY
- ☐ YOUR PERSONAL MEGA POWER SPELLS FOR LOVE, LUCK, PROSPERITY
- ☐ SIMPLE SPELLS USING AN ORDINARY DECK OF PLAYING CARDS
- ☐ CURSES AND THEIR REVERSALS: PLUS OMENS, SUPERSTITIONS AND REMOVAL OF THE EVIL EYE – Material by Maria and others.
- ☐ ANGEL SPELLS: ENOCHIAN OCCULT WORKBOOK OF CHARMS, SEALS, TALISMANS AND CIPHERS FOR CONTACTING ANGELS Material by Maria and others.

NOTE: Above books $20.00 each (add S/H)
☐ or all 10 just $179.00 + $12 S/H

Includes
1 Book by Maria
2 "Magic Lamp Incense Burner
3 Magickal Incense

Summon all you desire– as quickly as counting: One! Two! Three! For centuries the Aladdin's Lamp has been associated with power and success. King Solomon is said to have summoned and commanded the Genie to help construct Solomon's Temple. Beneficial Jinn can do your bidding. Lamp may differ from art.

☐ Send $35.00 + $5 S/H

THE COMPLETE SPIRITUAL AND OCCULT OILS WORKBOOK A-Z

☐ Here are over 1,000 magical powers of oils with easy to follow instructions for more than 1500 successful spells, recipes and rituals. Every conceivable formula and what purpose the oils are used for. **$18.00**

☐ Add kit of 5 spiritual oils Hex Breaking, Money Drawing, Commanding, etc. Add $25 + $5 S/H

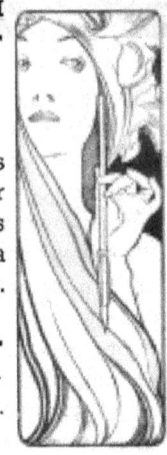

VIDEO WORKSHOPS

☐ Two Sets of DVDs, 6 mini workshops with instructions by Maria. Covers 25+ topics. Secret commands for Money. Power. Love. Spiritual Growth. Enjoy while you learn. **Both Sets $30.00 + $5 S/H**

MARIA'S "YES! YOU CAN " SERIES- $10 EACH
Easy to use reference manuals of various length (80-112 pages).
- ☐ "Sexy Medium's Love And Lust Spell Book."
- ☐ "Book Of Common Prayer."
- ☐ " Time Travel To Contact Beneficial Beings."
- ☐ "Supernatural Words Of Power"
- ☐ "Evocations To Evoke Summon Spirits."
- ☐ All 5 books $43.00 + $6 S/H

TIMOTHY BECKLEY, BOX 753, NEW BRUNSWICK, NJ 08903

DID A TOP-SECRET REPRINT OF A MYSTERIOUS MANUSCRIPT BY NAVAL INTELLIGENCE CAUSE THE SUICIDE OR MURDER OF A FAMOUS ASTRONOMER?

Was The Strange "Varo Edition" Of The Case For The UFO And The Allende Letters Penned By A Clan Of Gypsies Who Knew The Secrets Of Space Travel, Invisibility And Time Displacement?

SAUCER MAN SUICIDE
MIAMI, April 21 (JP) — Police said tonight that Morris K. Jessup, 59, widely known writer on flying saucers, took his own life with a hose linked to his automobile's exhaust pipe. Jessup, a mathematician and astronomer, was a former University of Michigan and Drake University instructor.

Only a dozen copies were reprinted of the paperback edition of the "Case For The UFO" authored by Dr. M.K. Jessup who eventually committed suicide or was murdered at the hands of a cabal known as the "Silence Group". The manuscript which had been laboriously typed out on offset stencils and printed by a Texas firm at the request of Naval intelligence, (one copy of which was known to have sold for $10,000.00 at auction) was run through their small office duplicator twice, once with black ink for the regular text of the book, then once again with red ink, the latter reproducing the mysterious annotations by individuals, who may have been gypsies or space people living among humankind.

☐ ORDER NOW! We have been selling this special VARO Edition of the "Case For The UFO" (with a unique introduction by the late Gray Baker, author of "They Knew Too Much About Flying Saucers" – and containing mysterious letters to the authors – for $39.00, but now offer it to our loyal mail order customers for $25.00 + $5 S/H

WANT TO LEARN MORE?

☐ "PHILADELPHIA EXPERIMENT REVELATIONS" expands on the concepts found in our Vero and Allende Letters U.S.S. Eldridge a mega-ton Destroyer Escort from its dry dock in the Philadelphia Naval Yard to Norfolk, Virginia - a distance of around 400 miles. Upon its return, most of the vessel's hand-picked test crew - all of whom had been left totally unprepared and unprotected - either "caught on fire," became literally frozen into the hull of the ship, went stark, raving mad, or vanished, never to be seen again. This is the "inside story" told by Commander X and Alfred Bielek, known to be the only survivor. $17.00 + $5 S/H

☐ Or BOTH VOLUMES for just $38.00 + $6 S/H

BOOK AND POWERFUL AMULET CAN NOW BE YOURS

CAN YOU ACQUIRE THE ABILITY TO WALK THROUGH WALLS? – LEARN THE SECRETS OF INVISIBILITY? – MASTER THE ART OF LEVITATION?

Book by military intelligence operative "Commander X" reveals secrets used by U.S. and other governments to master feats known to ancient scribes and now adapted by the elite.

"Kit" includes full length volume in which "sacred" techniques are readily given as well as a replica of "Seal of the Sun" amulet which may enable you to duplicate the amazing results of those who acquired the knowledge from a Heavenly source.

☐ Book and amulet $29.00 + $5 S/H

TIMOTHY BECKLEY, BOX 753, NEW BRUNSWICK, NJ 08903

THE TRUTH AT LAST! HARD-TO-FIND BOOKS
RADIONICS BOXES — MOLDAVITE — TREE OF LIFE

☐ **#1—NIKOLA TESLA 3-BOOK SUPER SPECIAL!**

"The Miracle of Tesla's Purple Energy." The benefits of the purple plates are said to be almost supernatural, yet are firmly rooted in scientific principles. *"Men of Mystery."* The untold story of Tesla and his student, Otis T. Carr, who claimed to be building an anti-gravity device to take us to space as early as 1959. *"Tesla's Death Ray and the Columbia Space Shuttle Disaster."* Earth shaking facts NASA wants kept under wraps. Who was responsible?
ALL THREE BOOKS—JUST $25.00

☐ **#2—2 BOOKS: MISSING DIARY OF ADMIRAL RICHARD BYRD & NAZI UFO TIME TRAVELERS**

Are there secret polar entrances leading to a paradice inside the Earth, inhabited by giants, as discovered by Admiral Byrd and revealed in his secret diary? Proof that the Germans developed a bell-shaped device capable of space and time travel based upon contacts with ETs, made as early as 1919. Hundreds of large-format, provacative pages.
2 VOLUMES—$25.00

☐ **#3 MATRIX CONTROL SYSTEM OF PHILIP K. DICK AND THE PARANORMAL SYNCHRONICITIES OF TIM BECKLEY**

Are we living in a computer simulation—mere robotic creations of ancient technology played upon an eternal chessboard? Can we reside in parallel univeses simultaneously, leading multiple lives? The role of bizarre "coincidences" that control our destiny fully revealed!
450 LARGE FORMAT PAGES—$23.00

☐ **ALL 6 BOOKS AND FREE UNCLASSIFIED DVD—$59.00**

☐ **RARE TRANSFORMATIONAL GEM FROM SPACE**

Moldavite opens multidimensional portals with its beautiful green extraterrestrial energy. This rare stone arrived in a meteor some million years ago and is found only in one place on Earth. Powerful aid for increasing sensitivity to guidance, intuition and telepathy, and ability to receive and understand messages from higher realms. COMPLETE MOLDAVITE KIT includes the stone in an elegant setting, a 178-page workbook, and "Divine Fire" audio CD. Individually crafted; stones and setting vary.
MEDIUM STONE—$79 • LARGE STONE—$92

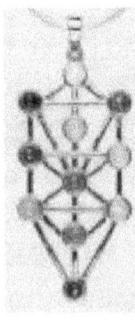

☐ **BLACK BOXES TWO ECONOMY VERSIONS OF OUR "WISH MACHINES"**

Other Rife, Harmonious or Radionics Machines sell for $2,000 or more! Our are two of the most economical, yet most powerful available. Includes comprehensive, *"Mind Machines"* book, and a dossier of scientific research describing their capabilities. No medical claims made. For experimental purposes. Actual box are custom-made and will vary.
MOST ECONOMICAL—$292
UPGRADED—$449 *(Plug-in model, antenna, light and toggle switch)*

☐ **TREE OF LIFE PENDANT ENERGY ACCUMULATOR**

The Tree Of Life was understood by Old Testament prophets as an energy accumulator. This beautiful, individually crafted pendant is cast in silver with ten faceted stones. It acts to ammplify your deepest desires, broadcasting them to the highest powers to bring awareness, wisdom and knowledge. Casts a deep reflection of the eternal mysteries. In the Kabbalah, the Tree Of Life represents a "telephone" to the heavens. Includes pendant, study guide and 70-minute audio CD. Designs, stones and settings may vary.
TREE OF LIFE PENDANT—$125

Check desired items. Include your name, postal address and ZIP. Check, Money Order or PayPal to Tim Beckley, 11 East 30th Street, #4R, New York, NY 10016. Secure Phone: 646-331-6777. Speak slowly and clearly name, address, items desired.

Timothy G. Beckley · Box 753 · New Brunswick, NJ 08903 · PayPal to mrufo8@hotmail.com
FREE CONSPIRACY JOURNAL · NO REFUNDS · email mrufo8@hotmail.com if paying via PayPal

www.ingramcontent.com/pod-product-compliance
Lightning Source LLC
Chambersburg PA
CBHW080358170426
43193CB00016B/2750